MAKE it WORK!
LIVING
HISTORY

MAKE it WORK!

LIVING
HISTORY

STONE AGE
PEOPLE

ANCIENT
EGYPT

THE
ROMAN
EMPIRE

NORTH AMERICAN
INDIANS

Created and published by
Two-Can Publishing
346 Old Street
London EC1V 9RB

Hardback ISBN: 1-85434-798-5

Hardback 10 9 8 7 6 5 4 3 2 1

A catalogue record for this book is available from the British Library.

Printed in Hong Kong by Wing King Tong.

Photographic credits:

Stone Age People

Ancient Art & Architecture Collection: p4 (t), p5 (tr), p36 (tr), p37 (t), p49 (t); CM Dixon: p28 (t), p40 (t); GeoScience Features: p10 (t); Historic Scotland: p23 (t); Magnum Photos Ltd: p21 (t); The Mansell Collection Ltd: p19 (t); Mary Evans Picture Library: p11 (t), p25 (tr); Musée Guimet/C Jarrige: p27 (t); Museum of London: p35 (l); Natural History Museum, London: p54 (t); Office of Public Works, Dublin, Ireland: p57 (t); Science Photo Library: p12 (t), p13 (t), p52 (t), p60 (l); South American Pictures: p43 (t).

All other photographs by Ray Moller

Ancient Egypt

British Museum: p4 (tr), p12, p15, p23 (tr), p24, p28, p31, p36, p40, p41, p50 (bl), p51, p55, p58 (r); Greg Evans International: p56, p58 (tl); Griffiths Institute: p11, p14, p37 (tr), p46, p60, p61; G.S.F. Picture Library: p39 (mr); Image Bank: p5 (tr); Mel Pickering: p4 (map); Metropolitan Museum of Art: p52 (l); Still Pictures: p9; Robert Harding: p23 (br), p37 (tl), p44, p50 (tl), p54, p58 (bl), RH/British Museum: p48; Science Photo Library: p39 (bl); Wernar Forman Archive: p35, WFA/University College London, Petrie Museum: p10, WFA/British Museum: p5 (bl), p18, p47, WFA/E Strouhal: p38, WFA/Egyptian Museum, Turin: p42, WFA/Egyptian Museum, Cairo: p52 (r).

All other photographs by Jon Barnes

The Roman Empire

AKG London/Erich Lessing: p38, p51, p59; Ancient Art & Architecture Collection: p49; British Museum: p42, BM/The Bridgeman Art Library: p60; CM Dixon: p12, p25, p44; Elsevier Archive/Atlas of the Roman World: p16; Michael Holford: p19, p28, p32, p36, p40, p48; Peter Clayton: p50; Planet Earth Pictures: p4 (tr); Scala: p4 (bl), p24; Tony Stone/Jean Pragan: p60; Zefa: p46.

All other photographs by Jon Barnes and John Englefield

North American Indians

American Museum of Natural History, courtesy Department of Library Services: p35 (tl), p56 (bl); Denver Art Museum: p18 (tr); Eric and David Hosking: p4 (ml); Mel Pickering: p60 (map), Peter Newark's Western Americana: p8 (tr), p24 (tr), p45 (tl), p60 (t); Phoebe A Hurst Museum of Anthropology, The University of California at Berkeley: p26 (bl); Range Pictures Ltd: p4 (tr), p5 (bl), p5 (tr), p5 (br), p61 (tl); Robert Harding: p61 (br); Smithsonian Institution, Museum of American History: p10 (tr), p16 (tr), p27 (tr), p30 (tr), p32 (tr), p34 (tr), p43 (tr), p46 (tl), p54 (tr); Zefa: p39 (tr).

All other photographs by Jon Barnes

STONE AGE
PEOPLE

Contents

Studying Stone Age life   4

Timeline   6

A frozen world   8

Back to our roots   10

Safety in numbers   14

Shelter from the elements   16

From fur to fabric   24

Hunting, fishing and farming   28

Ancient art   36

Special occasions   40

Understanding each other   42

On the move   44

Fighting off the enemy   48

Making magic   50

Burial beginnings   54

Digging up the past   58

Glossary   62
Words found in **bold** in the text can be found here

Index   64

Studying Stone Age life

All human beings need food and shelter to survive. They also have a system of beliefs that gives shape and meaning to their lives. From **prehistoric** times, people have created different ways of meeting these basic requirements. By studying Stone Age people, we learn how they used the resources around them to build shelters and find food, and how they developed a way of life that meant they could survive.

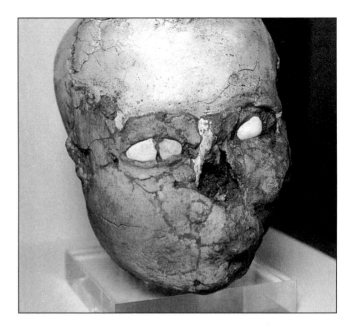

▷ *This plaster mould of a skull was found in Jericho, Jordan. It has shell eyes and dates from 7000 BC.*

THE PERIOD OF TIME covered in this book is vast – about three million years! **Archaeologists** normally divide up this time into three main periods: the **Palaeolithic** (Old Stone Age), the **Mesolithic** (Middle Stone Age) and the **Neolithic** (New Stone Age).

THE PALAEOLITHIC is such a long period of time (from three million BC to 10,000 BC) that it too is often divided up into Lower, Middle and Upper phases.

THE MESOLITHIC begins around 10,000 BC, but ends in different places at different times. The Neolithic dates from about 8000 to 3000 BC, but in some places it lasts longer. For example, in North America it continued until the arrival of the Europeans in the 15th century. Here, we have only traced Stone Age people down to about 3000 BC.

To make things clearer, we have given symbols to the Lower/Middle Palaeolithic, the Upper Palaeolithic and the Mesolithic/Neolithic. These act as a guide for when information relates to the time covered.

KEY FOR SYMBOLS

🐘 (mammoth) **Lower/Middle Palaeolithic** (3 million – 40,000 BC)

🏃 (spear-thrower) **Upper Palaeolithic** (40,000 – 10,000 BC)

🌾 (wheat grain) **Mesolithic/Neolithic** (10,000 – 3000 BC)

WRITING HAD BARELY BEEN INVENTED by 3000 BC, so we have to rely on objects we find to try and piece together what may have happened in the ancient past. As a result, we are never sure how Stone Age people lived, and experts often interpret the evidence very differently!

◁ *Female figurines may have been used by Stone Age people as symbols of fertility.*

ARCHAEOLOGISTS have the task of finding, digging up and trying to understand the evidence of Stone Age people, the world in which they lived and their way of life.

ANTHROPOLOGISTS studying the Palaeolithic are particularly concerned with understanding how, over hundreds of thousands of years, the human body adapted to a changing environment. They are called physical anthropologists.

stone helps to keep rotating stick steady

△ These amazing carved clay bison, found in caves in France, are at least 12,000 years old.

THERE IS PLENTY OF EVIDENCE about what early people made and what they ate. Stone tools, pottery, carvings, paintings and even food refuse have been found on sites all over the world. The way people built their houses and treated their dead provides clues about how they organized their societies. But trying to understand their beliefs about life, death and the supernatural is much harder (see page 50).

THE MAKE IT WORK! way of looking at history is to ask questions of the past and find answers by making replicas of the things people made. But you do not have to make everything in the book to understand Stone Age people's way of life.

△ A Stone Age man uses a bow-drill to make a fire.

Timeline

The Stone Age covers the most remote part of human history. By studying Stone Age people, we can try to understand the **biological** development of human beings across the world. We can learn how people have developed as social and spiritual beings, and how they have survived and spread out, in spite of frequently very harsh conditions.

LOOKING SO FAR BACK to investigate our early ancestors makes us realise how different their lives were. But it also shows us the characteristics that separate humans from all other animals.

HUMAN BEINGS DEVELOPED – in their physical build, the social groups they lived in and the tools and weapons they used – at a gradually increasing speed. As a result, there is more to record over the last 10 thousand years of the Stone Age than over the first three million years.

LOWER/MIDDLE PALAEOLITHIC

3 million BC

2m BC

1.5m BC

Australopithecus *in existence*

Homo habilis *appear*

First hand axes

Homo erectus *appear*

MIDDLE/UPPER PALAEOLITHIC

100,000 BC

50,000 BC

40,000 BC

Last ice age begins

Homo sapiens appear in Africa

Homo sapiens arrive in Australia

First sea travel

Mammoth bone huts

MESOLITHIC/ NEOLITHIC

10,000 BC

8000 BC

6000 BC

Making of pots in Near East

Farming in Europe and China

Farming and growth of permanent settlements in Near East (Fertile Crescent)

Earliest defended settlements, such as Jericho

THE ANCESTORS OF MODERN HUMANS first split off from the African apes between five and eight million years ago. But it took several million more years for *Homo sapiens,* or modern humans, to make an appearance (see page 12).

By that time, they were living in socially organized groups, had mastered hunting and gathering skills, discovered how to make fire, and equipped themselves with a basic, but effective, tool-kit made out of stones and pebbles.

THE CHART BELOW covers the entire Stone Age period we are looking at. However, the three bands relate to varying lengths of time:the top band spans three million years, while the bottom band covers just seven thousand years.

IN THIS BOOK we usually refer to the number of years BC (before the birth of Christ, nearly 2,000 years ago) to date an object or an event. There are times however, when we simply say the number of years ago that something happened.

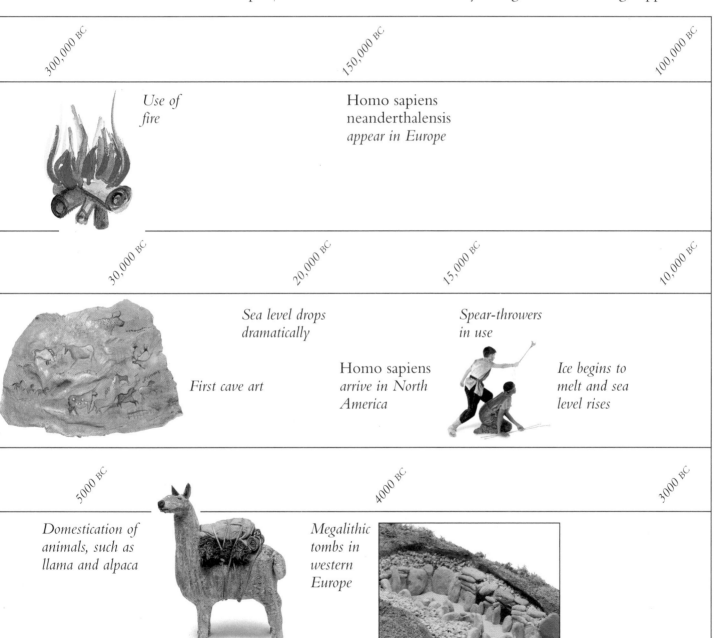

300,000 BC   150,000 BC   100,000 BC

Use of fire

Homo sapiens neanderthalensis *appear in Europe*

30,000 BC   20,000 BC   15,000 BC   10,000 BC

Sea level drops dramatically

First cave art

Homo sapiens *arrive in North America*

Spear-throwers in use

Ice begins to melt and sea level rises

5000 BC   4000 BC   3000 BC

Domestication of animals, such as llama and alpaca

Megalithic tombs in western Europe

A frozen world

About one and a half million years ago, the Earth started suffering periods of bitterly cold conditions known as 'glacials' or ice ages. *Homo sapiens* appeared roughly when the last ice age began, 100,000 years ago. This ice age is known as the Würm in Europe, or the Wisconsin glacial in the United States of America.

AS THE TEMPERATURE DROPPED during the last ice age, the ice sheets spread out to cover much of northern Europe and the mountains of North America. The ice was hundreds of metres thick. Freezing temperatures and strong icy winds made many areas uninhabitable.

THE SEA LEVEL lowered because so much water was locked up in the ice sheets. At the coldest point, around 20,000 BC, the sea was about 100 metres lower than it is today. As a result, land bridges existed to join Britain to Europe, North America to Asia and Australia to New Guinea.

▽ *These are some of the animals that lived during the last ice age and are shown on the map.*

Meadowcroft, USA

retreating ice sheet

Monte Verde, Chile

llama

wild boar

red deer

wild horse

cave bear

Homo sapiens

mammoth

musk ox

wild cow

reindeer

woolly rhino

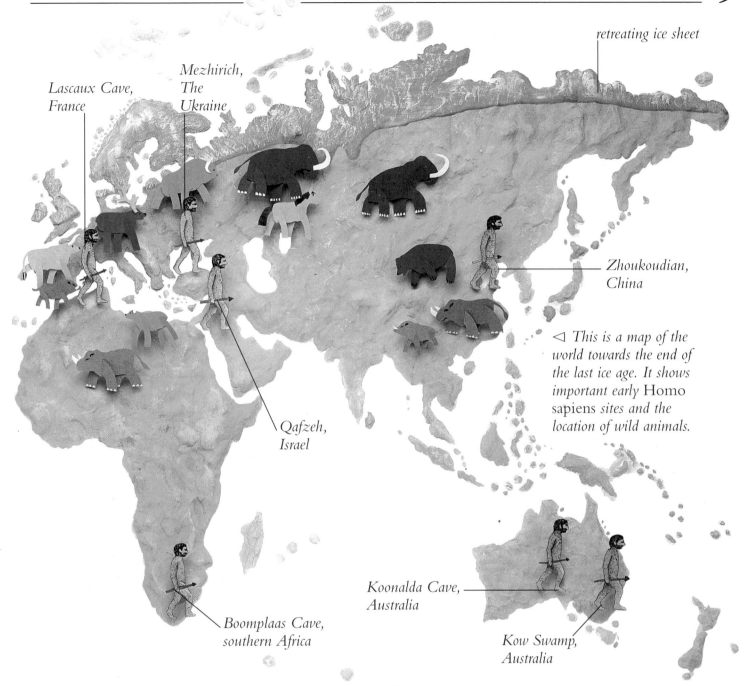

retreating ice sheet

Lascaux Cave, France

Mezhirich, The Ukraine

Zhoukoudian, China

◁ This is a map of the world towards the end of the last ice age. It shows important early Homo sapiens sites and the location of wild animals.

Qafzeh, Israel

Koonalda Cave, Australia

Boomplaas Cave, southern Africa

Kow Swamp, Australia

THE ICE BEGAN TO MELT and retreat and the sea level started to rise again around 15,000 years ago. The water slowly covered the existing land bridges, turning Britain into an island, and separating America from Asia and Australia from New Guinea.

LARGE ANIMALS that had adapted to the cold, such as the mammoth and woolly rhinoceros, followed the retreating ice sheets north. When the ice retreated further, they became **extinct**.

THE BARE, BLEAK LANDSCAPE at the edge of the ice sheets, which was covered in herbs and lichens and had very few trees, also moved northwards. With it went the reindeer who lived on these plants.

GRADUALLY, THE CLIMATE became warmer and wetter. This brought more grasslands and forests which suited the needs of smaller, faster animals such as deer and wild boar, and various birds, fish and edible plants.

Back to our roots

No-one is sure how or where *Homo sapiens* came into existence. We do know that humans and African apes once shared an ancestor and that between five and eight million years ago the first **hominids**, or human ancestors, separated from the apes.

STONE AGE PEOPLE date back to when these hominids, with human characteristics such as bigger brains, different jaws and **bipedalism**, or walking upright, emerged. By 100,000 years ago, while still living in the Stone Age, they had developed into what we call modern humans.

△ *This is the skull of an* Australopithecus, *found by famous anthropologist, Richard Leakey, at Lake Turkana in Kenya. Its jaw bone is missing.*

▽ *This is how Stone Age people developed.*

Australopithecus,
4 m years old

Homo habilis,
2 m years old

🐘 *AUSTRALOPITHECUS* were the first human ancestors. The oldest discovered fossils are around four million years old. They show that while this species had ape-sized brains, they walked upright. The most famous *Australopithecus* fossil is Lucy – surviving parts of her three-million-year-old skeleton were found in Ethiopia. The structure of her leg bones suggest that she was bipedal.

🐘 *HOMO* **IS THE SCIENTIFIC NAME** used for humans. The oldest discovered fossils referred to as *Homo* date back around two million years. The skeletons of **Homo habilis** resemble the *Australopithecus*, but they have larger brains, smaller jaws and are more lightly built. Also, *Homo habilis*, which means 'handy man', first developed the use of stone tools.

△ *Many cartoons printed in journals in the late 19th century made fun of Darwin's theory that humans descended from the apes.*

ONE OF THE FIRST PEOPLE to suggest that human beings descended from the apes was a man called Charles Darwin. Until the 19th century, it was generally accepted that God created human beings. But in 1859, Darwin caused an uproar in society when he published his theory of **natural evolution**.

In it, he claimed that groups of animals and plants changed as they struggled to exist. Nature selected which species succeeded in surviving, with the result that some died out completely while new species emerged. Human beings he said, evolved, or changed, in the same way and because of this our ancestors could be traced back to prehistoric times.

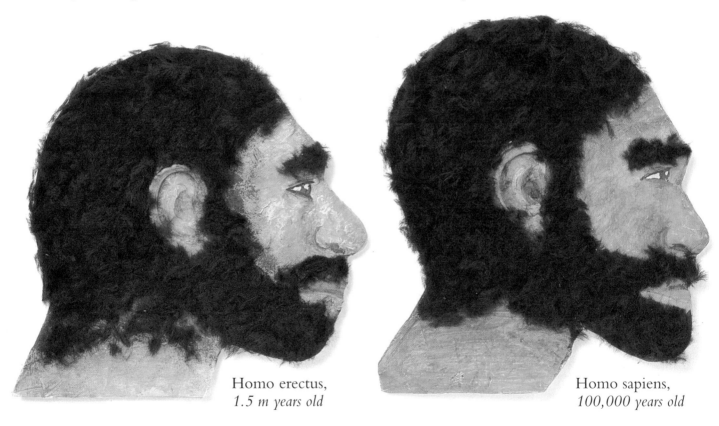

Homo erectus,
1.5 m years old

Homo sapiens,
100,000 years old

HOMO ERECTUS, which means 'upright man', appeared around 1.5 million years ago. *Homo erectus* had a bigger brain and body and smaller teeth than *Homo habilis.* Like modern humans they used fire. They were also the first early human form found in places outside Africa. By 700,000 years ago, they had spread to south-east Asia and later to northern Asia and Europe.

MODERN HUMANS belong to a species known as *Homo sapiens.* They had much larger brains and were more lightly built and less muscular than earlier species. It is perhaps partly because of this, that they could adapt to the Earth's changing climate and conditions more easily. *Homo sapiens* were the first species to inhabit all the continents in the world.

🦣 **THERE ARE DIFFERENT THEORIES** about how and where modern humans emerged. Some experts believe they appeared first in southern Africa, perhaps as far back as 150,000 years ago, and following this migrated to Europe, Asia, America and Australia.

Others believe it is more likely that *Homo sapiens* eventually developed separately in different parts of Asia from *Homo erectus*, who had spread to the Far East almost a million years earlier. From Asia and Africa, the species then spread to the other continents of the world. So far, the earliest modern humans outside Africa have been found on two sites in Israel and date back to around 90,000 years ago.

△ *This trail of footprints is 3.6 million years old. It proves that hominids were upright walkers by this time.*

HOW HUMAN BEINGS EVOLVED

▽ *This chart shows important landmarks in the development of modern humans and their ancestors.*

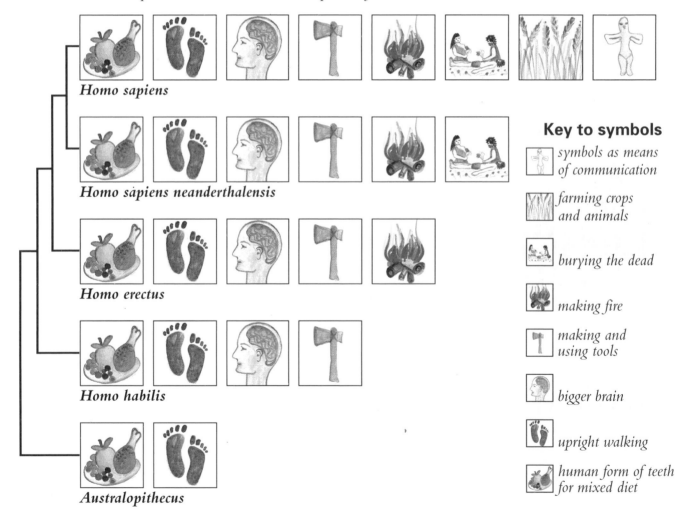

Homo sapiens

Homo sapiens neanderthalensis

Homo erectus

Homo habilis

Australopithecus

Key to symbols

symbols as means of communication

farming crops and animals

burying the dead

making fire

making and using tools

bigger brain

upright walking

human form of teeth for mixed diet

🐘 IN CHINA, *Homo sapiens* appeared by 70,000 years ago and in Australia by around 50,000 years ago. Although land bridges existed between New Guinea and Australia at that time, there was still almost 100 kilometres of sea to be crossed from Indonesia to New Guinea. So the arrival of *Homo sapiens* in Australia shows that they managed to make some sort of sea-going craft for the journey (see page 44).

🐘 🏃 THE NEANDERTHALS *(Homo sapiens neanderthalensis)* first appeared in Europe about 150,000 years ago, though no-one is sure exactly where they came from. Remains show that both sexes were stocky in build with a long, low skull, heavy jaw and receding chin. Neanderthals became extinct about 35,000 years ago.

🏃 A NEW TYPE OF EARLY human had arrived in central and western Europe by 40,000 years ago. They are called **Cro-Magnon** after the French cave where some of the earliest remains of the last century were found. The Cro-Magnons were tall and long-limbed and were similar in build to people who live in warm climates today.

Finally, around 15,000 years ago when the sea level was at its lowest, the first group of *Homo sapiens* walked across the land bridge in the Bering Straits from Asia to North America.

🐘 TOOL-MAKING was crucial to the development of the human species. Hand axes, which were first made around 1.5 million years ago were very successful tools.

WARNING! DO NOT MAKE OR USE A HAND AXE WITHOUT THE HELP OF AN ADULT.

▷ *A 700,000-year-old hand axe. It was probably used by* Homo erectus.

People continued to use these tools for over a million years. They were elongated and symmetrical with a sharp cutting edge. Today they are the earliest solid evidence experts have to help them understand the survival techniques of early hominids.

HOW A HAND AXE CAN BE MADE

1 *The first flake is chipped from the side of a stone to create a point.*

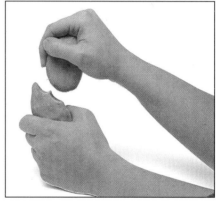

2 *A sharp edge emerges with the second blow to the same side.*

3 *The third blow lengthens the existing sharp, cutting edge.*

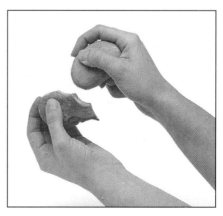

4 *Flakes are struck from the other side to sharpen the point.*

Safety in numbers

From the beginning, *Homo sapiens* seems to have understood that it was better to live and hunt with a larger group of people rather than just a single family. There was safety in numbers from dangerous wild animals and maybe even from other bands of hunters after the same food. Hunting in groups could also make it easier to trap and kill powerful creatures such as bison and mammoth.

✘ DIFFERENT PLANTS AND ANIMALS
were available as the seasons changed. This meant that many early hunters lived away from their base camp sometimes. In Denmark for example, some **hunter-gatherers** would move to different places at certain times of the year, setting up temporary camps along the way.

During the winter, they would camp inland, quite deep into the forest, near a stream or a lake. Some hunters would go in search of wild boar, elks and **aurochs** to kill for their meat. Smaller animals, such as beavers and foxes, were hunted for their warm pelts.

WHEN SPRING CAME, hunting continued inland as the groups relied mainly on red deer for their food supply. This was also the season when some members returned to the coast to hunt seals.

As the weather warmed up, the groups would move nearer to the sea and build a camp of branch huts by an inland stream or lake. This way they could travel easily to the coast to fish for cod and mackerel.

THE HUNTERS USED WEAPONS, such as bows and arrows, spears and clubs, which were made out of bone or wood. Harpoons for fishing were often carved from deer antlers. People gathered fruits, plants and nuts throughout the year. Supplies of these were stored for when meat and fish were scarce.

women gathering fruits and nuts

fishing from hollow tree-trunk boats

seals

✗ MAKE A HARPOON AND THROWING STICK

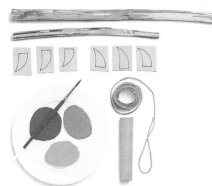

You will need: two sticks: one, 50 cm long, one, 22 cm long, thin card, cardboard tube, 10 cm long, paints, twine, glue, craft knife

1 Fit the cardboard tube on the longer stick, leaving half of it hanging over the end. Glue in place. Draw six blades onto the card and cut out.

2 Ask an adult to help you cut three slits, spaced out, down each side of the shorter stick. Insert a blade into each slit and glue.

3 Now ask an adult to help you sharpen each end of the harpoon into a point.

4 Bind twine around the end of the tube. Bind more further up where the tube is over the stick and leave enough twine to wind around and attach the harpoon as shown right. Paint the harpoon and the shaft browny-grey.

WARNING! NEVER THROW THIS HARPOON AT A LIVING THING.

▽ *Moving from spring into summer: hunter-gatherers in Denmark set up camp near the coast to fish and hunt during the warmer weather.*

red deer

hunter with wooden spear hunting deer

fisherman with harpoon

branch hut in summer base camp

Shelter from the elements

Even the earliest **nomadic** humans needed shelters to survive. At first, these were basic dwellings such as caves and huts made from branches and leaves. As people began to lead more settled lives, they wanted more permanent homes. The place where they lived, the climate and the raw materials and tools at hand, affected the types of houses they built.

EARLY HUMANS sheltered in caves that they came across as they wandered in search of food. Caves protected them from the rain and kept them warm in the winter and cool in summer. Fossilized remains of some of the earliest hominids have been found in the limestone caves of southern Africa.

EVIDENCE OF some of the oldest man-made shelters has been discovered in those areas of southern Africa where caves are rare. Here, early people stuck small branches into the ground and supported them by piling stones around their base. By bringing the branches together at the top and perhaps weaving grass among the leaves and twigs, these shelters provided shade from the blazing African sun.

ABOUT 13,000 YEARS AGO, a group of hunter-gatherers made a riverside settlement at Monte Verde in southern Chile. The walls of the 12 rectangular dwellings were made of a wooden framework covered by the hides of **mastodons** (extinct elephants). Inside each hut there was a shallow, clay-lined pit for holding coals for warmth. Cooking probably took place at large communal hearths outside.

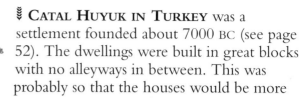

CATAL HUYUK IN TURKEY was a settlement founded about 7000 BC (see page 52). The dwellings were built in great blocks with no alleyways in between. This was probably so that the houses would be more secure, but it meant there was no way in at ground level. Therefore people had to walk across the rooftops and climb in by wooden ladder. The roofs were supported by wooden beams which rested on the mud brick house walls. Inside each house there were fitted benches and platforms, a hearth and a built-in clay oven.

BY THE RIVER DANUBE in Serbia, are the remains of Lepenski Vir, a settlement of tent-like **trapezoidal** houses dating from about 6000 BC. Up to 100 people may have lived there. The walls of the houses were made of wooden poles fixed to a central ridge and then covered with reed thatch. Inside, beyond a stone threshold, the floor was plastered with limestone and a hearth was near the door.

AROUND 6000 BC, BANPO, a settlement in northern China, was built (see page 39). The dwellings were either pyramid-shaped or circular and sunk four steps down below ground level. People entered them by a long, low porch. Thatched roofs were supported on four large posts set in a square. Most of the houses had clay-plastered floors and a sunken fire pit set into the centre.

A SHORTAGE OF RAW MATERIALS never stopped early *Homo sapiens* from building shelters. Some of the most amazing homes lived in by Stone Age hunters are the mammoth bone huts of southern Russia and The Ukraine. These were built between 15,000 and 40,000 years ago.

UP TO SIX HUNDRED MAMMOTH BONES, including skulls, jaw bones, tusks, leg and toe bones, went into the construction of each hut. It is thought that the largest hut used bones from more than a hundred different mammoths.

These bones would have come from both mammoths that had died naturally and those that had been hunted. Primarily, mammoths were killed for the mountains of meat they provided. It was so cold that people could store any surplus meat in holes they dug in the ground. There was enough flesh on one mammoth to feed a family for a whole year.

JAW BONES, SKULLS AND LEG BONES were used to build a base for the huts. They were also a support for the tusks and wooden poles which formed a roof that was probably arched.

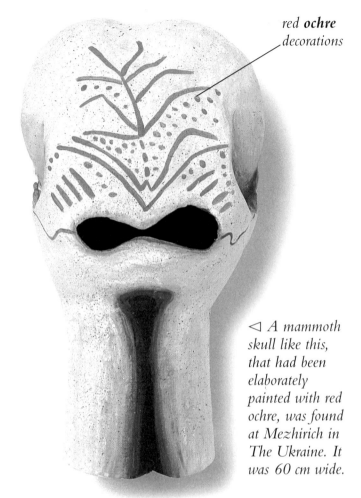

red **ochre** decorations

◁ *A mammoth skull like this, that had been elaborately painted with red ochre, was found at Mezhirich in The Ukraine. It was 60 cm wide.*

MAKE A MAMMOTH BONE HUT

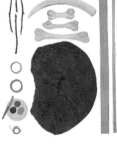

You will need:
3 m brown fur fabric, thick card, twigs, double-sided sticky tape, paints, string, large pebbles

1 Cut four card strips, 2.6 m x 5 cm and seven strips, 52 cm x 5 cm. Cut a number of thinner strips, 52 cm x 3 cm. Cut out the bone and tusk shapes as shown left. Paint these off-white. Cut out the fabric into big, rough shapes.

2 Lie one of the large card strips flat on the floor. Place the other three large strips over it spacing them out to make a star. Tape to secure. Get a friend to hold this up to create a dome. Tape the seven shorter 5 cm wide strips around the base.

THE GAPS BETWEEN THE BONES were probably packed with grass and moss. Animal hides would have been stretched over the framework and held down with mammoth jaws to stop them from tearing in the wild winds. Turf may also have been used on the outer layer.

△ *Mammoths looked like hairy elephants with huge curvy tusks. They lived in cold parts of the world.*

ARCHAEOLOGISTS BELIEVE that it may have taken four people a week to build one of these huts. And it would have been hard work: some of the tusks weighed up to 200 kilogrammes.

3 Now, working upwards, tape the thinner strips horizontally around the dome to reinforce its shape and make it stronger. You will probably need three or four rows of struts. Make sure there is an equal distance between each row.

4 Tie together a small bundle of twigs with string. Attach it to top of the hut with tape. Next, use tape to stick the pieces of fabric to the hut frame. Work from the bottom upwards to make sure that the fur overlaps and there are no gaps.

5 Using string, tie together one pair of tusks at the tip so that they cross over each other. Tape them over the hut entrance. Add another tusk either side. Lean the bones around the base of the hut. Finally, use the pebbles to build a hearth inside.

MAMMOTH BONE HUTS may have been kept warm inside by lining them with hides. At the mammoth bone hut site in Mezhirich in The Ukraine, evidence of hearths containing ash and charcoal were found. As well as being used to cook over, these would have helped to heat the dwellings too.

The inside area of the huts was about seven or eight metres in diameter. This was just large enough for four or five people to live fairly comfortably, but still a small enough space to keep reasonably warm.

bones hold down hides to prevent tearing in the wind

FLINT TOOLS, BONE NEEDLES and **awls**, and simple ornaments of bone and amber, have all been found on the sites. They indicate that these huts really were homes where people lived.

AS PEOPLE SETTLED in one place more permanently, and particularly as they learned to farm crops and breed animals, they began to live in larger communities of hamlets and villages (see page 30). Some of these may have been no bigger than hunter bands, while others were villages with populations of a few hundred.

IN THE UKRAINE, villages of 20 to 40 long houses were emerging by 4000 BC. Each one was 20 to 40 metres long and probably housed extended families of perhaps 10 to 15 people.

▽ *Mammoths provided all the necessary materials to build a hut: bones for a strong and sturdy framework and hides for warm walls.*

hairy hides keep out the cold

hearth

decorating a mammoth skull with red ochre (a real life skull is about half the size of a human!)

In some cases, the houses were arranged in a rough circle with one or two buildings in the centre – perhaps the home of a chieftain, or even a communal hall. Similar long houses are found in villages in eastern and central Europe.

▷ *Mammoth bone huts and later, long houses, kept out the severe cold of an icy Russian climate.*

≋ **IN NORTHERN CHINA** during the same period, villages were made up of individual round and square dwellings, each only large enough to house a single family. Here, too, there were sometimes larger buildings which may have been a ceremonial centre for the entire village.

≋ **MAKE A LONG HOUSE**

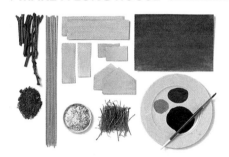

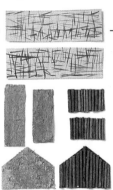

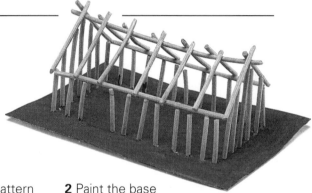

You will need: twigs, cut to 4cm, wooden skewers, paints, hay, plaster powder, grit, glue, cardboard pieces: two, 18 cm x 6 cm, two, 5 cm x 4 cm, one, 13 cm x 4 cm, one, 11cm x 4 cm, two end sections: 9 cm wide x 7 cm at point, base: 25 cm x 14 cm

1 Paint a brown criss-cross pattern onto two roof sections (18 cm x 6 cm). Glue twigs to two smallest side sections of house and to one end section. Mix plaster with grit and water and apply to larger side sections and the other end section.

2 Paint the base brown. Mark house outline, 18 cm x 9 cm, and using the skewer, make holes about every 2 cm around it. Cut skewers to match height of side and end sections. Glue in holes. Cut more for rafters and glue in position.

3 Glue twig and plaster-covered sides to framework as shown. One of the plastered sections is shorter to leave space for a doorway. Glue on roof sections. Glue hay on top.

4 Smear glue on base surround and sprinkle grit or earth on top, so long house looks like it is in a rural setting.

IN 1850, THE REMAINS OF SKARA BRAE, a 5,000-year-old settlement on the west coast of the island of Orkney, off northern Scotland were exposed by a violent sea storm. This semi-subterranean village consists of seven houses linked together by narrow alleyways. These were surrounded by a mound of **midden**, made up of rotten vegetables, dung, bones, stones and shells. This must have been very smelly, but it protected the houses from rough weather.

▷ *One of the houses of Skara Brae.*

dresser used for storage and display

thick walls built from stone slabs collected from the beach

watertight stone box for shellfish

box bed with bracken mattress and skin canopy

THE ROOFS were probably made of turf, perhaps over an underfelt of animal skins, and were supported on whalebone rafters. In the centre, a hole must have been left open to allow smoke to escape from the family hearth below.

INDIVIDUAL HOUSES were roughly square and consisted of one main room with alcoves set into the walls. These may have been for storage, though some have drains running underneath them so could have been used as toilets. Doorways, only one metre high and half a metre wide, were closed by a stone slab held in place with a wooden or whalebone bar. Their small size was probably the best way to keep Orkney's freezing winds at bay.

△ *Today, a narrow stretch of sand separates Skara Brae from the sea. But when people lived there, sand dunes kept the village some distance from the water.*

FURNITURE from the Stone Age is rare, but it survives at Skara Brae because it was built of stone. The large boxes against the wall are thought to be beds. People may have used bracken and heather to make mattresses and animal-skin blankets to keep warm.

WALL CUPBOARDS or recesses above the beds may have been where personal trinkets were kept. A dresser, with stone slab shelves and legs, was found facing the door in every house. It was most likely to have been the main place to store things such as cooking pots, large containers and animal hides.

THE HEARTH in the middle of the main room would have both heated the house and been used to cook over. Wood was probably too precious to burn, so fuel would have been a mixture of animal dung, dried seaweed and grasses, and even whalebone.

THE BOXES by the hearth have been sealed with clay to make them watertight. As the people of Skara Brae would have fished a lot, they could have been used for soaking limpets for fishbait.

From fur to fabric

Stone Age people first wore clothing to provide protection from the elements, especially the bitter cold. Skins and furs were best for this, but they also acted as a means of camouflage for hunters and warriors. Later, as clothing became more sophisticated, it could show a person's rank in society. Clay figurines, cave paintings and remains found in well-preserved burials, give us some idea of what Stone Age people wore.

SKINS AND FURS were worn by early people because they were warm and available. First, flint scrapers were used to clean the fat, grease and dried blood off the inside of the skins. They were then washed and stretched as they dried. By rubbing with smoothed stones and bones, the skins could be kept soft and supple.

TAILORING GARMENTS from skins involved flint knives to cut them up, and flint or bone awls to punch holes for sewing the pieces together. Bone needles and twine made from sinews or vegetable fibre were used to stitch the skins together.

MAKE A STONE AGE OUTFIT

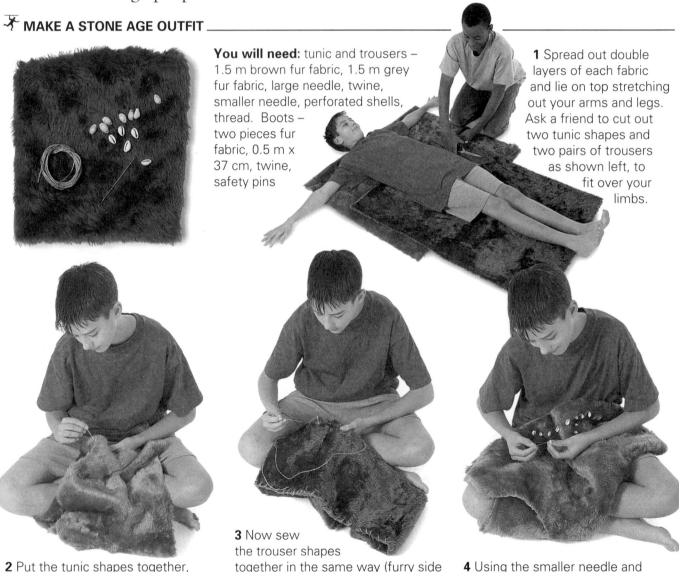

You will need: tunic and trousers – 1.5 m brown fur fabric, 1.5 m grey fur fabric, large needle, twine, smaller needle, perforated shells, thread. Boots – two pieces fur fabric, 0.5 m x 37 cm, twine, safety pins

1 Spread out double layers of each fabric and lie on top stretching out your arms and legs. Ask a friend to cut out two tunic shapes and two pairs of trousers as shown left, to fit over your limbs.

2 Put the tunic shapes together, with the furry side facing out. Thread the large needle with twine and sew the two together.

3 Now sew the trouser shapes together in the same way (furry side out). Your stitches can be large and uneven as this is how Stone Age people would have sewn them.

4 Using the smaller needle and thread, sew some shells onto the front of tunic and, if you like, down outside edges of the trouser legs.

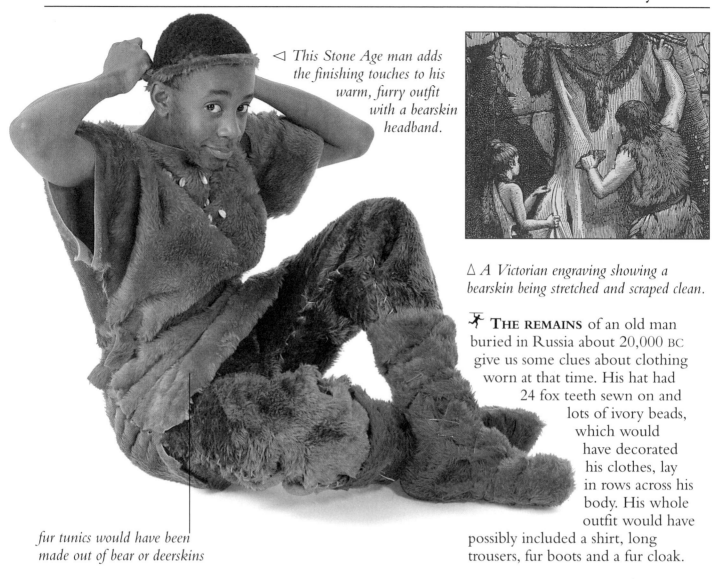

◁ *This Stone Age man adds the finishing touches to his warm, furry outfit with a bearskin headband.*

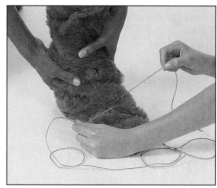

△ *A Victorian engraving showing a bearskin being stretched and scraped clean.*

THE REMAINS of an old man buried in Russia about 20,000 BC give us some clues about clothing worn at that time. His hat had 24 fox teeth sewn on and lots of ivory beads, which would have decorated his clothes, lay in rows across his body. His whole outfit would have possibly included a shirt, long trousers, fur boots and a fur cloak.

fur tunics would have been made out of bear or deerskins

MAKE THE BOOTS

1 Place one piece of fur on the floor (furry side down). Slip 1.2 m twine under it near the front leaving even lengths on both sides. Put your foot on the fur towards the front.

2 Ask a friend to help you fold the fur securely over your foot, starting at the front. Pin to hold in place. Continue to fold and tuck the fur up your leg until you reach the top.

3 Cross twine over your foot and ankle and criss-cross all the way to the top of fur, pulling in tightly (but so boot feels comfortable) as you go. Tie and cut off surplus twine.

MAKING FABRIC WAS A BIG STEP forward in producing clothes. It offered lots of new and different textures and the opportunity to dye in various colours and to make patterns within the material. Along with jewellery, it meant that Stone Age people could decorate themselves and think more about their appearance.

🌾 **THE EARLIEST FIBRES** used by humans to make clothing may have been the plant fibres made into cord about 10,000 BC in Peru and Utah, USA. By stitching long lengths of it to a belt, cord could be used to make a skirt.

▷ *A Neolithic woman spinning wool. She is wearing a linen dress and a decorated purse. It is believed that people sometimes used clay stamps to apply patterns, similar to the one on this purse, to plain cloth.*

🌾 **MAKE A PATTERNED PURSE**

stone bead and tooth nekclace

undyed wool

spindle with weight

purse with stamp

coloured border

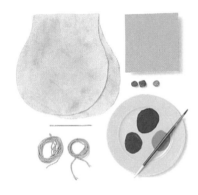

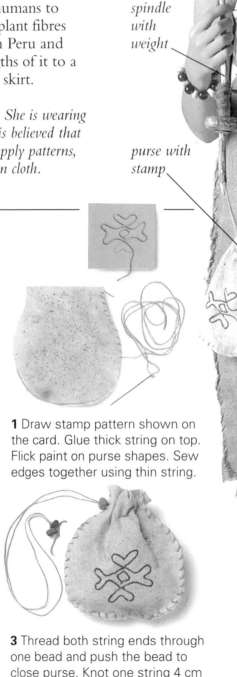

You will need: two pieces calico cut in purse shape as shown, stiff card, 12 cm square, beads, thick and thin string, paints, glue

1 Draw stamp pattern shown on the card. Glue thick string on top. Flick paint on purse shapes. Sew edges together using thin string.

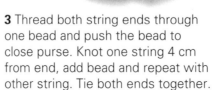

2 Paint stamp pattern red and print it on the purse. Thread thin string through the top with long stitches, leaving long lengths at either end.

3 Thread both string ends through one bead and push the bead to close purse. Knot one string 4 cm from end, add bead and repeat with other string. Tie both ends together.

❧ **IN TURKEY BY 6000 BC,** wool was being spun on simple spindles with weights (or whorls), and flax was being harvested to make linen. Further east in China, a plant fibre called **hemp** was being used to make cloth by 2000 BC.

❧ **DYEING AND WEAVING** were probably invented as early as spinning. On simple looms which lay flat rather than stood upright, wool was woven into cloth. Flowers, leaves and tree bark were used to dye materials in reds, yellows and browns. Minerals produced greens and blues. Figurines showing women in dresses and skirts with zig-zag and chequered patterns, suggest that the Stone Age weavers soon learned how to make good use of their coloured wools.

JEWELLERY, worn by men, women and children, consisted mainly of necklaces. People made these by stringing perforated seashells, animal teeth or beads of soft stone, such as amber, on cord or twine. Sometimes, pendants were hung from the centre of a necklace.

SOME SEASHELLS were so valued they were traded over great distances. The teeth of wolves and bears may have been worn to demonstrate the skill and bravery of hunters.

△ *This jewellery from Mehrgarh, India, was made around 7000 BC from bone, shell and limestone beads.*

BODY PAINTING was probably common but there is little evidence to prove it. The 'paint' would have been made by grinding up ochre and black pigments mixed with animal fat, and then adding water. A lump of red ochre found with some sharp needles in a cave in the Pyrenees suggests that tattooing may have been practised since 9000 BC.

MAKE A NECKLACE

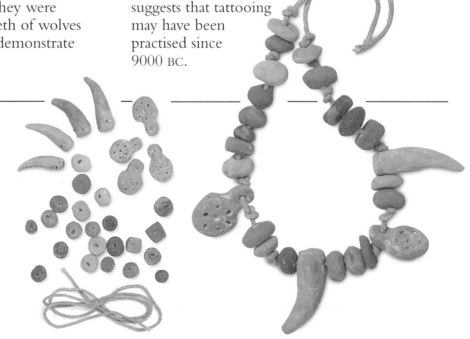

You will need: self-hardening clay, string, paints (natural colours), thick needle

1 Roll the clay into rough bead and teeth shapes as shown. Make holes in the beads with a needle. Leave to dry. Paint the beads, rubbing the wet paint to give wishy-washy look.

2 Paint the string yellow. Thread beads, knotting at irregular intervals. Make a knot before the first bead and another after the last. Leave enough string at both ends to tie.

Hunting, fishing and farming

Prehistoric rubbish dumps are important sources of information about what Stone Age people ate. Butchered bones tell us the creatures that were used for meat. Seeds, shells and charred cereal grains reveal what plants and fruits were gathered or grown. Human skeletons may show wear and decay in teeth revealing the food that was eaten.

🐘 OUR MOST ANCIENT ANCESTORS were partly scavengers and partly hunters. In the beginning, they probably obtained most of the meat in their diet by scavenging the remains of animals that had been killed by other carnivores. They would have used their stone hand axes more to cut up carcasses than to make a kill.

△ *These Neolithic stone spearheads and arrowheads were found in different parts of Britain.*

🏃 MAKE A SPEAR AND SPEAR-THROWER

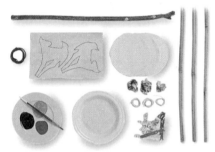

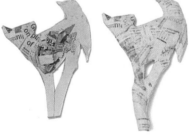

You will need: newspaper, flour and water paste, string, glue, three calico circles, card, three pieces bamboo, 67 cm long, wood, 50 cm long, paint, paper, craft knife, leather thong

1 Cut out the deer and bird shapes from card, and glue together. Build up with papier-mâché using tiny strips of newspaper. Use enough layers to make the bird's tail solid but still able to fit in bamboo.

2 Ask an adult to help you cut a slit in the top of the wood using a craft knife. Insert the animal shape and glue. Blend the join with papier-mâché. Paint. Tie thong to the other end.

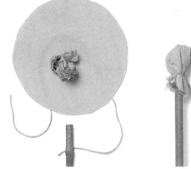

3 For the spears, glue a ball of newspaper on the end of each bamboo pole. Place a calico circle on top and tie with string to secure.

4 Slot tail of the bird into hollow bamboo. To throw spear, wrap the leather thong around your wrist, hold spear-thrower up above your shoulder and hurl spear at a target.

TAKE CARE – NEVER THROW SPEARS AT A LIVING THING.

To use: make a target of some wild animals you have painted, such as mammoths, woolly rhino and cave bears. Pin them to a tree or a tall fence, stand back and fire!

▽ *The remains of a fishtrap like this, dating from 4000 BC, were found in a bog site in Denmark.*

🏃 **WEAPONS AND WAYS FOR CATCHING** animals were gradually developed by early humans. The first spears were made of wood with a tip hardened by charring in a fire. By 15,000 BC, wooden and bone spear-throwers were being used to give hunters greater power and range. Often, these were carved with animal designs.

🌾 **BOWS AND ARROWS** came increasingly into use after the ice age. Bows of yew and elm, about two metres long, and feather-flighted pine arrows, have been found in northern Europe from 8000 BC.

Spears and bows and arrows were used for fishing too, but after the ice age new methods were developed. In Denmark around 5000 BC, basketwork traps were laid in rivers and bone hooks on lines were used. In Scandinavia and Japan, nets made of twine were weighted with stone rings to catch sea fish.

spear-thrower attached to wrist

SHELLFISH were another source of seafood, and dumps or middens of shells are found around coastal zones all over the world. Shell middens can be huge. Some discovered in Europe measure 100 metres by 40 metres and are up to three metres deep.

hunter launches spear using spear-thrower

🏃🌾 **A SEASONAL CYCLE** involved gathering shellfish as well as collecting summer fruits, nuts and edible plants. Communities in eastern Japan followed a cycle like this from 10,000 BC. Middens indicate that over 30 species of shellfish were eaten. Plant food was an important part of the diet too: over 180 types of plant have been identified from various Japanese settlements.

◁ *Spear-throwers enabled Stone Age hunters to kill bigger prey from further away.*

❦ **THE CHANGE FROM HUNTING** to farming was a long process and happened at different times everywhere. It first occurred 10,000 years ago in the **Fertile Crescent** – an arc of land from southern Iraq and Iran northwards, through Syria and down through Lebanon and Palestine. Farming emerged separately in Europe, North Africa, China and New Guinea before 6000 BC and in South America in 5000 BC.

▽ *A central European farming village in autumn.*

fields being ploughed for the next sowing

rubbish pit

△ *Cereals grew wild in the Fertile Crescent which may have encouraged farming to develop there first.*

long house where families live

WILD FORMS OF WHEAT AND BARLEY grew naturally around the Fertile Crescent, so people may have started sowing these near to their homes where they could be looked after easily. Watering and weeding, and selecting the best grains to sow, eventually led to bigger grains and more crops. Later, where conditions allowed, pulses and legumes, such as lentils and peas, were grown in the Fertile Crescent too.

THE FIRST CROPS TO BE FARMED varied from country to country. Millet and rice were grown in China, taro (a root crop) and bananas in New Guinea, maize (corn) in South America and squash, peppers and avocados in Mexico.

FARMING HAD A MAJOR impact on people's lifestyles. It meant they had to settle in one place and tend their crops. They also had to look after their newly domesticated, or tamed, animals in order to breed or rear them for meat and milk.

In winter, food supplies had to be stored and protective shelters built. As a result, early farming was often accompanied by the growth of permanent settlements – either farms or villages.

But in some areas where there was lots of wild food to support the population, the switch to farming was very gradual. Hunting and gathering was so successful in southern Africa for example, that people continued to practise it there up until just a few hundred years ago.

wooden trackway

fishing net drying

animal skin drying

covered working area

river for water and fish supplies

sheep pen

LEARNING HOW TO MAKE FIRE was one of the human race's major discoveries. Early hominids would have found animals cooked by bush fires and may even have used the embers of these fires for light and heat. But evidence of hearths, in caves and open sites in Europe and Asia, show that it wasn't until 300,000 years ago that fire-lighting was discovered.

BY GATHERING TINDER – dry grass and small pieces of dry wood and bark – and rubbing two sticks vigorously against each other in the centre of the tinder, a fire can be started in minutes.

BY PERHAPS 4000 BC, in both Eurasia and America, the process of making fire had become easier as people were using bow-drills. These were small bows (about 30 cm long). The string was twisted around a stick standing upright in the tinder, which was rotated back and forth very fast. Fragments of these bow-drills have been found in the Guitarrero Cave in Peru.

COOKING WITHOUT USING POTS was common for Stone Age people. Meat was either roasted on a spit over a fire, or baked in the embers by wrapping it in large leaves.

▷ *Preparing a cooked meal in Neolithic Europe – the use of a bow-drill made fire-lighting easier*

bow-drill being used to light fire

bark container

tinder made up of dry wood and bark

❧ MAKE A BOW-DRILL

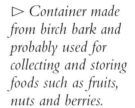

You will need: string, dowelling, self-hardening clay, block of wood, bendy willow twig, paints, craft knife

NEVER USE A BOW-DRILL WITHOUT AN ADULT. FIRES CAN CAUSE ACCIDENTS.

1 Mould the clay into an oval blob. Make a dent in the side. When dry, paint it to look like a stone. Ask an adult to help you cut a small hole in centre of the wood and to sharpen one end of the dowel to fit into this.

2 Tie string to one end of the twig. Lie twig across middle of the dowel. Wrap string around dowel and tie it to the other end of the twig, allowing twig to bend a bit.

3 Hold the clay stone, dent side down, and fit it into top of dowel. Place pointed dowel end in hole in wood. Twist it fast to make fire.

▷ *Container made from birch bark and probably used for collecting and storing foods such as fruits, nuts and berries.*

clay pots used for storing fruit, vegetables and grains

PRE-HEATED STONES, known as pot boilers, were also used. They could heat water in skin containers before food was boiled in them. Or they could be placed in shallow ground with food and then covered with earth.

❧ **CLAY POTS** for cooking or storing food were another great step forward. People started making them soon after the beginnings of farming. Because clay pots do not catch fire, they could be put directly on a hearth or in an oven and food could be safely left to cook in them for long periods at an even temperature.

🌾 **ONCE PEOPLE SET UP FARMS,** they could eat meat more regularly. Sheep and goats were the earliest domesticated animals reared for their meat, though they continued to live wild around the Fertile Crescent. The wild pig and wild forms of cattle were domesticated across Eurasia by 6000 BC.

EVEN WITHOUT MEAT, the prehistoric diet was surprisingly varied. And with the use of fire, food could be prepared in different ways too. Vegetables and plants could be boiled together into stews, and fruit could be poached or preserved in jams and jellies.

◁ *Early digging sticks were weighted at one end and used to dig up edible plants.*

🌾 **TRANSFORMING THE EARS** of edible grasses into flour to make bread is one of the many achievements of early farmers. The first fields were dug with hoes from forked branches or digging sticks with one pointed end and a stone weight at the other. But by 3000 BC, cattle-drawn ploughs usually made of branches with a hardened tip of wood, were in use in Europe, the Near East and China.

goat   *cow*

pig   *sheep*

△ *These wild creatures are believed to look very similar to the earliest domesticated animals.*

🌾 **SICKLES FOR HARVESTING** wild grasses appeared in Egypt around 15,000 BC. They had bone or wooden handles with short flint blades set in them. The same models remained in use for thousands of years in many parts of the world.

🐘 **MAKE A WILD FRUIT COMPOTE**

You will need: blackberries, redcurrants, sloes, plums, apple, honey, small saucepan, wooden spoon

1 Wash the fruit. Ask an adult to help you peel, core and chop the apple and to chop the plums. Put all the fruit in the pan and, with an adult present, cook gently for 10 minutes until the fruits soften.

2 Stir in honey to sweeten (one or two tablespoons will be enough) and continue stewing for another few minutes. Eat warm or cold by itself or with cream or yoghurt.

◁ *This flint sickle was found in the River Thames in London. It could be as much as 6,000 years old.*

AFTER THE CORN was **threshed** and **winnowed**, the grains were ground down. Neolithic farmers everywhere used a quern, a large flat stone, and a smaller oval stone pestle for doing this. The daily grinding of grain into a coarse flour by rubbing it backwards and forwards on the quern using the pestle, gradually wore down the centre of the millstones. That is why they are sometimes referred to as saddle-querns.

Stone Age people probably used large shells as dishes where they were available

BAKING OVENS WERE AN EARLY invention of Neolithic farmers and they appear at Abu Hureyra in Syria around 9000 BC and Jarmo in Iraq around 6000 BC. Made of mud or mud-brick, they are usually round or horseshoe-shaped and have a dome roof.

FLOUR WAS MIXED WITH WATER to make dough which was moulded into loaves and baked in these ovens. The same dough was used to make smaller, flat drop scones. These were cooked on a stone hot-plate over an open fire.

▷ *Enjoying a tasty compote: fruits used would have varied according to the season.*

Ancient art

Some of the finest Stone Age art still survives today in the cave and rock paintings and engravings in parts of Europe, Asia, Africa and Australia. In Europe alone, over 200 caves with examples of this art have been found.

🏃 **THE EARLIEST CAVE PAINTINGS** are from France, possibly dating back to 30,000 BC. Examples found in Saharan Africa were first painted around 20,000 BC, while the earliest Australian rock art may be even older.

Many cave paintings in Spain or France are found deep in caves where there is no natural light. The painters must have worked in the flickering light of brushwood torches, or lamps made by burning fur or moss soaked in animal fat. They applied their paint with either their fingers or 'brushes' made of hair.

△ *Hunters armed with bows and arrows were painted on the rocks at Valltorta, Spain around 6000 BC.*

THE EARTHY COLOURS they used – red, yellow, brown and black – came from minerals such as ochre, manganese and charcoal. These were ground to a powder and mixed with animal fat to make a sticky paint which stuck to cave walls and ceilings. The colours are still bright even though they were painted 30,000 years ago.

PICTURES OF ANIMALS, similar to those painted on the walls, are sometimes found carved on stone slabs or bone. They may have been sketches that the artists used to paint from.

IN EUROPE, the cave artists painted animals far more than humans (hunters feature more in later Spanish rock art). Horses, bison, deer and mammoths are the most common, but woolly rhino, cave bears and boars are also depicted.

🌾 **LATER, SAHARAN** rock art reflects the move from hunting and gathering to farming. Paintings dating from 6000 BC show domestic cattle and dogs rather than hunting scenes and wild animals.

▽ *Cave art creatures.*

horse

reindeer

ibex

auroch (wild cow)

▷ *A painted bull and horse in the Lascaux caves in south-west France. The magnificent paintings there were discovered by four boys and their dog in 1940.*

THE MYSTERY OF THE MEANING of cave paintings still remains. Some archaeologists believe cave art was involved in magical ceremonies related to hunting. This is because many images are of animals, some with spears in them, that Stone Age people hunted. Other less clear images could be male and female symbols which were linked to **fertility rites**.

▽ *A copy of a European cave painting showing commonly hunted animals.*

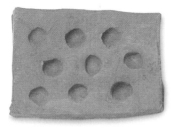

🐘 **STONE WAS THE FIRST MATERIAL** that our ancestors learned to make things with, as far back as two million years ago. The first carved wooden implements known are a spear from England dating from around 300,000 BC and a club from Kenya from about 200,000 BC.

🏃 **BONE AND IVORY** started to be used by hunters in Southern Europe towards the end of the last ice age. Mostly, this was for tools and weapons such as awls, spatulas and harpoons. They also made ivory figurines of women that were often fat with exaggerated features. These are known as Venus figurines because they are thought to represent the mother goddess. Bone and ivory were used for modelling animals too.

🌾 **NEOLITHIC FARMERS** continued the tradition of carving by making animal-headed sickles. They also carved everyday artefacts out of bone, such as fish-hooks, needles, combs and pendants.

△ *Here are some of the different designs and patterns used to decorate Stone Age pots. They include cuts, grooves, holes, strokes and thumb prints.*

🌾 **THE EARLIEST KNOWN POTTERY** comes from Japan and dates back to about 10,500 BC. The Chinese started making pots soon after. Because pottery is both heavy and breakable, it only appears where people lived in settled societies.

The first pottery vessels were made by pressing a lump of clay between thumb and fingers and gradually shaping it. People soon started making larger, stronger pots by coiling a strip of clay into a spiral to build up the walls, and then smoothing the sides. Initially, they experimented with firing their pots briefly in their ovens or in bonfires, but the first kilns appeared before 6000 BC in Iran.

🌾 **MAKE A COIL POT**

You will need: self-hardening clay, plastic knife or spatula

1 Roll out long sausages from the clay. Coil these into a round base.

2 Now coil another sausage up from the base, smoothing the outside so that the coils merge. Repeat to build up your pot. Make a pattern around top using a knife edge.

STONE AGE POTTERS decorated their pots in different ways. They made markings by pressing a shell edge, a pointed stick, a length of cord or their fingertip into the soft clay before it was fired. Alternatively, they would make a pattern with a bone point or flint blade, or draw a bone comb across the clay to give it a ridged surface.

MANY NEOLITHIC POTTERS painted their pots, usually in red or black, in a wide variety of patterns. Others polished the surface to make them less porous. At the Neolithic site of Banpo in northern China (see page 17), about 500,000 pieces of pottery were recovered. Six kilns were also discovered on the settlement. Many of the bowls and jars were painted with vivid black designs.

▷ *A potter uses a pointed stick to decorate her unfired pot.*

WOODEN BOXES and baskets provided an alternative to pottery containers. However, because these materials are perishable, it is hard to tell how common they were. Rectangular boxes of wood, as well as shallow bowls, were in use at Catal Huyuk in Turkey before 6000 BC. By this time, hunters and fishers in north-west Europe, Mexico and Oregon, USA were weaving baskets of vegetable fibres or twigs. Woven matting, made from reeds, was also known at this time in the Near East.

▷ *Examples of the characteristic designs of Neolithic northern Chinese pottery.*

red clay —

black paint —

Special occasions

The music, dancing and feasting practised by later Stone Age people were not purely for entertainment. People probably believed that music and dance would ensure a good hunt or a plentiful harvest. Feasting meant people could get together and individuals could gain prestige by providing the food.

🏃 **THE OLDEST MUSICAL** instrument yet found is a bone whistle of about 45,000 BC from Libya. Similar whistles, with just one finger hole and blow hole bored into an animal's toe bone, were used in Europe by 30,000 BC. These could only give out a single, high-pitched sound.

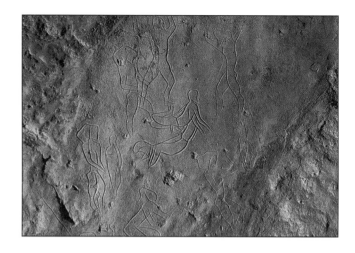

△ *This is a rock engraving from Addaura, Sicily that dates from 9000 BC. The swaying figures are thought to be men and women performing a ritual dance.*

⚜ MAKE A GOURD RATTLE

You will need: balloon, paper strips, flour and water paste, paints, needle and twine, pasta, glue, newspaper, sandpaper, craft knife

1 Cover blown-up balloon in three layers of papier-mâché.Once dry, pop the balloon. For a stalk, roll a piece of newspaper and wrap it with papier-mâché. Glue to gourd. When dry, smooth gourd with sandpaper.

2 Paint white undercoat, dry, then paint yellowy-green. Ask an adult to help you cut a curvy line around the top. Remove the lid and put a scoop of pasta into the rattle. Oversew lid to the main shell, keeping stitches long and loose. Finally, pull stitches tightly to secure the lid in place.

⚜ MAKE A NEOLITHIC DRUM

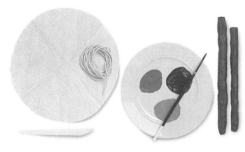

You will need: self-hardening clay, large needle, twine, circle of calico, paints, plastic knife, twigs

1 Make a pot as shown on page 38. Cut the twigs to make drumsticks.

2 Speckle paint on the calico so it looks like skin. Paint pattern around edge. Thread the needle with long length of twine. Sew through near edge of fabric, take under drum and up through the fabric on the other side. Continue until skin sits tightly on drum and knot.

rattles made of gourds

🏃 **RUSSIAN** archaeologists believe that the oldest group of musical instruments in existence may be the painted mammoth bones found at Mezin in The Ukraine. A shoulder blade, played with an antler hammer, sounds like a drum. A hip bone could be played like a xylophone and jaw bones could make an effective castanet. This collection of possible musical instruments dates from 15,000 BC.

🎵 **DRUMS OF WOOD** with skin stretched across their necks were probably used by Neolithic musicians. It is thought that tall, Neolithic pots with broad necks and cord-like decoration around their shoulders may be imitations of wooden drums. Extra rhythm may have been added by rattles made out of gourds filled with gravel, dried beans or fruit stones.

🏃 🎵 **STONE AGE MUSIC** was almost certainly created to accompany dancing. A careful study of the footprints of Palaeolithic teenagers in a French cave suggests they were performing a dance. And a rock engraving on a cave wall at Addaura in Sicily, from about 9000 BC, depicts swaying people who were probably dancing.

decorated drum played with twig drumsticks

Understanding each other

The earliest hominids had ape-like voice boxes and could not speak as we do. They must have communicated, like apes and monkeys, by a combination of sounds, facial expressions and hand gestures. Very gradually, as the human brain and skull developed, came the need and ability to speak.

✳ **HOMO SAPIENS** was the first of our ancestors with a larynx (containing the vocal chords) in a similar position to ours. So although there is no proof, experts usually agree that early humans were speaking to each other by 50,000 BC. Some argue that the amount of knowledge which one generation was clearly passing to the next by around 250,000 BC must have been through speech, although it would have been very basic.

CAVE AND ROCK PAINTINGS were a way of communicating by different kinds of images, either with the spirits or other living people. The idea of drawing pictures of a creature or an object is behind all the earliest forms of writing. But the cave artists of 20,000 BC went a step further when they drew the symbols which archaeologists believe they used for male and female. In doing this, they created a primitive **ideogram**, where a sign represents an idea.

◁ *Painted pebbles that looked like these may have been used as counters.*

✳ **RECORDING NUMBERS** of things may have been the first written records that humans kept. From around 30,000 to 10,000 BC, many bones from human occupation sites in Europe carry man-made marks.

✳ ﾞ These are usually in groups of dots or short straight lines. They look like tallies, where ancient man has kept a record of numbers. Around 8000 BC in the Pyrenees, painted pebbles may have been tallies, although the signs on these could have been magic symbols.

ﾞ MAKE A PAINTED CAVE WALL

You will need: fine chicken wire, 1 m x 0.5 m, flour and water paste, newspaper strips, paints, diffuse tube, jam jar, sticky tape

1 Turn the edges of the wire under all round and work the wire to create a slightly uneven surface to resemble a rough cave wall.

2 Cover the wire with three layers of papier-mâché. Leave to dry.

3 Tape newspaper to a wall and tape the cave wall on top. Paint surface greyish. Water down orange paint in a jam jar. Ask a friend to place his/her hand on cave wall. Put diffuse tube in paint and blow out over hand to leave outline. Repeat.

✗ ❦ **PERSONAL IDENTITY** may have been expressed by cave artists when they spray-painted around their hands on cave walls. One cave in Argentina has a wall covered in hundreds of hand outlines. They are thought to have been done by horse hunters, between 9000 and 7000 BC.

❦ **A SIMPLE CLAY OR STONE STAMP** with a distinctive design on it which may have been a personal mark was carried by some people in the Neolithic. These stamps have been found in Turkey and south-east Europe before 5000 BC. Shortly after this, potters in south-east Europe began to sign pots with engraved marks and this may have led to an early written sign language seen on circular clay tablets about 4000 BC.

△ *Spray-painted hands found in Cave of the Hands in Argentina. They are at least 9,000 years old.*

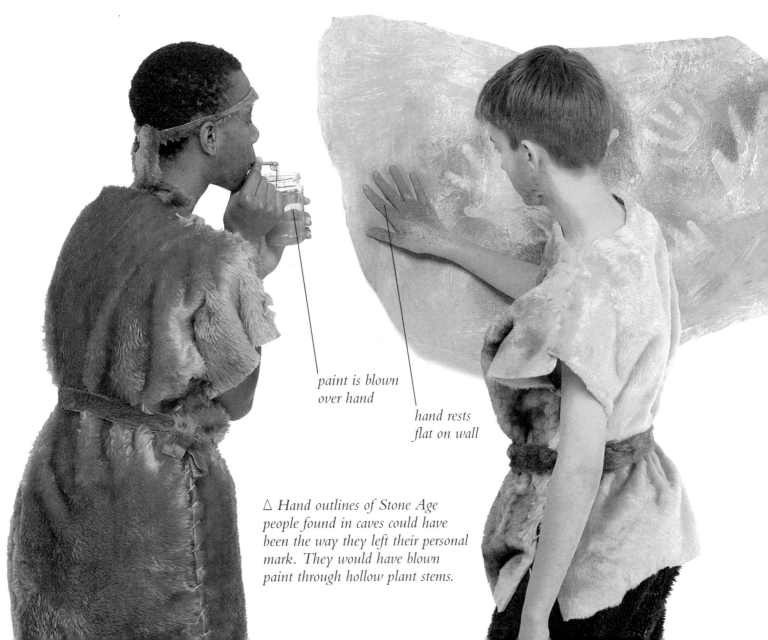

paint is blown over hand

hand rests flat on wall

△ *Hand outlines of Stone Age people found in caves could have been the way they left their personal mark. They would have blown paint through hollow plant stems.*

On the move

By 50,000 BC the first humans had reached Sahul – the land mass made up of what is now New Guinea and Australia – by island-hopping from south-east Asia. At that time the sea level was much lower than it is today, but the journey would still have involved sea-crossings of up to 100 kilometres.

✗ **SIMPLE OUTRIGGER CANOES** were probably used by these earliest seafarers. By 30,000 BC they were making longer crossings of over 100 kilometres to colonize New Britain and New Ireland (off the coast of New Guinea). For this, the outriggers had probably been fitted with a sail and a riding platform, and could carry eight or 10 people and their essential supplies.

❧ **HOW STONE AGE BOATS** were constructed depended mainly on the raw materials that were available. In southern Mesopotamia (now Iraq) there were no trees, but reeds grew abundantly.

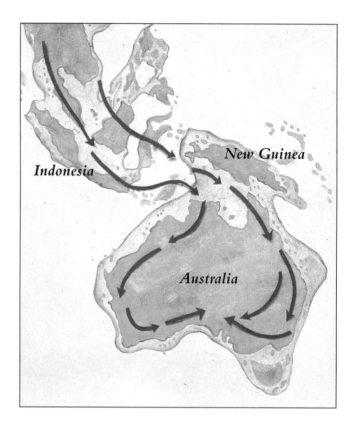

△ *These are the two possible land and sea routes the first humans took to reach New Guinea and Australia.*

△ *An arctic kayak with sealskin covering over wooden frame. Seal oil was applied to make vessel waterproof.*

These were gathered and tied into bundles, and the bundles then skilfully lashed together to make a boat which was basically a raft with upturned ends. By the end of the Neolithic, similar boats in Egypt had been improved by adding a mast and a small square sail.

❧ **WOOD WAS SCARCE** in arctic North America too. So the people there used it carefully, building narrow kayaks for single fishermen and umiaks (larger boats) for groups of fishers.

Both boats were covered with sealskins sewn together and stretched over a light frame made out of driftwood or whalebone. They were easy to manoeuvre and probably propelled with wooden paddles.

bow

❧ MAKE A REED BOAT

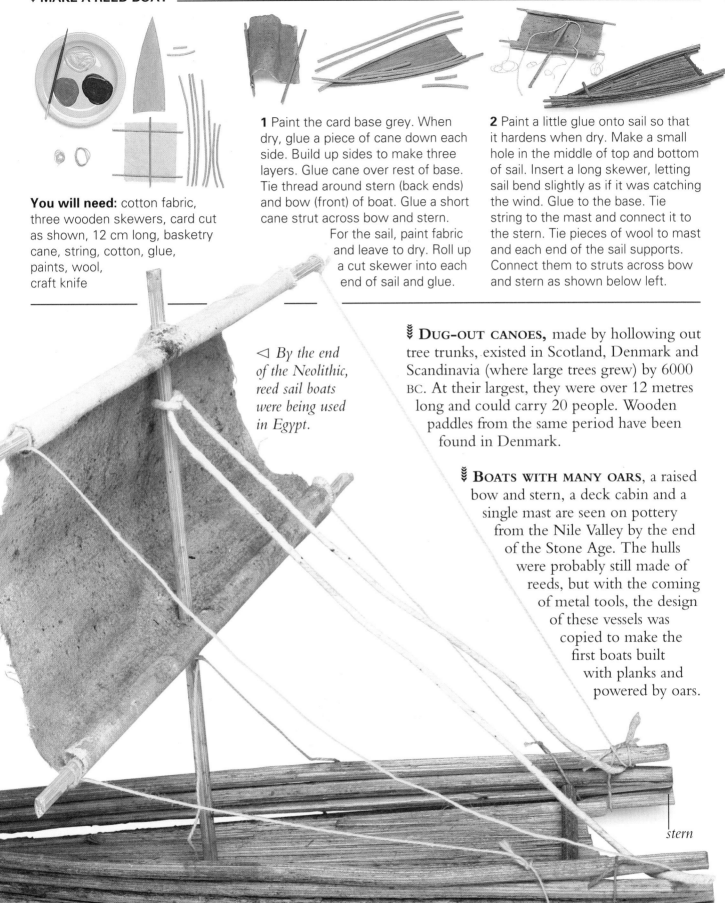

You will need: cotton fabric, three wooden skewers, card cut as shown, 12 cm long, basketry cane, string, cotton, glue, paints, wool, craft knife

1 Paint the card base grey. When dry, glue a piece of cane down each side. Build up sides to make three layers. Glue cane over rest of base. Tie thread around stern (back ends) and bow (front) of boat. Glue a short cane strut across bow and stern.
For the sail, paint fabric and leave to dry. Roll up a cut skewer into each end of sail and glue.

2 Paint a little glue onto sail so that it hardens when dry. Make a small hole in the middle of top and bottom of sail. Insert a long skewer, letting sail bend slightly as if it was catching the wind. Glue to the base. Tie string to the mast and connect it to the stern. Tie pieces of wool to mast and each end of the sail supports. Connect them to struts across bow and stern as shown below left.

◁ *By the end of the Neolithic, reed sail boats were being used in Egypt.*

❧ **DUG-OUT CANOES,** made by hollowing out tree trunks, existed in Scotland, Denmark and Scandinavia (where large trees grew) by 6000 BC. At their largest, they were over 12 metres long and could carry 20 people. Wooden paddles from the same period have been found in Denmark.

❧ **BOATS WITH MANY OARS**, a raised bow and stern, a deck cabin and a single mast are seen on pottery from the Nile Valley by the end of the Stone Age. The hulls were probably still made of reeds, but with the coming of metal tools, the design of these vessels was copied to make the first boats built with planks and powered by oars.

stern

OUR REMOTE ANCESTORS tended to walk great distances as the changing seasons and climates sent them in search of food. This travelling became more demanding as they acquired belongings and had to find ways of carrying them. Once people began to settle permanently in one place, they came to rely on others who would travel to find raw materials not available locally.

PACK ANIMALS were important as there were no roads and this made walking with heavy goods hard. Creatures that carried loads on their backs were domesticated later than those first reared for meat. Animals all over the world were tamed for back-packing: the ass in north-east Africa in 3500 BC, and the horse in The Ukraine and the llama in the Andes, both 500 years later.

WOODEN SLEDGES were used by hunters and farmers in northern Europe and The Ukraine. Wooden runners from long, narrow sledges that are 8,000 years old have been found in Norway. Clay models of sledges made by Ukrainian farmers around 4000 BC show that the runners were made from planks set on edge and small, round tree trunks. Many of these wooden sledges would have been pulled by humans, but dogs were used once a harness had been devised, perhaps by 2000 BC.

THE FIRST WHEELED VEHICLES appear between 3500 and 3000 BC. They are mostly associated with people who, by that time, had acquired metal wood-working tools. But in western Europe, Neolithic farmers were using wheeled wagons by 3000 BC.

Two-wheeled carts with wheels carved from a single piece of wood are found in Holland and Denmark, and four-wheeled wagons have been discovered in Switzerland. The wheels of the Swiss vehicles are made from three separate pieces of wood held together by cross-pieces.

Ancient clay models from eastern European countries, such as Hungary, show high-sided wagons that farmers may have used to carry large loads of hay or grain.

MAKE A WAGON CUP

You will need: self-hardening clay, rolled out to 0.5 cm thick; paints, plastic knife or spatula, glue

1 Cut four side sections from the clay, 5 cm across bottom, 10 cm deep and fluting out to 7 cm across top. Cut handle, 1.5 cm x 10 cm, and four wheels, 2 cm in diameter.

2 When clay has hardened slightly, mark the cup sides and wheels as shown above.

3 Glue sides to base. Shape handle and glue to the cup. Leave to dry.

4 Glue the wheels to the cup. Paint the cup metallic yellow. Use orange to highlight the pattern.

◁ *A pottery wagon cup similar to this was found in a grave in Hungary dating from 4000 BC.*

CROSSING MARSHY ground using wagons or sledges would have been difficult. In south-west England and Holland, roads or trackways built between 4000 and 3000 BC would have made the task quite a lot easier.

◁ *The South American llama was used as a pack animal and could carry heavy loads of up to 60 kilogrammes.*

❧ **THE EARLIEST ROADS** were rather flimsy walkways of planks, pegged onto a narrow raft of wooden stakes, about one metre wide. Others are lengths of hurdle-work (interwoven branches and twigs) laid across a marshy area. The most hardy, that could have been used for cattle-driving, were made of small tree-trunks laid edge to edge on a brushwood foundation.

◁ *A purpose-built track makes a long trek across marshy land easier for this Stone Age man, especially as he's taking his belongings too.*

cloth and hides

tree trunks laid on brushwood foundation form a solid track

Fighting off the enemy

Once people started making weapons, they had the means of attack as well as defence. Then, as populations grew and conflict between groups of people competing for food and land increased, defended settlements began to spring up.

❧ **THE RESULT OF A BATTLE** fought in the Nile Valley about 10,000 BC was unearthed at Jebel Sahaba. Of 58 skeletons buried in a communal cemetery, over 20 had died violently. Fragments of spear or arrowheads were still embedded in their bones, and deep cut marks suggested that they were finished off with flint knives or axes.

❧ **MORE SOPHISTICATED WEAPONS** started to appear during the Neolithic. Danish farmers began to make superbly crafted flint daggers and impressive battle-axes. So much trouble was taken over these that they were probably used more as status symbols than as weapons.

▽ *The late Neolithic defended settlement of Dimini in East Thessaly, Greece.*

❧ **DEFENDED SETTLEMENTS** appear in south-east Europe in the late Neolithic. They were often built on hilltops so the inhabitants could spot attackers quickly. In Thessaly in Greece, villages such as Dimini and Sesklo were defended by stone walls. These were a deterrent more because of their complex layout and the many gates and enclosures, than because of their size.

Dimini, which was built around 4000 BC, bears the standard features of a **fortified** village of this period, including main gates at each end and a courtyard around the main hall.

main hall with columned entrance and a central hearth inside

main courtyard

❦ **THE OLDEST BUILT DEFENCES** in the world are the stone walls built around the settlement of Jericho about 8000 BC. These were over two metres wide and still stand almost four metres high. In at least one place, a stronghold had been built – a huge tower over nine metres high and 10 metres in diameter. Later, a great ditch eight and a half metres wide was added.

We'll never know who the potential enemy was, though some archaeologists believe that the impenetrable defences may have been against flooding rather than groups of invaders.

△ *The round tower of Jericho lies inside the settlement walls. It may have been a watch-tower, built on the highest point to give the widest view.*

gate situated at one end of the settlement

Making magic

Archaeologists are convinced that Stone Age people believed in a spirit world because towards the end of the last ice age they started to deliberately bury their dead. Evidence of food, and remains of tools and weapons found in prehistoric grave sites, shows that they thought these would help the dead survive in the afterlife. It also seems as if Stone Age people expressed their belief in the **supernatural** through art. They may have believed their paintings and pottery had magical powers.

△ *Copies of stone objects found in the prehistoric village of Skara Brae, Orkney. They were probably used in religious rites.*

❦ **SOME HUMAN SKULLS** look as if they were chosen for special treatment before burial. In Jericho, burials dating from around 7000 BC show that skulls were often removed. Stone Age people used these to make portrait skulls by covering them with carefully moulded plaster. To represent eyes, they put cowrie shells in the eye-sockets. These skulls may have been a way that early people worshipped their ancestors. They may also have used them to communicate with gods, displaying and using them in rituals.

❦ **PREHISTORIC BRAIN SURGERY** shows that Stone Age people believed in curing through magic rather than medicine. Skulls with a carefully cut hole in them have been found in western Europe. They first appear in 3000 BC. Stone Age people may have thought that conditions such as severe headaches, epilepsy or madness were caused by evil spirits in the head which needed to be released. Amazingly, many patients are known to have survived the horrific hole-in-the-head operation.

☃ MAKE A REINDEER HEADDRESS

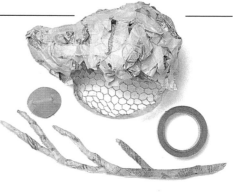

You will need: 1.5 m fur fabric (painted like deerskin), 1.5 m white felt (painted like skin), chicken wire, paper nose and eye shapes, paints, thread, newspaper, flour and water paste, masking tape, glue

1 Cut out fabric and felt to match shape above. Glue felt to underside of fur. Cut out ear shapes as shown. To make reindeer head, mould chicken wire to fit over your head. Fix with masking tape.

2 Tape balls of newspaper all over wire frame to make deer-shaped face. Build up nose with papier-mâché. Roll up newspaper to make two long antlers and shorter branches. Tape together. Build up with newspaper and paste. Paint when dry.

✗ **CAVE PAINTINGS** in France suggest an ancient belief in hunting magic. Some show animals that have been attacked with spears. Others show men, thought to be **shamans**, wearing bison and deer masks. No-one is sure what these figures mean, but perhaps Stone Age people thought that a big hunt would be more successful if they went through the ritual of painting it first.

▷ *A dancing shaman. It is believed that antlers were worn as headdresses during rituals.*

THE SHAMAN, or medicine man, was probably an important figure in hunter-gatherer societies. He may have been chosen for his supernatural powers which he would have probably used to communicate with the dead and nature. He may also have been looked to for curing illnesses. Shamans may have dressed up in skins and antler headdresses to perform their 'magic'.

✗ **VENUS FIGURINES,** found in Europe between 28,000 and 12,000 BC, suggest a belief in female fertility magic. They show that Stone Age people knew how important fertility was for their survival.

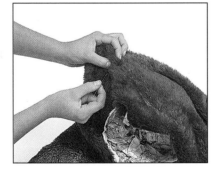

3 Fold up nose and tape. Paint nose and eyes. Fit fur over mask and sew together as shown, tucking in fabric where necessary. Glue on nose and eyes. Sew on ears. Cut holes above ears and secure antlers firmly into headdress.

antler headdress

red ochre was used to decorate different parts of the body

leather anklet adorned with shells

THE EARLIEST SACRED PLACES known to us are the caves and rock shelters where paintings and engravings were made. But almost certainly, the first humans held special ceremonies in and around caves, trees and rock formations. During the Neolithic, rituals started to take place by water beside lakes and rivers, and the first purpose-built shrines and temples appear.

❧ OVER FORTY SHRINES were found in the settlement at Catal Huyuk in Turkey, each one decorated differently. Dating from around 7000 BC, Catal Huyuk is the largest Neolithic site yet discovered (see page 17).

The most impressive features of the shrines are plastered bulls' heads, stone benches with lots of bulls' horns set into them and wall paintings of bulls.

RELIEF models of a fertility goddess, figurines and paintings were also found in the same shrines. The bull and the goddess were probably male and female representatives of a fertility **cult**, or special form of worship.

SOME DECORATIONS also suggest a death cult. In one shrine, pictures show vultures with human legs, thought to be priests in disguise, with a headless corpse lying nearby. In reality, it is possible that priests dressed up as vultures to perform certain rituals.

△ *The trilithons of Stonehenge are arranged around the original prehistoric henge of a ditch and a bank.*

❧ STONEHENGE in England is one of the most famous prehistoric temples. The great stone **trilithons** were erected after the end of the Stone Age in Britain, but the earliest monument at Stonehenge was built before 3000 BC. The first **henges** were oval or circular enclosures with a high earth bank and a very deep ditch. Some henges had stone circles built inside them.

Inside these were circular timber shrines or halls which are believed to have been used for seasonal meetings of large groups of people.

◁ *A vulture headdress like this may have been worn in Catal Huyuk to perform death rituals.*

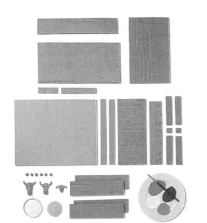

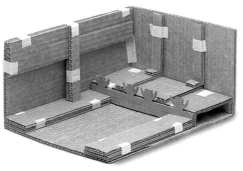

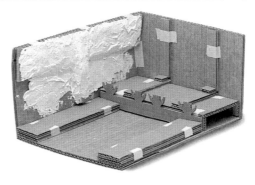

You will need: self-hardening clay, paints, double-sided sticky tape, plaster of Paris, sand, glue, corrugated cardboard cut into: floor, 30 cm x 20 cm, two walls, 30 cm x 15 cm, and 20 cm x 15 cm, altar top, 20 cm x 10 cm, two supports, 20 cm x 3 cm, bench, 20 cm x 6 cm, extra corrugated cardboard for strips

1 Tape together floor and walls to make the shrine shell. Then tape altar supports to each side of altar top. Glue into corner of the shrine. Draw outline of the bulls' heads on the bench and cut around. Glue the bench to the altar front.

2 Cut out more strips of cardboard. Tape them to the shrine to act as wall supports and steps on the floor as shown above.

3 Plaster the walls roughly. Leave to dry. Make the clay bulls' heads and paint when dry. Paint walls creamy-yellow and leave to dry. Then paint on bulls and patterns copying the colours shown. Glue bulls' heads to back wall. Sprinkle sand over floor.

▽ *A decorated shrine similar to the many shrines found at Catal Huyuk in Turkey.*

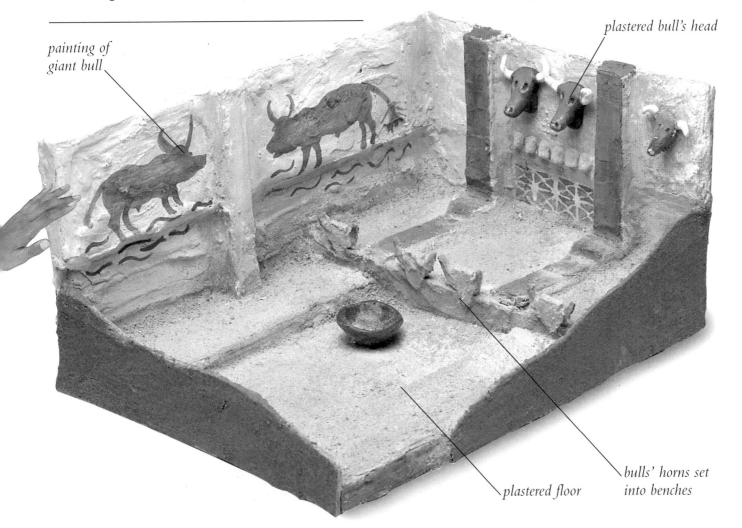

painting of giant bull

plastered bull's head

plastered floor

bulls' horns set into benches

Burial beginnings ___

The earliest human burials were made by Neanderthal man during the last ice age, around 60,000 years ago. These were either in a dug grave or pit, or beneath a mound of earth or stones. They may have been intended both to protect the living from the spirits of the dead and to show respect to the dead.

✣ **A WELL-KNOWN NEANDERTHAL GRAVE SITE** at Shanidar Cave in Iraq, shows that some of the people found there were killed by rocks falling from the roof. However, other bodies there may have been deliberately buried – ashes and food remains discovered among stones heaped over them seem to suggest this. Pollen found in the soil around one 30-year-old man came from eight varieties of early summer flowers, including hollyhocks. It could be that these were picked and sprinkled around his body as part of the funerary rituals, though archaeologists still argue about the evidence!

△ *A Neanderthal male skeleton, about 60,000 years old, found in a deliberately dug pit in Kabara, Israel.*

✣ **A MAN AND TWO YOUNG BOYS,** buried at Sungir near Moscow, were probably highly respected people. The man was in a grave of his own and his clothes were decorated with 3,000 mammoth ivory beads. The two children were buried with ivory spears and ornaments in a single grave just three metres away. Their clothes were decorated with over 5,000 ivory beads. All three bodies had been sprinkled with red ochre.

✾ **PEOPLE FIRST CAMPED** at Roonka Flat Dune in Australia 18,000 years ago. But the earliest burials found there – a series of 12 graves – are thought to be 4,000 to 7,000 years old. The bodies were placed vertically in a shaft hole. Shell and bone pendants were found with them.

◁ *A body is prepared for a Neanderthal burial. The preparations are an important part of the burial ritual.*

man decorates body with powdered red ochre

body is laid out flat while ochre is applied

over the years, ochre decorations may stain bones

❦ **OVER 1,500 NEOLITHIC BURIALS** and graves have been found at the village of Peinan on Taiwan. Here, it was common for people to bury their dead below the floors of their houses in rectangular graves lined with slate. The bodies were laid out with the heads to the west. Most of the adults were accompanied by grave goods.

❦ **VILLAGE CEMETERIES** were becoming common by the end of the Neolithic period. At Tiszapolgar in Hungary, over 150 burials were laid out in rows of rectangular graves.

▷ *This Hungarian pot with a face at the top dates from 4500 BC. This kind of pottery was buried in graves during the Neolithic.*

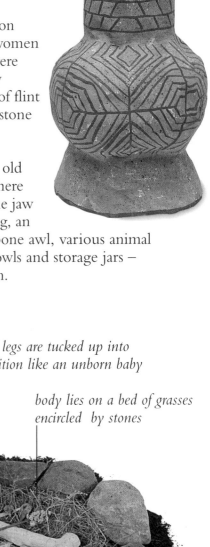

Men were laid out on the right side and women on the left. They were buried with pottery vessels, tools made of flint and **obsidian**, and stone and shell beads.

In the grave of one old man for example, there were flint blades, the jaw of a wild boar, a dog, an antler axe-head, a bone awl, various animal bones, and cups, bowls and storage jars – probably all his own.

flowers are laid all over dead man's body

arms and legs are tucked up into foetal position like an unborn baby

body lies on a bed of grasses encircled by stones

❧ **MEGALITHIC TOMBS** – tombs built with huge stone slabs – emerged in western Europe during the Neolithic, and this represents an important change in burial customs. They allowed successive burials to be carried out in a single chamber over many centuries.

❧ **AT LEAST FORTY-SIX PEOPLE WERE BURIED** in the West Kennet **long barrow,** or tomb, in southern England. It was built about 3500 BC. The wedge-shaped mound which covers the burial chambers, is over 100 metres long and faces east. Behind a forecourt, a passage gives access to side chambers and an end chamber.

When the last burials were made, the chambers and passage were filled with rubble. Then the forecourt was filled with boulders and a facade of **megaliths** built across the front of the tomb.

north-west burial chamber

north-east burial chamber

SOME VERY REMOTE MEGALITHIC TOMBS, such as those found in Ireland, were built by 4500 BC, long before those in the Mediterranean.

❧ NEWGRANGE IN IRELAND is a spectacular circular mound over 80 metres in diameter. It is enclosed by 97 massive boulders, each over three metres long. Many are carved with elaborate spiral and zig-zag designs. The entrance to a long passage was originally blocked by a closing slab. This passage and a chamber shaped like a cross leads to three burial side chambers. Each one contains a stone basin which held the cremated bones of the dead.

❧ IN BOTH BRITTANY AND SPAIN some of the megalithic slabs used to build the tombs were decorated with mysterious symbols. The French engravings include axes, shepherds' crooks, yokes and boats. In contrast, the Spanish symbols often include stylized human faces.

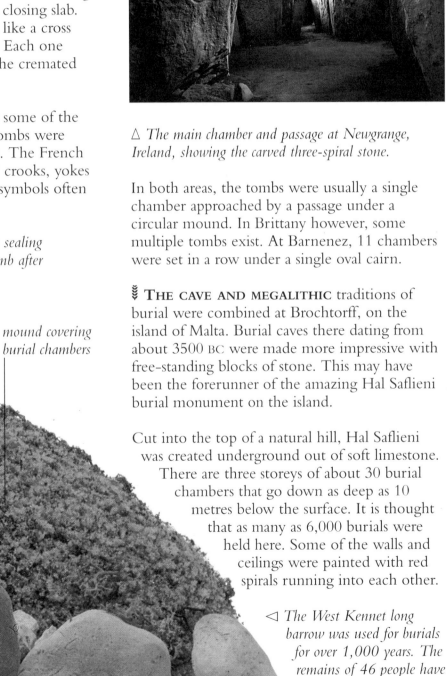

△ *The main chamber and passage at Newgrange, Ireland, showing the carved three-spiral stone.*

In both areas, the tombs were usually a single chamber approached by a passage under a circular mound. In Brittany however, some multiple tombs exist. At Barnenez, 11 chambers were set in a row under a single oval cairn.

❧ THE CAVE AND MEGALITHIC traditions of burial were combined at Brochtorff, on the island of Malta. Burial caves there dating from about 3500 BC were made more impressive with free-standing blocks of stone. This may have been the forerunner of the amazing Hal Saflieni burial monument on the island.

Cut into the top of a natural hill, Hal Saflieni was created underground out of soft limestone. There are three storeys of about 30 burial chambers that go down as deep as 10 metres below the surface. It is thought that as many as 6,000 burials were held here. Some of the walls and ceilings were painted with red spirals running into each other.

blocking stone sealing entrance to tomb after final burial

mound covering burial chambers

◁ *The West Kennet long barrow was used for burials for over 1,000 years. The remains of 46 people have been found there.*

Digging up the past

Archaeologists spend many hours working in the open air, the laboratory and the study to try and piece together how early people lived. Their work involves four main stages: discovering archaeological sites, recovering evidence by **excavation**, analysing the evidence and understanding what has been found.

THE DISCOVERY OF archaeological sites often happens by accident – they are dug up by builders or farmers. Other sites are found by studying aerial photographs which may show crops growing differently over buried features.

▷ *This shows members of an excavation team on the site of a typical archaeological dig. They are led by a director who plans the dig, selects the team members and checks that the work is carried out properly.*

ONCE A SITE IS FOUND, archaeologists may search for more remains buried in the unexcavated part of the site. A **magnetometer** is used to measure the magnetic field. It reveals certain objects, such as iron tools, that contain magnetic minerals which change the strength of the Earth's magnetic field. Others, such as stone walls, are free of these minerals and are less magnetic than the soil.

SMALL TROWELS are used to gradually dig away layers of soil and retrieve finds. Little brushes and teaspoons are used to recover really tiny objects.

draughtswoman drawing plan of site

stratigraphy

photographer

stone hut foundation

ancient oven

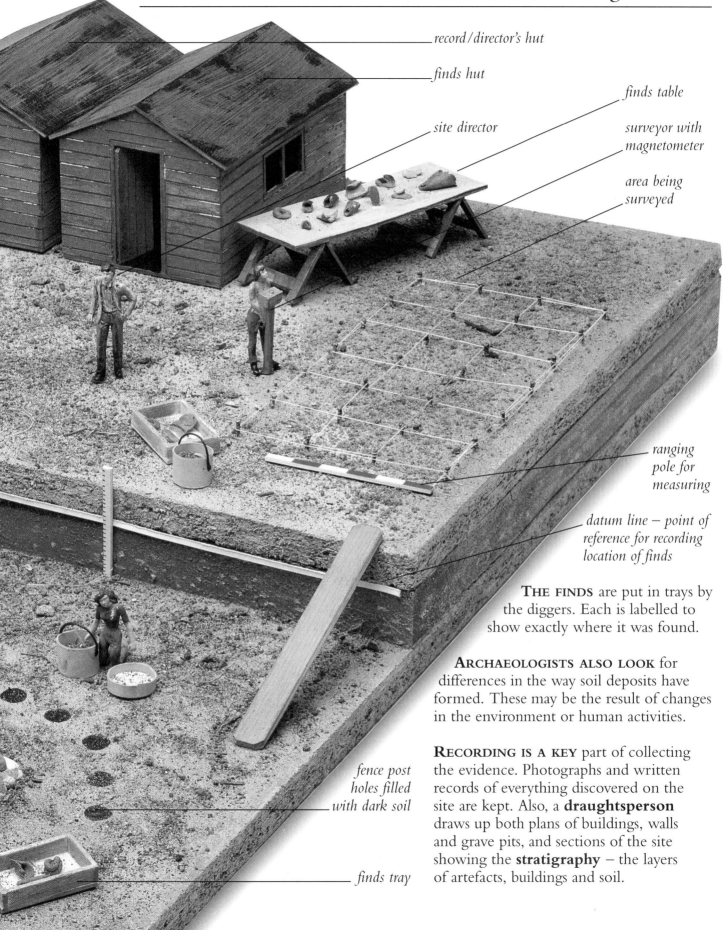

record/director's hut

finds hut

finds table

site director

surveyor with magnetometer

area being surveyed

ranging pole for measuring

datum line – point of reference for recording location of finds

fence post holes filled with dark soil

finds tray

THE FINDS are put in trays by the diggers. Each is labelled to show exactly where it was found.

ARCHAEOLOGISTS ALSO LOOK for differences in the way soil deposits have formed. These may be the result of changes in the environment or human activities.

RECORDING IS A KEY part of collecting the evidence. Photographs and written records of everything discovered on the site are kept. Also, a **draughtsperson** draws up both plans of buildings, walls and grave pits, and sections of the site showing the **stratigraphy** – the layers of artefacts, buildings and soil.

THE ARCHAEOLOGICAL LABORATORY is where all the evidence found in a dig is cleaned up and studied to extract as much information as possible from it.

CARBON 14 is one way scientists date the remote past. C14 measures the amount of radioactive carbon left in a dead organism. From this, the date a plant or animal died can be calculated. Some remains can be dated as being up to 100,000 years old.

DENDROCHRONOLOGY, or tree ring dating, uses the annual growth rings of trees to tell us when a wooden post or timber track was built. One tree trunk may carry 6,000 years worth of tree rings.

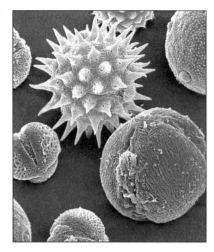

△ *Pollen grains from ancient plant remains can be identified by examination under a microscope.*

POLLEN GRAINS shed by plants and spread by the wind are preserved in buried soils. Peat bogs and very dry areas are where plant remains survive best. Different plants have differently shaped pollen and this allows us to identify the various types of trees, shrubs and grasses that were growing in the past. It can also tell us which ones were the most dominant during any particular time.

rim sherds are the easiest pieces to sort out first

△ *The **sherds**, or pieces, of a copy of a Neolithic Chinese pot. They have been cleaned and spread out to help with putting them together.*

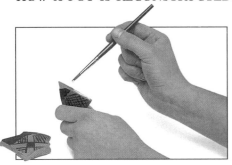

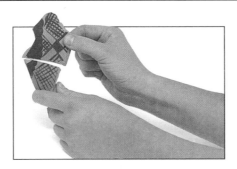

1 *A very, very thin layer of glue is carefully applied to the edge of a cleaned sherd.*

2 *Two matching sherds are stuck together gently, but firmly. Only one of the sherds has glue on it.*

3 *The reconstructed pot is supported in sand and left to dry. Masking tape strengthens the joins.*

PLANT REMAINS, such as seeds and roots, tell us what wild plants were collected for food and at what time of year people lived on a site. Remains of cereal grains can reveal what crops Neolithic farmers were able to grow.

ANIMAL BONES are identified to tell us what species were in the area and what Stone Age people hunted or reared for food purposes. The age of mature farm animals, for instance, helps us to understand why the farmers were keeping them – for meat, wool or milk.

HUMAN SKELETONS can tell us the sex and age at death of Stone Age people. We can also see if they contracted various diseases, suffered broken bones, and if their diet lacked vitamins and minerals.

POTTERY can be used as evidence of materials that communities traded in. This is because scientists can often identify the source of the small grits they find in the clay that the pots were made from. Looking at pieces of pottery under the microscope may reveal traces of what the pots once contained and therefore what people probably used them for.

4 *Enough sherds have been recovered to allow the pot to take shape properly.*

5 *The masking tape is removed once the glue is dry. The gaps can be filled with plaster of Paris.*

Glossary

anthropologist A person who studies the culture, language, origins and behaviour of different peoples around the world.

archaeologist A person who studies the way people lived in the past by looking at remains of buildings, artefacts and other evidence they left behind.

auroch A recently extinct form of wild cow with long horns, thought to be one of the ancestors of modern cattle.

Australopithecus An ape-like creature that was the earliest ancestor of modern humans.

awl A pointed tool with a blade used for piercing tough materials such as leather.

biological Relating to the make-up of a living organism, such as a plant or animal, and the way that it functions.

bipedalism Walking upright on two feet.

Cro-Magnon An early type of modern human who lived in Europe during the late Palaeolithic period. They are named after the Cro-Magnon cave in France where their remains were first found.

cult A specific system of religious worship, usually involving certain rites and gods.

draughtsperson A person who prepares detailed scale drawings of machinery, building devices and various artefacts. These will usually be located on a plan by the draughtsperson, indicating where they are situated.

excavation The digging up of buried objects to try and discover information about the past.

extinct An animal or plant species that has died out and no longer exists.

Fertile Crescent An area of fertile land extending in a semicircle from Israel to the Persian Gulf. This was where people first started growing crops during the Neolithic period.

fertility rites Special ceremonies held in the past at certain times of the year. People believed these would help to bring them good harvests and healthy children.

fortified When a place has been given a form of defence such as high walls or deep trenches.

hemp A strong-smelling Asian plant with tough fibres that are used to make canvas and rope.

henge A circular area consisting of a bank and a ditch, that often contains a circle of stones or wooden posts.

hominid Any member of the family known as Hominidae, which includes all humans and their ape-like ancestors.

Homo erectus An extinct species of modern humans that preceded early *Homo sapiens*, appearing around one and a half million years ago. The scientific name means 'upright walker'.

Homo habilis An extinct species of modern humans that preceded *Homo erectus*, appearing around two million years ago. The scientific name means 'handy man'.

Homo sapiens The scientific name given to modern humans.

Homo sapiens neanderthlensis A form of early humans who lived in Europe. They are named after the Neander Valley in Germany where the first Neanderthal fossils were found.

hunter-gatherers Humans who move around in search of food. They hunt wild animals and gather edible plants, fruits and nuts. It is believed that early humans lived like this.

ideogram A sign or symbol used in a written language that represents an object or an idea.

long barrow An elongated mound from the Neolithic period that usually covers one or more burial chambers.

magnetometer An instrument that measures the Earth's magnetic field and can be used to detect buried features such as ancient fireplaces and metal objects.

mastodon An extinct elephant-like mammal.

megalith A massive stone that often forms part of a prehistoric monument.

Mesolithic The period between the Palaeolithic and the Neolithic which begins around 12,000 years ago, but ends at different times in different parts of the world.

midden A pile of past people's rubbish.

natural evolution A theory put forward by Charles Darwin. It states that nature chooses the animals and plants that, over a long period of time, change so that they can survive. Others die out which allows new species to evolve.

Neolithic The period marked by the emergence of early farming – crop growing and rearing animals – from 10,000 to 5,000 years ago in most parts of the world.

nomadic When a tribe or group of people move around in search of food and grazing land for their animals.

obsidian A dark, glassy volcanic rock made of hardened lava.

ochre Various natural earths containing minerals that can be used as yellow or red pigments.

Palaeolithic The period of the appearance of early humans and the use of the first stone tools. It lasts from more than three million years to about 12,000 years ago.

prehistoric The period relating to the development of human beings before writing was invented.

shaman A priest or medicine man representing a religion that is based on a belief in good and evil spirits. The shaman is believed to be able to control these spirits.

sherd A broken piece of pottery or china.

stratigraphy The composition and study of layers of rocks and other deposits left by humans to discover their geological and human history.

supernatural Involving forces and events that are out of the ordinary and often believed to be controlled by a god.

thresh and winnow The act of separating the grain from husks and straw by first beating it and then circulating air or wind through it.

trapezoidal A four-sided structure with neither of the pairs of sides running parallel.

trilithon A structure of two upright stones with another placed on top.

Index

Africa 6, 11, 12, 16, 30, 36, 46;
African apes 7, 10
anthropologists 4, 10, 13, 42
archaeologists 4, 13, 19, 37, 41, 42,
    49, 50, 54, 58-59, 60-61
Asia 8-9, 11, 12, 32, 36, 44
Australia 6, 8-9, 12-13, 36, 44;
    Roonka Flat Dune 54
Australopithecus 6, 10

Bison 14, 36; clay bison 5
boats 13, 44-45
bow-drills 5, 32-33
brain 10, 12, 42; brain surgery 50
burials 12, 24, 50, 54-57

Canoes 44-45
Carbon 14, 60
Catal Huyuk 17, 39, 52-53
caves 13, 16, 36, 42, 52, 57;
    Cave of the Hands 43; Guittarero
    cave 32; Lascaux cave 37;
    Shanidar cave 54;
    cave paintings 36-37, 42-43
China 6, 13, 17, 21, 27,
    30-31, 34, 39
clay 38-39, 43, 46, 61; clay oven 17
Cro-Magnons 13

Dancing 40-41
Darwin, Charles 11
dendrochronology 60
Denmark 14-15, 29, 45, 46

Egypt 34, 44-45
Eurasia 32, 34
Europe 6, 7, 8, 11, 12, 29,
    30, 32, 34, 36, 38-39, 40, 43,
    46, 48, 50-51, 56
excavation 58

Farming 6, 12, 30-31, 34-35; farms
38, 46, 48, 61
Fertile Crescent 6, 30-31, 34
fertility 4, 37, 51, 52
figurines 4, 24, 38, 51-52
fire 5, 7, 11, 12, 29, 32-33, 35
France 36-37, 51

Glacials 8
grave sites 50, 54, 55

Henges 52
hominids 10, 12, 16, 32, 42
Homo erectus 6, 11, 12-13
Homo habilis 6, 10
Homo sapiens 6-7, 8-9, 10-11,
    12-13, 18, 42
Homo sapiens neanderthalensis 13;
    Neanderthals 13, 54

Ice ages 6, 8-9, 38, 50, 54
Iran 30, 38
Iraq 30, 35, 54
Israel 12, 54
ivory 25, 38, 54

Japan 29, 38
Jericho 4, 6, 49, 50
jewellery 26-27

Kayak 44
Kenya 10, 38
kilns 38-39

Language 42-43
Leakey, Richard 10
llamas 7-8, 46-47
long houses 21, 30

Magic 42, 51
magnetometer 58-59
mammoths 8-9, 14, 18-19, 36, 41;
    mammoth bone huts 6, 18-19,
    20-21
megaliths 56
Mesolithic 4, 6
Mesopotamia 44
Mexico 31, 39
middens 22, 29
musical instruments 40-41

Natural evolution 11
Neolithic 4, 6, 26, 28, 32, 35,
    38-39, 41, 43, 44-45, 46, 48,
    52, 55, 56, 60-61
Newgrange 57

New Guinea 9, 13, 30-31, 44
Nile Valley 45, 48
North America 4, 7, 8, 26, 39, 44

Pack animals 46-47
Palaeolithic 4, 6, 41
Peru 26, 32
pollen 54, 60
pottery 5, 6, 23, 32-33, 38-39,
    43, 45, 46, 50, 55, 57, 60-61
Pyrenees 27, 42

Quern 35

Red deer 8, 14-15
reindeer 8, 50
rituals 50-51, 52; funerary rituals 54
Russia 18, 25

Scandinavia 29, 45
shamans 51
shells 4, 27, 29, 35, 39, 54-55
shrines 52, 53
Skara Brae 22-23, 50
skeletons 48, 54, 61
skulls 4, 42, 50
Spain 36, 57
Stonehenge 52
supernatural 5, 50-51
Syria 30, 35

Tallies 42
tattooing 27
temples 52
tools 5, 6-7, 10, 12-13, 20, 24,
    28-29, 38, 55, 58; awls 20, 24,
    38, 55; axes 6, 13, 48, 57;
    digging sticks 34; sickles 34-35, 38
trilithons 52
Turkey 17, 27, 39, 43, 52-53

Ukraine, The 18, 20, 41, 46

Wagons 46
weapons 6, 48, 50; battle-axes 48;
    harpoons 14-15, 38; spears 28-29,
    37-38, 51; spear-throwers 7, 28-29
West Kennet 56-57

ANCIENT EGYPT

Contents

Studying ancient Egyptian life	4
Timeline	6
The fertile River Nile	8
Cool clothes	10
From pharaoh to labourer	16
Homes and villas	18
Everyday life	24
Work on the land	26
Food and drink	28
Fun and games	30
Arts and crafts	34
Reading and writing	40
Egyptian inventions	42
Boats and chariots	44
Guarding the frontiers	50
Gods and the afterlife	52
Pyramids and burial	56
An amazing discovery	60
Glossary	62

Words found in **bold** in the text can be found here

Index	64

Studying Egyptian life

All human beings need food and shelter to survive. They also need things to look forward to that give their lives hope and meaning. Throughout history, different groups of people around the world have come up with their own ways of meeting these basic requirements. Studying past **civilizations** can tell us how people used the resources around them to build shelters, how they found or farmed food, and how they met their spiritual needs and hopes for a better future.

△ *Some simple farming methods used by the ancient Egyptians are still used today.*

▽ *This map shows modern-day Egypt and nearby countries, some of which were of major importance to ancient Egypt.*

IN THE COURSE OF HISTORY civilizations have risen and eventually fallen because of internal troubles or pressures from outside. The story of the ancient Egyptian civilization is a very long one. It lasted for over 3,000 years. The great Roman Empire rose and fell in half that time, and the Greek civilization lasted less than 1,000 years.

TO HELP people make sense of this vast stretch of time, the greatest period of Egyptian history is usually divided into three periods, or kingdoms. In this book we have given each kingdom a symbol, which is used purely as a guide, when information relates to that time.

KEY FOR SYMBOLS
- Old Kingdom 2686 BC – 2181 BC
- Middle Kingdom 2055 BC – 1650 BC
- ⌇⌇⌇ New Kingdom 1550 BC – 1069 BC

EGYPT'S GEOGRAPHICAL LOCATION plays a vital part in understanding its development as a civilization. During the period covered in this book, foreign trade and travel grew with the discovery of valuable raw materials from abroad.

THE EGYPTIANS travelled to nearby countries by sea or overland. As the wealthiest country of the ancient world, Egypt had much to offer its neighbours, such as gold from the Eastern Desert, in exchange for what it lacked. This made for good trading relations at first, but later led to invasion by foreign countries keen to exploit Egypt's fine natural resources.

EGYPT'S LEGACY to the world lies in some of the most spectacular monuments ever built. The **pyramids** at Giza, the Great Sphinx, and magnificent temples, are all wonderful technological achievements. In fact, many experts are still trying to understand how the Egyptians were able to build such massive constructions with the use of only very simple tools.

△ *The magnificent temple at Abu Simbel was carved out of sandstone cliffs, for Queen Nefertari, on the orders of Ramses II.*

ARCHAEOLOGISTS AND ANTHROPOLOGISTS have, however, been able to explain a lot about the daily lifestyle of the ancient Egyptians by the wall-paintings, documents, treasures, personal possessions and household items that have been discovered in the remains of such tombs and temples.

THESE FINDINGS also reveal much about the Egyptians' religious faith and their views on death and what followed. Experts have been able to work out a lot about their belief in the **afterlife** from the discovery of tomb models buried with the dead, coffins covered with written spells to protect against danger and **mummies** – perfectly preserved bodies for burial.

◁ *This wall-painting shows the type of boats the ancient Egyptians used, the birds found on the banks of the Nile and the tools that noblemen used for hunting.*

THE MAKE IT WORK! way of looking at history is to ask questions of the past and to find the answers by making the things people made, as close as possible to the way they made them. You do not need to make everything in the book to understand the ancient Egyptian's way of life. Simply by looking at the step-by-step instructions, you will be able to see how they put things together and made them work efficiently.

Timeline

In this book we look at history by finding out how ancient Egyptians lived. Another way to look at history is to study the events and political changes that occurred over time. You can see from this chart, for instance, which dynasty of **pharaohs**, or kings, was on the throne, when Egypt started trading with other countries and when foreign invaders arrived.

EGYPTIANS WERE RULED by pharaohs and the throne was passed down the family from generation to generation. A dynasty, or family line, continued until the male line died out and an outsider, possibly with the support of the army or court, married the queen or heiress. There was rarely a struggle. Each dynasty had its own traditions and character. Some built monuments, some encouraged the arts, some were weak and lazy and others financed powerful armies which carried out impressive military campaigns.

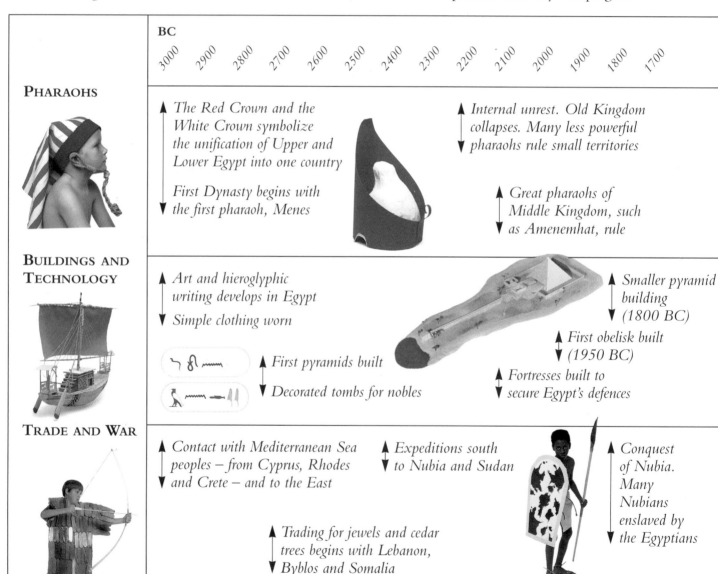

BC

3000 2900 2800 2700 2600 2500 2400 2300 2200 2100 2000 1900 1800 1700

PHARAOHS

▲ The Red Crown and the White Crown symbolize the unification of Upper and Lower Egypt into one country

▼ First Dynasty begins with the first pharaoh, Menes

▲ Internal unrest. Old Kingdom collapses. Many less powerful pharaohs rule small territories

▲ Great pharaohs of Middle Kingdom, such as Amenemhat, rule

BUILDINGS AND TECHNOLOGY

▲ Art and hieroglyphic writing develops in Egypt

▼ Simple clothing worn

▲ First pyramids built

▼ Decorated tombs for nobles

▲ Smaller pyramid building (1800 BC)

▲ First obelisk built (1950 BC)

▲ Fortresses built to secure Egypt's defences

TRADE AND WAR

▲ Contact with Mediterranean Sea peoples – from Cyprus, Rhodes and Crete – and to the East

▲ Expeditions south to Nubia and Sudan

▲ Trading for jewels and cedar trees begins with Lebanon, Byblos and Somalia

▲ Conquest of Nubia. Many Nubians enslaved by the Egyptians

𒀭 OLD KINGDOM
(2686 BC–2181 BC)

INTERMEDIATE PERIOD

🦅 MIDDLE KINGDOM
(2055 BC–1650 BC)

EACH KINGDOM – Old, Middle and New – witnessed a succession of ruling dynasties. Between the kingdoms themselves there were periods of chaos and conflict. This was because of political unrest within Egypt, with a number of different rulers fighting for control of the country, and foreign invasion. After the New Kingdom had ended, there were only brief periods of calm and prosperity as repeated raids from Sudan, Persia and Macedonia became increasingly threatening and disruptive.

EGYPT FINALLY FELL to the Greeks in 332 BC. For the next 300 years the Ptolemy family ruled the country and important people adopted Greek **culture** and learned to speak Greek. By 30 BC, Egypt had become a province of Rome. Over the next several hundred years the gradual erosion of Egyptian culture and religion continued. An Arab invasion of AD 7 saw the arrival of Islam, and in AD 324 Egypt officially turned to Christianity, replacing all the country's temples with **Coptic churches** and monasteries.

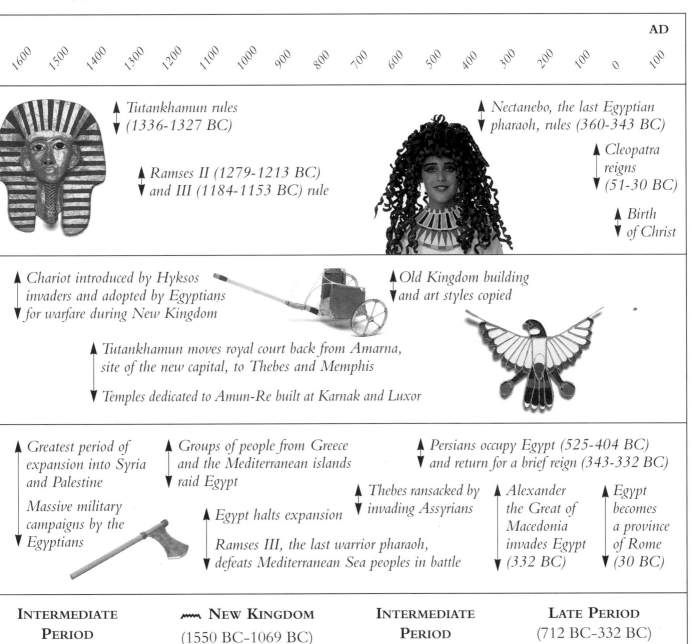

AD

1600 1500 1400 1300 1200 1100 1000 900 800 700 600 500 400 300 200 100 0 100

▲▼ *Tutankhamun rules (1336-1327 BC)*

▲▼ *Ramses II (1279-1213 BC) and III (1184-1153 BC) rule*

▲▼ *Nectanebo, the last Egyptian pharaoh, rules (360-343 BC)*

▲▼ *Cleopatra reigns (51-30 BC)*

▲▼ *Birth of Christ*

▲▼ *Chariot introduced by Hyksos invaders and adopted by Egyptians for warfare during New Kingdom*

▲▼ *Old Kingdom building and art styles copied*

▲ *Tutankhamun moves royal court back from Amarna, site of the new capital, to Thebes and Memphis*

▼ *Temples dedicated to Amun-Re built at Karnak and Luxor*

▲▼ *Greatest period of expansion into Syria and Palestine*

Massive military campaigns by the Egyptians

▲▼ *Groups of people from Greece and the Mediterranean islands raid Egypt*

▲▼ *Egypt halts expansion*

Ramses III, the last warrior pharaoh, defeats Mediterranean Sea peoples in battle

▲▼ *Thebes ransacked by invading Assyrians*

▲▼ *Persians occupy Egypt (525-404 BC) and return for a brief reign (343-332 BC)*

▲▼ *Alexander the Great of Macedonia invades Egypt (332 BC)*

▲▼ *Egypt becomes a province of Rome (30 BC)*

| INTERMEDIATE PERIOD | 〰 NEW KINGDOM (1550 BC-1069 BC) | INTERMEDIATE PERIOD | LATE PERIOD (712 BC-332 BC) |

The fertile River Nile

The first Egyptians were **Stone Age** hunters, followed by settlers from the south and east who were attracted by the river valley's fertile soil. The ancient Egyptian civilization began over 5,000 years ago and lasted for 3,000 years, before being wiped out by foreign invasions. Initially Egypt was divided into Upper and Lower Egypt (the valley and the **delta**). These were united in 3118 BC and ruled by a pharaoh called 'Lord of the Two Lands'.

▽ *The compass shows the direction of the flow of the Nile: south to north.*

▽ *Lower Egypt (Ta-mehu)*

Giza

Memphis

Nile Delta

THE MARSHY, TRIANGULAR DELTA of Lower Egypt, where the river divides into separate branches, was known as *Ta-mehu* – land of the papyrus plant. Upper Egypt, the long, narrow valley just 11 kilometres wide, was called *Ta-shema* – land of the reed. Ancient Egyptian civilization developed in these two fertile areas.

MEMPHIS was one of the most inhabited areas, not only of Egypt, but of the ancient world. It was the capital of Egypt during the Old Kingdom and its harbour and workshops played a key part in the country's foreign trade. Just north of Memphis is Giza, the site of the largest pyramid of all – the Great Pyramid.

THE NILE starts high in the mountains of Central Africa and springs of Ethiopia. From there it flows north to the Mediterranean Sea. Summer rains caused the Nile to flood, covering the valley floor with a layer of mud and water. When the floodwaters went down, a rich layer of soil was left behind. This soil made excellent farming land.

▷ *Today, the floodwaters of the Nile are controlled by a dam at Aswan, but a lush green corridor of rich farm land still runs along both sides of the river's banks.*

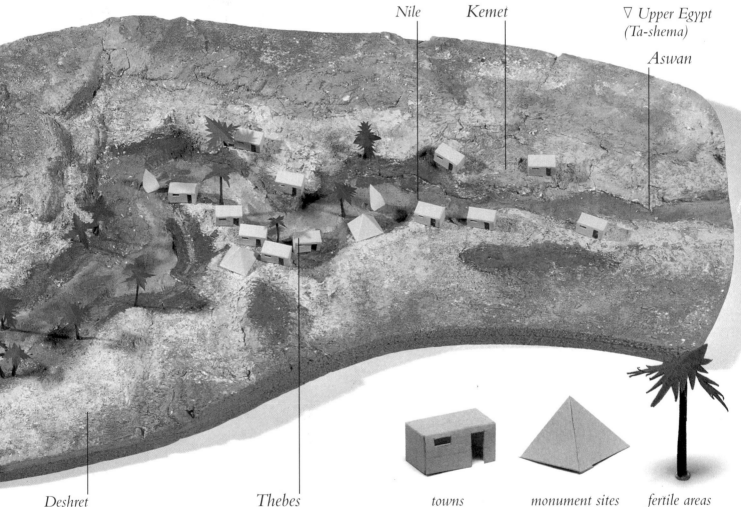

Nile Kemet ▽ *Upper Egypt (Ta-shema)*

Aswan

Deshret *Thebes* *towns* *monument sites* *fertile areas*

THE RED LAND or *Deshret* was the desert that surrounded the river valley. There was nothing to sustain life and nobody lived there. For the ancient Egyptians however, it provided several things: a barrier against invasion, safe trade routes to the rest of Africa, sandstone for building monuments and gold for making jewellery.

THE BLACK LAND, known as *Kemet*, was the narrow strip of **silt** that runs along the river valley. It took its name from the rich, fertile soil in which crops flourished. The Egyptians called themselves *remet-en-Kemet* – people of the black land – and their language, *medet-remet-en-Kemet*, meant speech of the people of the black land.

Cool clothes

The clothes worn by the ancient Egyptians were light and cool. They were made from fine, undyed linen cloth and needed very little stitching as they were simply draped around the body. Colour and decoration came in the form of elaborate jewellery, wigs and make-up. Because it was so hot for most of the year, children often wore nothing at all.

OLD KINGDOM WOMEN wore a simple tube dress made from a rectangle of linen sewn down one side with straps attached to the top edge. To help them keep cool the linen was often very fine and no-one wore underwear. This simple dress style did not change, although during the Middle Kingdom colourful, patterned collars started being worn by both the rich and poor. New Kingdom fashion was more elegant, with a pleated, fringed robe worn over the tube dress.

MEN WORE SHORT KILTS to the knee during the Old Kingdom. The linen cloth was pleated and fastened at the waist, either with a knot or buckle. In the Middle Kingdom, the style of kilts changed to become straight and longer for all. Full-length cloaks kept winter chills at bay.

△ *This pleated dress is possibly the oldest existing garment in the world. It dates from the period of the first pharaoh, which was around 3000 BC.*

By the New Kingdom, fringing and pleating became popular, adorning the sashes and aprons that men now wore.

MAKE A TUNIC

You will need: needle and thread, felt-tip pen, scissors, safety pin, rectangle of fabric

1 Wrap the fabric around the person you are making the tunic for, from under their arms to the knees.

2 Allow an overlap of at least half the width again. Mark the fabric and cut it. Use the leftover material to make two straps.

3 Use a safety pin to hold the tube together, by pinning it carefully at the top of the back (so that you can take it off and put it on).

MAKE A PAIR OF SANDALS

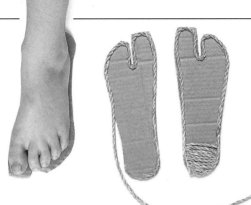

You will need: cardboard, pen, scissors, thin string and bodkin, glue, plaited raffia

1 Place feet on the cardboard, draw around them carefully and cut out.

2 Glue the raffia around the edge of the sole and cut lengths to fit across the centre, filling in the sole shape as shown.

3 Use the thin string to sew the raffia straps into place. Fix the centre of the strap between the toes and either side of the heel. Leave the rest to tie around the ankle.

PLEATING was the main form of decoration. The pleats were probably made by pressing the fabric on to a grooved board and then fixing them firmly in place with a form of starch.

▷ *This is the kind of tunic dress that would have been worn by a servant in a noble household.*

4 Sew the straps on to both shoulders and even up the hem using a pair of scissors.

5 By adding some elaborate decoration to the basic tunic you can transform it into a costume fit for royalty. Popular decorations of the time included feathers, rosettes and sequins. A fringed border was also used to embellish the robes of noblewomen.

▷ *The soles of these royal sandals are decorated with images of the traditional enemies of ancient Egypt. This was so that they could be trampled underfoot with every step!*

LINEN WAS A COMMON material at the time because **flax** – the plant that produces linen threads – grew easily in the rich Nile silt. Also, cotton did not grow in Egypt and Egyptian sheep were not the wool-bearing variety.

WHITE WAS THE COLOUR OF PURITY and white linen cloth was mostly used for dress during the Old and Middle Kingdoms. At this time, the Egyptians sometimes used brown and blue dyes to colour the linen, but were unable to use other, brighter colours such as red and green, as they needed a special fixative to colour the cloth. By the New Kingdom the method for fixing dyes had been discovered. After this clothes became much brighter and designs more elaborate.

ANCIENT EGYPTIANS LIVED in the north-east corner of Africa. They had dark eyes, straight, black hair and coppery-coloured skin.

MAKE-UP and perfumed oils were used by men and women and kept in beautiful caskets. Oils softened their skin and stopped it from burning and cracking in the sun and sandy winds.

EYELIDS were coloured with green pigment, made from a crushed soft stone called malachite. Eyes were outlined with black **kohl**, made of lead ore mixed with water, to make them look larger, and to protect them from the sun's glare.

CHEEKS AND LIPS were stained red with **ochre**. Henna, made from the powdered leaves of a plant, was used to colour hair as it still is today.

MIRRORS WERE ESSENTIAL for all this making-up and hairdressing. Egyptian mirrors were round, and made from highly polished metal discs, usually bronze. Their shape and brightness made the ancient Egyptians think of the life-giving sun, and so mirrors were important as religious objects too. By the New Kingdom the back of the mirror was often decorated with sacred motifs.

▷ *This bronze mirror dates from the New Kingdom. The handle is in the shape of a papyrus plant.*

🦅 〰 MAKE A WIG

You will need: 3 sheets of black craft paper, scissors, glue, ruler, thin dowelling, thick dowelling and modelling clay or wig stand

1 Make wig stand using thick dowelling as shown. Cut long paper strips for wig base, about 3cm wide. Fit, cut and glue base band. Make cross pieces as shown. Glue.

2 Cut long thin strips of paper. Wrap each strip around the thin dowelling and run your hand along it. Remove the dowelling and you will have a tightly curled ringlet.

CHILDREN'S heads were shaved, except for one long, plaited lock which hung at the side. It was known as the 'lock of youth'.

◁ *On important occasions, the pharaoh wore a false beard of plaited and knotted hair, hooked around the ears.*

FACIAL AND BODY HAIR was thought by many to be unclean. Women used tweezers to pluck their hair and shape their eyebrows. Noblemen at court sometimes wore short beards, although most men were clean shaven. Priests kept their heads and bodies completely hair-free.

∿∿ MAKE-UP FOR A QUEEN

You will need: black kohl pencil, green eye shadow, red lipstick

1 Make sure that your face is clean and tie your hair back. Apply eye shadow from the eyelid to the brow.

2 Draw a heavy line around the eyes with the kohl pencil, taking care to avoid any smudging.

3 Darken the eyebrows with kohl to form a straight line.

4 Apply lipstick carefully, following the outline of your mouth.

5 To remove the make-up, wipe with cotton wool dipped in an oily make-up remover.

3 Put the base on the wig stand and glue ringlets to base, starting at the base band. Use shorter ringlets for the front and trim the fringe with scissors.

READY-DRESSED WIGS
were worn by many Egyptians who shaved their heads or kept their hair short. Elaborately curled and beaded wigs were worn on special occasions. The base was made from a net of woven hair with individual strands looped into the netting.

◁ *The higher a person's status, the more make-up and clothes they wore. Servants were scantily dressed.*

JEWELLERY WAS WORN by rich and poor, men and women, and even some sacred animals. Elaborate costume jewellery was worn to adorn otherwise plain clothing, and as a sign of social position.

GOLD AND SEMIPRECIOUS STONES were used to make expensive jewellery. Cheaper versions were made of glass and **faience**, a glazed composition made by heating powdered quartz, or sand, in moulds. Jewellery often served a dual purpose: as decoration for the body and as **amulets**, or charms, to protect the wearer from harm. From earrings to anklets, the ancient Egyptians decorated almost every part of the body.

STONES such as carnelian, lapis lazuli and turquoise were thought to have charmed powers.

△ *This collar was found on the mummy of the pharaoh Tutankhamun. Made of coloured glass, it shows Nekhbet, the vulture goddess of Upper Egypt.*

∿ MAKE A PECTORAL

You will need: paper, compass, pencil, thin card cut into strips about 2cm wide, glue and sticky tape, Plasticine, plaster of Paris, paints

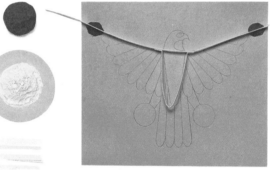

1 Using a compass for the circles, copy the shape above on to a piece of paper. Next, stick the strip that runs across the top of the wings and body with Plasticine.

2 Starting with the body, cut, curve and glue the card strips so that they follow the lines of the drawing. Secure with tape if necessary.

3 Roll out the Plasticine using a rolling pin. This will be the base for pouring the plaster, so make sure it is completely flat.

4 Place the card outline on the Plasticine, pushing down gently so that no plaster can escape under the card walls. Prepare the plaster.

5 Pour the plaster into the mould and leave to dry overnight. Remove the Plasticine, turn the pectoral over and paint as shown right.

MAGIC MOTIFS included figures of the gods and, most significantly, the **scarab** – a representation of the dung beetle. To the ancient Egyptians, this was a powerful symbol of the sun god and life being reborn from dust. Children sometimes wore a fish pendant in their plaits to protect them from drowning. Pregnant women wore figures of the hippopotamus goddess Taweret, meaning 'the great one', to help them in childbirth.

GOLD-WORKING TECHNIQUES were quite varied. Most gold jewellery was made by hammering out thin sheets which were then cut to shape. These were decorated by punching on designs with a sharp chisel and making indentations to hold stones or jewels. The sheets were also cut into thin strips to make gold wire. Expensive, solid pieces of jewellery were made by pouring molten, or liquid gold into moulds.

▷ *This falcon pectoral with outstretched wings shows the god Re-Harakhty, the sun god in one of his many forms.*

talons clutch the 'shen' symbol, meaning eternity

PECTORALS were worn on the chest for protection as well as decoration and often took the shape of falcons or scarabs. They were made using a technique now known as **cloisonné**, where semiprecious stones or coloured glass are held in place by fine metal strips.

▷ *These gold bracelets show the god Horus as a child sitting on a lotus flower, between two cobras.*

From pharaoh to labourer

Egyptian **society** was well-ordered and administered by law-enforcers, courts and judges. All classes paid their taxes in goods or services, which were then used to pay government officials and the army. Scribes were the only members of society who could possibly rise through the ranks to become noblemen. Yet despite this, ancient Egyptian society remained stable and secure.

THE PHARAOH, meaning 'great house', was absolute ruler. He could have many wives, but only one queen could be the Great Royal Wife. His symbols of office were the double crown of Upper and Lower Egypt, the **crook** and the **flail**, an implement used for threshing grain.

COURT OFFICIALS AND NOBLEMEN held high office in ancient Egypt and helped the pharaoh to rule the country. The pharaoh would often reward loyal nobles with gifts of land, so that they would have their own income from taxes.

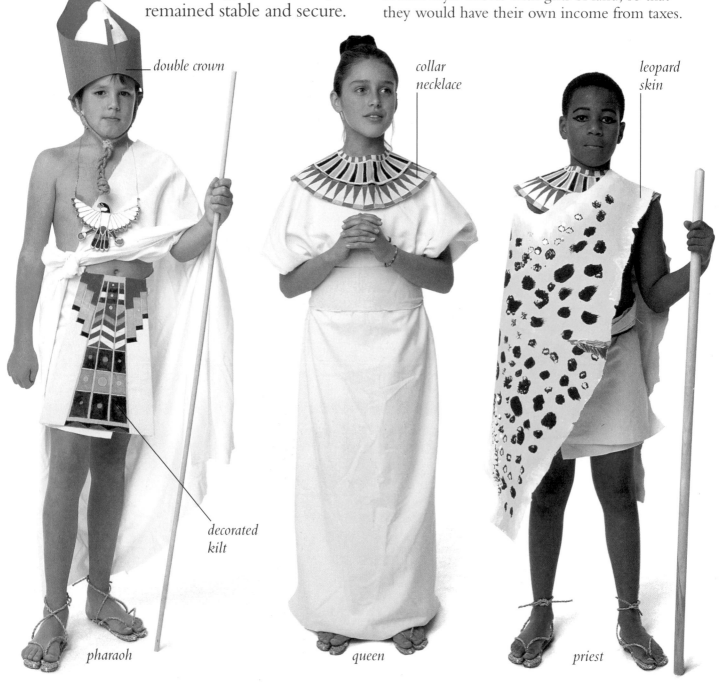

double crown

collar necklace

leopard skin

decorated kilt

pharaoh

queen

priest

PRIESTS AND PRIESTESSES looked after the temples and held religious ceremonies. The high priest ran his temple with the help of musicians, dancers and assistant priests. Taxes were paid directly to the temples, for their upkeep.

SCRIBES were the civil servants of ancient Egypt. They administered the law, collected taxes and oversaw government projects. Parents were keen to send their children to scribal school (see page 41) so they would learn to read and write. They could then enter government or royal service where they might become rich and powerful.

ARTISTS AND CRAFTSMEN worked in organized workshops using simple techniques and tools, and were employed by the pharoah, the government or the temples. During the Old Kingdom, blind men often worked as musicians and dwarves were traditionally employed as jewellers.

FOOT SOLDIERS AND UNSKILLED LABOURERS were amongst the poorest members of society, unlike officers who were the equivalent of nobles. Labourers paid their taxes by joining the army, or working on government projects during the flooding season, when farm work stopped.

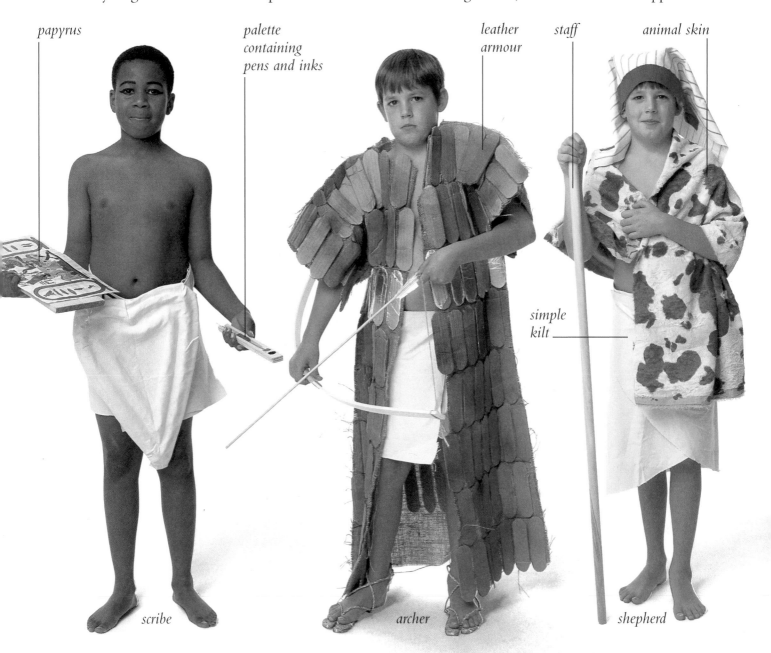

papyrus

palette containing pens and inks

leather armour

staff

animal skin

simple kilt

scribe

archer

shepherd

Homes and villas

The majority of Egyptians lived in towns and villages strung out along the Nile Valley. To escape the effects of the annual flooding, towns were built on the edge of the desert and on patches of high ground within the cultivated valley. Until the New Kingdom, houses, palaces, government offices and even temples were built from dried mud bricks, quite a fragile building material. As buildings crumbled, the occupants would knock them down and rebuild on top of the remains, so that gradually the high ground became even higher and therefore safer from the floods.

△ *This model 'soul house' is based on a typical village house. It was placed in a burial tomb to provide a home for the deceased in the afterlife.*

〰 **GRANARIES, BAKERIES AND BREWERIES** were important features of any town. Models of these buildings were made and buried with people when they died, as it was thought that they would need sustenance in the afterlife.

sun shield

silos for storing grain

silo

external stairs leading to roof

courtyard

outside granary

TOWN HOUSES were built with a shelter on the roof to catch cool north breezes. Families would sometimes live there during hot weather. Inside, houses were often cramped and quite dark as windows were small and high up to keep out the sunlight. Kitchens were usually situated on the top floor so that the heat and cooking smells could drift out through an opening on to the roof terrace.

△ *The earliest homes and temples found in Egypt were made of reeds. The houses were shaped like beehives.* — *temple*

SUPPORTING BEAMS and pillars were made of wood, covered in plaster and then painted. Columns were made of several tree trunks bound together with a rope made of **papyrus**, a tall reed. Houses were covered with white limestone plaster to deflect the heat of the sun.

'TO START A HOUSE' was the Egyptian term for marriage, which was not marked with any kind of ceremony. Families would get together to arrange their children's marriages, and once a written agreement had been drawn up, the couple set up house together (see page 24).

∧∧∧ MAKE A VILLA

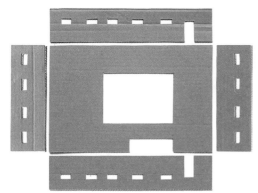
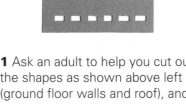
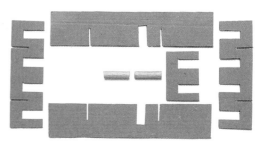

You will need: corrugated cardboard, craft knife, masking tape, dowelling, base board, plaster of Paris, spatula

1 Ask an adult to help you cut out the shapes as shown above left (ground floor walls and roof), and above (top floor) from cardboard.

2 Cut out interior walls for the top floor as shown above. Cut two pieces of dowelling to the height of each ceiling. This is the pillar.

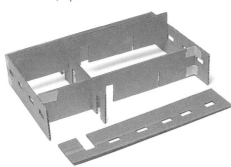

3 Assemble the ground floor and internal walls as shown. Fix the corners with masking tape. Glue pillar in position as shown overleaf.

4 Add the ground floor roof, then assemble and attach the upper storey with masking tape. Glue pillar in place (see over) and add the roof.

5 Prepare the plaster of Paris and apply a thin layer with a spatula. When dry, trim plaster from doors and windows with a craft knife.

~~~ **A NOBLEMAN'S VILLA** was home to family, servants and livestock, as well as being a place of business. Like most Egyptian buildings, it would have been a low, white-plastered construction with a flat roof. Usually, this would have been approached through beautiful landscaped gardens with terraces, ponds, shady trees and flowers. The vegetable gardens, stables and granaries were situated around a courtyard at the back of the house with the servants' quarters and the kitchen.

▷ *The finished villa (see previous page) with part of the roof and walls cut away to reveal the interior. You could paint your villa, make simple palm trees or use sand to decorate it.*

PRIVATE ROOMS were at the back of the house and were much more simple. This is where the bedrooms were situated and where children could play by themselves.

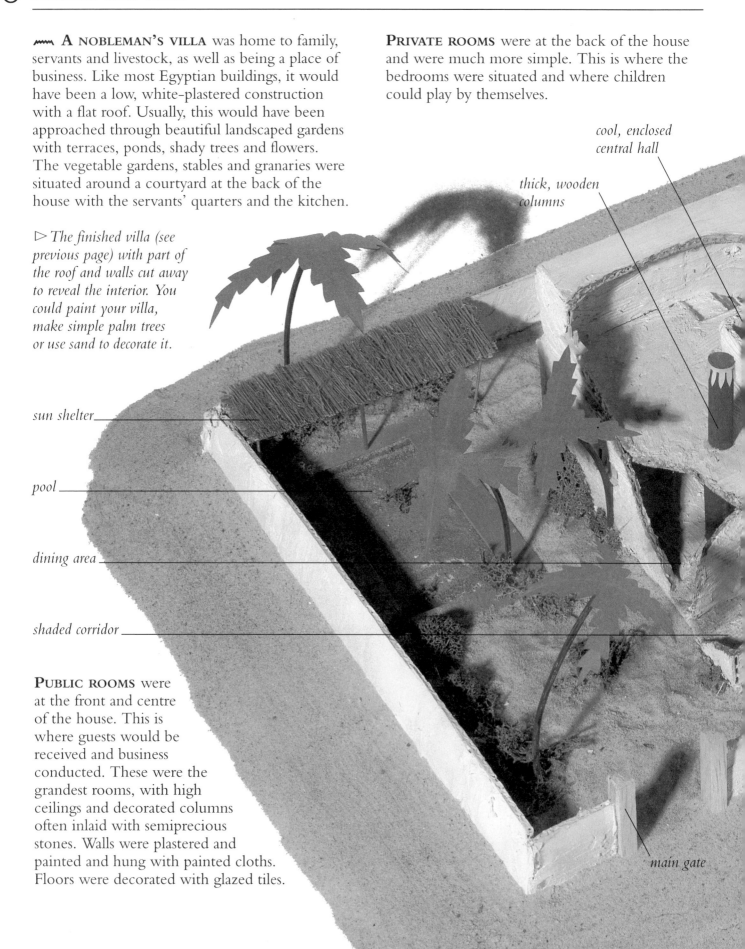

cool, enclosed
central hall

thick, wooden
columns

sun shelter

pool

dining area

shaded corridor

main gate

PUBLIC ROOMS were at the front and centre of the house. This is where guests would be received and business conducted. These were the grandest rooms, with high ceilings and decorated columns often inlaid with semiprecious stones. Walls were plastered and painted and hung with painted cloths. Floors were decorated with glazed tiles.

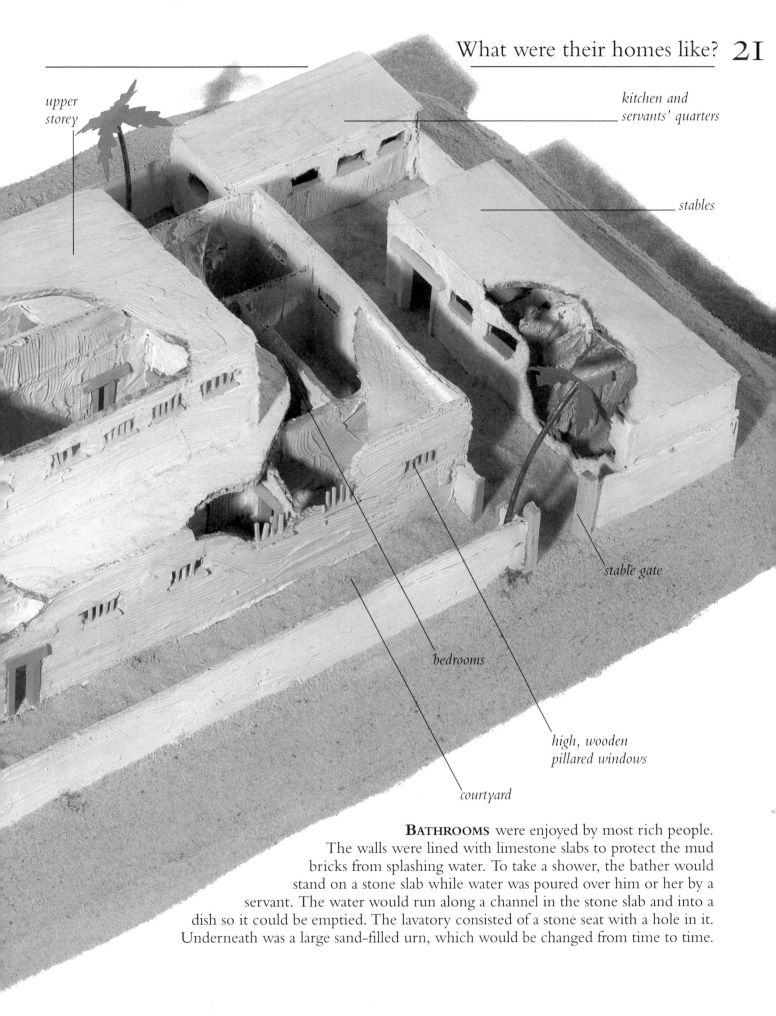

upper storey

kitchen and servants' quarters

stables

stable gate

bedrooms

high, wooden pillared windows

courtyard

BATHROOMS were enjoyed by most rich people. The walls were lined with limestone slabs to protect the mud bricks from splashing water. To take a shower, the bather would stand on a stone slab while water was poured over him or her by a servant. The water would run along a channel in the stone slab and into a dish so it could be emptied. The lavatory consisted of a stone seat with a hole in it. Underneath was a large sand-filled urn, which would be changed from time to time.

FURNITURE such as stools, tables, beds and chests was simple and made in workshops by carpenters. Poorer people either made their own basic furniture, or squatted on the floor on mats or cushions.

CHAIRS had carved wooden frames and low seats made from plaited cord. The legs were often carved to resemble a lion's paw or a bull's hoof.

roof beams

woven wall hanging

doorway

plaster wall over mud brick

folding stool

water pot

simple bed

STOOLS came in a variety of styles from simple, low structures to elaborately decorated models with carved legs. Everybody, from the pharaoh down, used stools. Chairs, which had very short legs and no arms, were only used by royalty and people of considerable social rank.

LAMPS were stone or pottery bowls filled with palm-nut oil and a wick made of flax. They were lit in the evenings, only for the short time between sunset and bedtime, as people went to bed as soon as it got dark and got up at sunrise to make the most of the daylight.

MATS AND CURTAINS were made of woven reeds and decorated with coloured fabric.

〜〜 **SHRINES** to household gods were often a feature of Egyptian living rooms. Among them were Bes, the dwarf god of marriage and family prosperity, and Imhotep, god of medicine.

CHESTS were used to store everything as there were no cupboards. Some were made of wood – sycamore, fig or imported ebony – and some of woven reeds. They ranged from the plain and simple, to finely carved pieces, inlaid with ivory and faience.

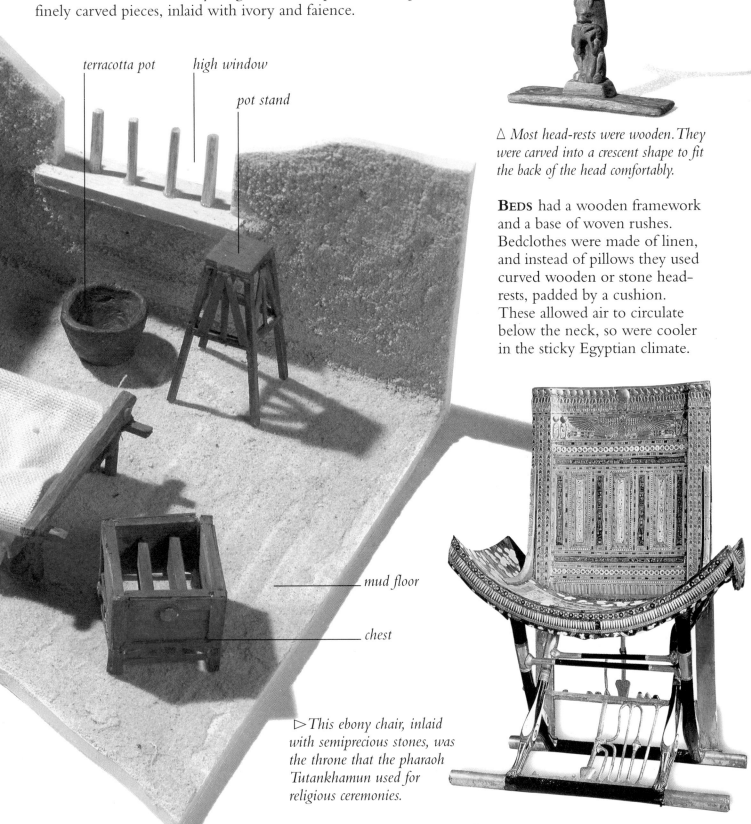

terracotta pot

high window

pot stand

△ *Most head-rests were wooden. They were carved into a crescent shape to fit the back of the head comfortably.*

BEDS had a wooden framework and a base of woven rushes. Bedclothes were made of linen, and instead of pillows they used curved wooden or stone head-rests, padded by a cushion. These allowed air to circulate below the neck, so were cooler in the sticky Egyptian climate.

mud floor

chest

▷ *This ebony chair, inlaid with semiprecious stones, was the throne that the pharaoh Tutankhamun used for religious ceremonies.*

Everyday life

Ancient Egyptians had a strong sense of family, and usually married someone from their own social group or extended family. Historians once thought that brothers and sisters sometimes married, but apart from the royal family, it seems that this was not true. The words 'brother' and 'sister' in ancient Egyptian were simply terms of affection. Marriage was fairly straight-forward and divorce was legal, but costly.

△ *This Old Kingdom tomb model of a woman and her husband, Hetepheres and Kaitep, dates from 2500 BC.*

INTER-MARRIAGES often took place within the extended family, such as between cousins. Children played an important role in society and were thought to be a great blessing. Parents prayed to the gods for many children who were then expected to look after their parents during old age.

CHILDHOOD was short as children were sent to learn a trade, or the privileged few to be educated at scribal school, when they were only eight or nine years old. Girls married when they were as young as 12 years old and boys at 14. The average life expectancy was 40 years, although mummies of officials and rulers show that some lived much longer.

DAILY LIFE centred around the market place, with stalls filling squares and lining streets. This is where the wealthy would send their servants to shop. The ancient Egyptians did not use money, relying instead on a **barter** and exchange system of trade. They used everything for this – from storage jars and furniture to grain, flax or copper ore. Prices rarely went up, which meant that the value of things tended to remain the same. As a result, people knew what to expect in exchange for their goods.

cattle

market stall

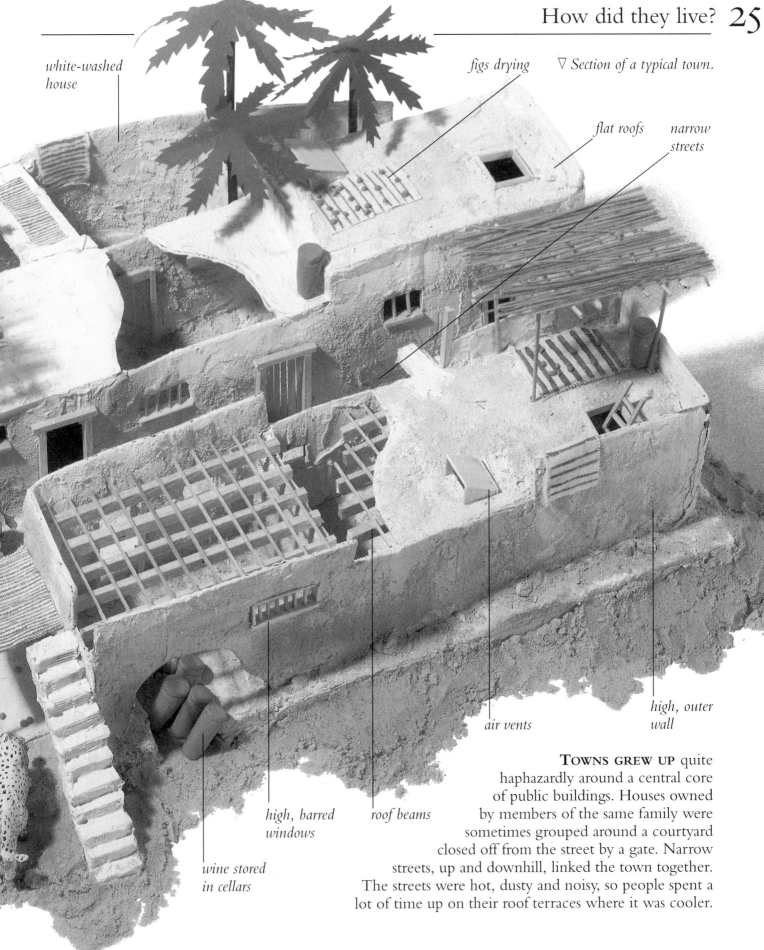

white-washed
house

figs drying

▽ Section of a typical town.

flat roofs

narrow
streets

high, outer
wall

air vents

roof beams

high, barred
windows

wine stored
in cellars

TOWNS GREW UP quite
haphazardly around a central core
of public buildings. Houses owned
by members of the same family were
sometimes grouped around a courtyard
closed off from the street by a gate. Narrow
streets, up and downhill, linked the town together.
The streets were hot, dusty and noisy, so people spent a
lot of time up on their roof terraces where it was cooler.

Work on the land

Ancient Egypt was a wealthy country because most years the rich and fertile soil yielded magnificent crops. This was due to the annual flooding of the River Nile between July and October. During this time, little farmwork was done and poorer families paid their taxes in labour by working on government projects.

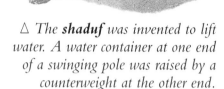

△ The **shaduf** was invented to lift water. A water container at one end of a swinging pole was raised by a counterweight at the other end.

AKHET was the name given to the season when the Nile flooded the river plain, soaking the dry soil and leaving behind a fertile layer of black silt. If too little water covered the land, crops would suffer, while too much severely damaged houses.

WORK STARTED when the flood waters began to recede. **Irrigation** channels had to be repaired and boundaries re-established. Farmers marked out their fields to avoid ownership arguments and to make it easier to calculate what they owed in taxes each year.

Nile

The annual flooding of the Nile irrigated and fertilized the soil of nearby fields.

Irrigation channels allowed the flood waters to reach those fields further away from the river.

PERET was the growing season and ran from November to February. Water had to be kept flowing in the irrigation channels to supply the crops. Small boys chased off birds, but plagues of insects and flash storms were a constant threat to the crops.

SHEMU was the period between March and June, during which crops were harvested. Children worked too, picking up the ears of wheat or barley missed by the harvesters. The work was overseen by tax assessors or scribes who calculated how much the farmers owed in taxes and rent.

THE LAND WAS PLOUGHED, once it had been cleared, by a simple wooden plough pulled by cows. The most important seeds sown were wheat and barley for making bread and beer, flax for making linen cloth and linseed oil, and emmer, an ancient variety of wheat.

HARVESTED CROPS were taken away to be stored in granaries once all dues had been paid to the government. Those who did not pay were often beaten without mercy. Finally, offerings were made to Renenutet, goddess of the harvest, to give thanks for a plentiful crop.

The parched soil of the plains was covered with a fine layer of silt.

Deeper channels had to be dug, in order to irrigate higher ground.

Towns and villages were located on high, dry ground to avoid flooding.

Food and drink

The Egyptians loved good food and drink. Almost all their food was home-grown and the staple food was bread. Most people drank beer, brewed from barley, and the rich drank wine. Even poor people enjoyed a healthy diet of vegetables, fruit and fish from the Nile, while the wealthy supplemented their diet with meat – mainly from calves and oxen – and poultry such as duck, pigeon, goose and stork. Meat was expensive because there were few grazing pastures as land was needed for growing crops.

△ *This coffin painting of a man offering a feast to the gods gives us an idea of what the Egyptians used to eat.*

EGYPTIANS DINED at low tables and ate with their fingers. Ordinary people ate off earthenware dishes, but the rich were attended by servants who served them on dishes of silver, bronze, gold or faience.

During banquets the servants would tie a cone of scented grease on the head of each guest. These would melt and run down their hair and wigs, leaving them sweetly perfumed.

MAKE FIG·CAKES

You will need: blender, 200g fresh figs, water, ground cardamom, honey, 50g walnuts, 50g almonds

1 Using a blender, grind the almonds and walnuts separately and set them aside.

2 Chop the figs roughly and put them in the blender, adding just a little water.

BEER WAS MADE by first half-baking loaves of barley bread, then crumbling the loaves into a mixture of barley and water. The jars were sealed and left to ferment, and the resulting thick, lumpy beer was strained through a sieve before being served.

THE VINE was one of the main garden crops, and was used mainly for wine. Grapes were trampled to extract the juice in troughs big enough to hold six men. It was poured into clay jars and sealed and labelled with the date and the name of the vineyard, much as it is today.

▷ *Once grain had been harvested, it was threshed (trampled by oxen) and winnowed, to separate the grains from the chaff, or casing. Then it was stored in silos, until ground down for cooking.*

COOKING was done outside or on the rooftops, because it was too hot and dangerous to cook over an open fire indoors. Fires were started by rubbing a bow string vigorously against a stick.

MEAT from cows and sheep was grilled over the open fire or stewed. Some pigs were kept, although priests associated them with the evil god Set, and so refused to eat them. Fish and duck caught from the Nile were sometimes salted and dried to preserve them. Bees were kept in clay pots to produce honey which was used as a sweetener in baking.

storing grain in silos

threshing grain

3 Add the walnuts and cardamom and blend again, adding a little water if the mixture is too sticky.

4 Spoon the mixture out of the blender on to a clean surface. Shape the mixture into balls.

5 Roll the balls in honey and sprinkle with ground almonds.

BREAD was the mainstay of most people's diet, but it was a bit of a mixed blessing. The texture of Egyptian bread was fairly tough as it was often full of sand and grit that became mixed up in the grinding of the grain. Studies on mummies show that it was so coarse that it wore down the teeth of those who ate it!

Fun and games

Tomb paintings and the **artefacts**, or man-made implements, that were buried with the ancient Egyptians, show that they enjoyed themselves in many ways. Music was very popular, and performers were in great demand at celebrations.

MUSICIANS were in great demand for public festivals. During the Old Kingdom they were mostly men, but mainly female by the New Kingdom. Children of rich families were taught to play an instrument for their own pleasure. But there is also evidence to suggest that ordinary Egyptians enjoyed music and singing on an everyday basis.

∿ MAKE A HARP

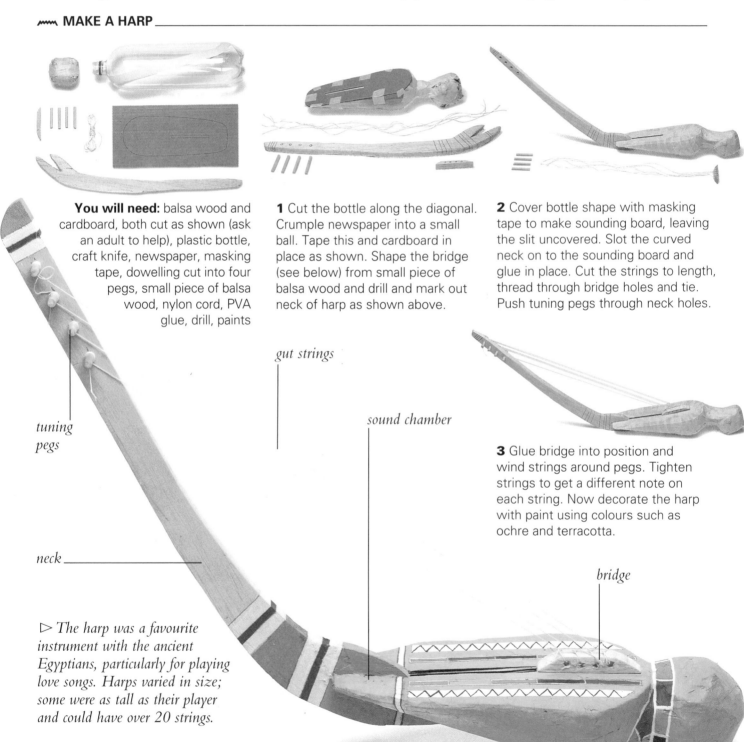

You will need: balsa wood and cardboard, both cut as shown (ask an adult to help), plastic bottle, craft knife, newspaper, masking tape, dowelling cut into four pegs, small piece of balsa wood, nylon cord, PVA glue, drill, paints

1 Cut the bottle along the diagonal. Crumple newspaper into a small ball. Tape this and cardboard in place as shown. Shape the bridge (see below) from small piece of balsa wood and drill and mark out neck of harp as shown above.

2 Cover bottle shape with masking tape to make sounding board, leaving the slit uncovered. Slot the curved neck on to the sounding board and glue in place. Cut the strings to length, thread through bridge holes and tie. Push tuning pegs through neck holes.

3 Glue bridge into position and wind strings around pegs. Tighten strings to get a different note on each string. Now decorate the harp with paint using colours such as ochre and terracotta.

gut strings

sound chamber

tuning pegs

neck

bridge

▷ *The harp was a favourite instrument with the ancient Egyptians, particularly for playing love songs. Harps varied in size; some were as tall as their player and could have over 20 strings.*

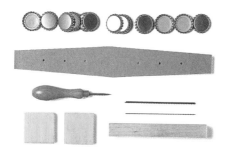

You will need: balsa wood, cut as shown (ask an adult to help), PVA glue, saw, bradawl, pliers, thin wire, thick card cut and drilled as shown, bottle tops, paint

1 Glue both squares of wood on to handle as shown. Use bradawl to pierce a hole in each bottle top. Using pliers, cut the wire into three and bend up one side. Make saw cuts into top of handle as shown above right.

2 Push straight ends of each wire through holes in card. Thread on bottle tops, shape card round and bend wire to secure. Push rattle head into slots in handle and glue. Paint.

MUSICAL INSTRUMENTS fell into three groups: strings, wind and percussion. They became more complex during the New Kingdom as new musical ideas arrived from the East. The harp, lyre and lute were the main string instruments; early forms of the flute, oboe and clarinet made up the wind section; rattles, castanets and tambourines were popular percussion instruments.

△ Dancing girls and musicians are in full swing at a banquet in this wall-painting. The hieroglyphs show the song being performed.

EGYPTIAN BANQUETS were rowdy and fun, and religious festivals were equally lively. Enormous amounts of food and wine were consumed, and for guests who over-indulged, a servant was always on hand with scented water or a sick bowl!

PROFESSIONAL DANCERS, acrobats, magicians and storytellers were attached to the royal court and to noblemen's homes. The dancers were mainly women who started their training when young. Other performers worked in troupes for hire.

△ Noblewomen and priestesses carried a sacred rattle, or sistrum at ceremonies.

~~~ **HUNTING** was a favourite pastime of men. The pharaoh and his nobles hunted lions, wild bulls and leopards. Accompanied by professional hunters, they took off into the desert in horse-drawn chariots in pursuit of prey. Alternatively, they would lie in wait around a water hole, ready to attack with bows and arrows.

IN THE MARSHY RIVER DELTA, water birds were killed with throwing sticks, and hippopotami with lassoes and harpoons. Hippos were a menace to farmers as they flattened crops. Only the brave hunted crocodiles!

▷ *Hippo-hunting on the river.*

THE RIVER was also a place to relax. Egyptians would take their reed boats down to the water, enjoy a picnic, go fishing or catch water birds.

CHILDREN played leap-frog and tug-of-war, and practised wrestling and gymnastics. **Senet** was a favourite board game played by everyone.

~~~ MAKE A SENET GAME

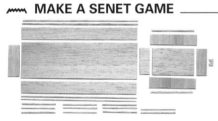

You will need: balsa wood, craft knife, PVA glue, paint, felt-tip pens, self-hardening clay, ruler, sandpaper

1 Ask an adult to help you cut the balsa wood as shown. The larger pieces on the left are for the board, the smaller (right) are for the drawer.

2 Make five pieces each for both players (and a couple of spares), from the clay. When the clay is dry, paint five of the pieces black and the other five white.

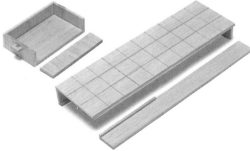

3 Glue together the drawer and handle from balsa wood as shown. Then glue the drawer runners to the bottom edge of the side pieces. Mark the top board into 30 squares.

TO PLAY SENET

The object of the game is for one player to get his or her pieces around and off the board before their opponent. Players throw the four dice sticks to find out how far to move when it is their turn:

One flat side up = 1
Two flat sides up = 2
Three flat sides up = 3
Four flat sides up = 4
Four round sides up = 6

RULES

● Throwing a 1, 4 or 6 wins a player another throw.
● Pieces move up and down the board lengthways: row one, left to right; row two, right to left; row three, left to right.
● Landing on a square occupied by an opponent means the opponent's piece must move back to the square his attacker has come from.
● Two pieces of the same colour cannot occupy one square, but next to each other they cannot be attacked.
● Three pieces in a row cannot be passed by an opponent.
● The square marked 〰 means a player must go back to the square marked ⚷, and if that is occupied, go back to the start.
● The squares marked 👌, 🛶 and 👥 are safe from attack.
● A player cannot move a piece off the board until all his pieces are off the first row.

START OF PLAY

1 Place a white piece on every other square of the first row and five black pieces on the squares in between.

2 The first player to throw a 1 moves the last black piece on the first row one square down. Then he throws again, free now to move any of the black pieces.

start

finish

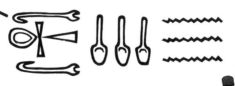

3 When the white player makes his first move, he must use the last white piece in the first row.

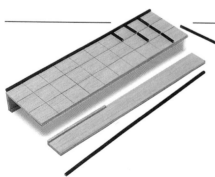

4 Paint the long vertical strips and shorter dividing sticks black. Cut the dividing sticks into short strips and glue firmly in between the vertical ones as shown above.

5 Copy the images above on to the top of the board. It is important that each sits on the correct square as shown right. Decorate the board's sides with felt-tip pens and paint.

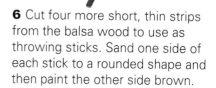

6 Cut four more short, thin strips from the balsa wood to use as throwing sticks. Sand one side of each stick to a rounded shape and then paint the other side brown.

Arts and crafts

Many beautiful objects have survived from ancient Egypt, indicating that the Egyptians were skilled and creative. They made papyrus sheets to write on, and the rich adorned their houses with ornaments and fabrics. Many workers were employed solely as craftsmen to meet these needs.

WEAVING was one of the earliest Egyptian crafts. Scraps of woven linen have been discovered that date back 6,000 years. Linen fibres come from the flax plant. The stems were soaked in water until only the fibres were left. These were combed into fine strands and spun to make a continuous thread.

TO MAKE PAPYRUS SHEETS, papyrus reeds, which grew abundantly along the Nile, were harvested. First the green outer skin of the stem was peeled away. The inner core was then cut into strips and soaked in water. The wet strips were placed in a frame, side by side and just overlapping, and an alternate layer of strips was placed on top. Lastly, the paper sheet was pressed, dried, rolled and polished.

MAKE A LOOM

You will need:
chipboard for base, drilled as shown, dowelling, cut as shown, balsa wood, cut and drilled with holes as shown, string, black and beige wool, scissors

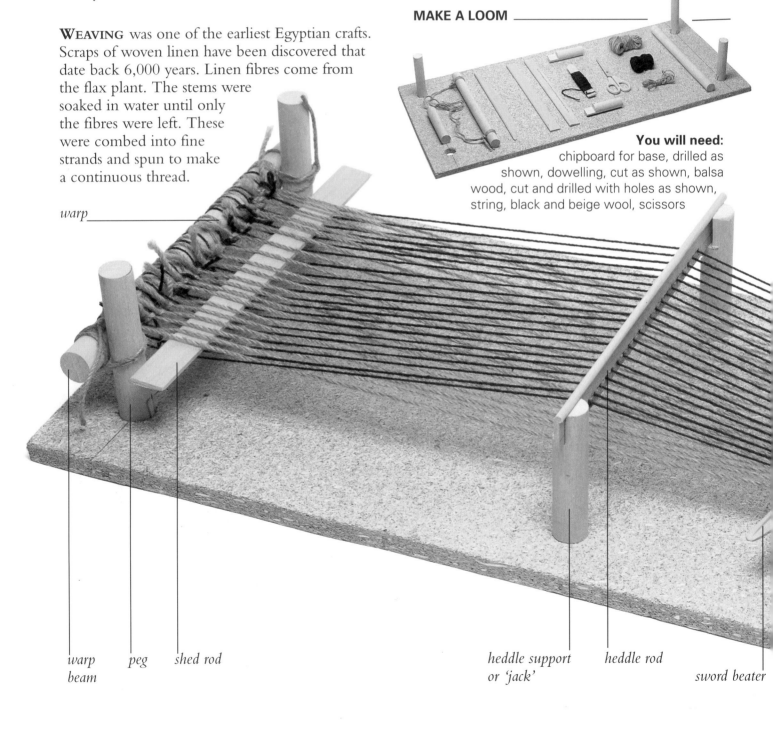

warp

warp beam *peg* *shed rod*

heddle support or 'jack' *heddle rod* *sword beater*

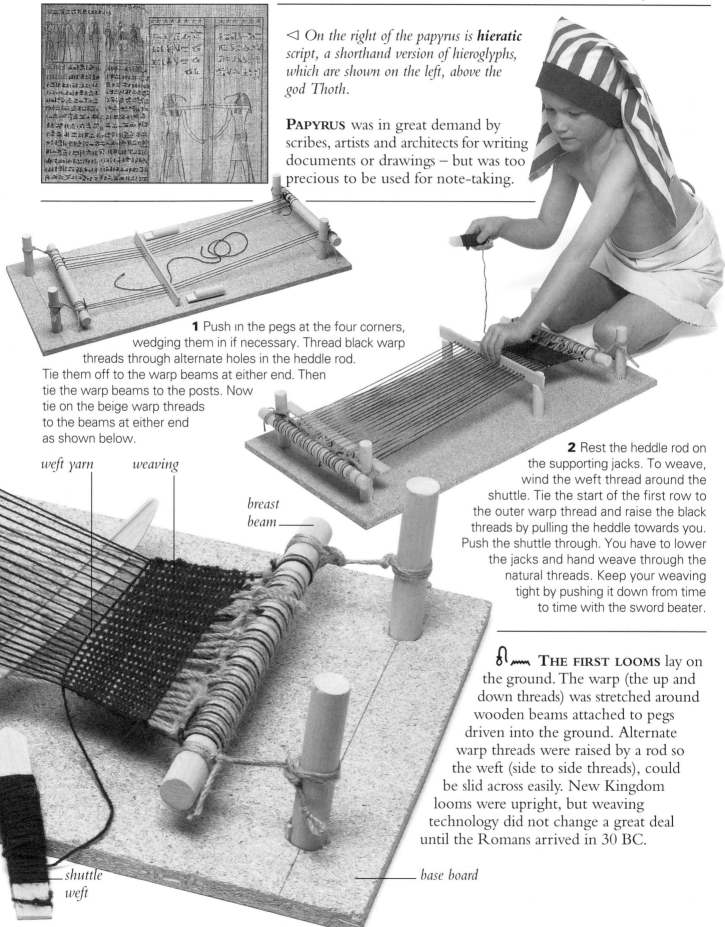

◁ *On the right of the papyrus is* **hieratic** *script, a shorthand version of hieroglyphs, which are shown on the left, above the god Thoth.*

PAPYRUS was in great demand by scribes, artists and architects for writing documents or drawings – but was too precious to be used for note-taking.

1 Push in the pegs at the four corners, wedging them in if necessary. Thread black warp threads through alternate holes in the heddle rod. Tie them off to the warp beams at either end. Then tie the warp beams to the posts. Now tie on the beige warp threads to the beams at either end as shown below.

weft yarn   *weaving*

breast beam

2 Rest the heddle rod on the supporting jacks. To weave, wind the weft thread around the shuttle. Tie the start of the first row to the outer warp thread and raise the black threads by pulling the heddle towards you. Push the shuttle through. You have to lower the jacks and hand weave through the natural threads. Keep your weaving tight by pushing it down from time to time with the sword beater.

THE FIRST LOOMS lay on the ground. The warp (the up and down threads) was stretched around wooden beams attached to pegs driven into the ground. Alternate warp threads were raised by a rod so the weft (side to side threads), could be slid across easily. New Kingdom looms were upright, but weaving technology did not change a great deal until the Romans arrived in 30 BC.

shuttle weft

base board

◁ *This Middle Kingdom jug shows a kneeling woman suckling a baby. Scholars believe that it could even be a representation of the goddess Isis feeding her son Horus. A mother's milk was thought to be a potent remedy for illness and was often stored in jars and pots.*

HOUSEHOLD POTS were made from river clay. The clay was first prepared by adding fine sand to make it easier to work. The potters then shaped the vessels using the coil method and smoothed them inside and out to a remarkably even thickness. The outsides of the pots were often rubbed with a flat stone before firing to give them a shiny red look. Others were painted with black designs or rippled by dragging a comb across the surface.

WOOD-BURNING KILNS were used to fire the pots. They were beehive-shaped and made from mud bricks. They needed constant attention to keep the temperature high and even.

MAKE A CLAY POT

You will need: self-hardening clay, sharp pencil, paints

1 Knead the clay until it is easy to work. Make a flat, round base for your pot. Keep the remaining clay in a ball so it does not dry out.

2 Take some clay from the ball and roll out two long coils of the same thickness. Score the rim of the base with a pencil so the clay will stick properly.

3 Use the coils to build up the sides of the pot as shown. Make a third coil before using the second, and so on, to ensure they are all the same length. Score every layer as you go.

◁ *Decorate your pots with bold geometric patterns.*

A TAPERING BASE was given to many vessels. This meant they could be rested in a stand or fitted into a depression in the ground. Early on, they were decorated with geometric patterns on a red surface, or spiral and mottled designs to mimic vessels that had been carved from stone.

DECORATIVE VASES and stylized sculptures of human and animal figures were made in the New Kingdom period. Instead of the red and black decoration of earlier times, pots were also painted with a bold shade of blue, a pigment extracted from copper or cobalt.

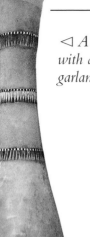

◁ *A New Kingdom alabaster vase with a long neck inlaid with floral garlands made of glass paste.*

△ *This calcite 'wishing cup' was one of the first finds by the excavators venturing into Tutankhamun's tomb.*

METAL VASES, BOWLS and open containers were made of gold, bronze and copper by hammering sheets of metal around an anvil, a heavy wood or stone block. Statues, tools and weapons were cast by pouring the molten metal into a pottery or stone mould. All metals were considered rare and precious because, even if there was an adequate supply, mining was an expensive, difficult and lengthy process.

4 When you get to the widest point, stop and smooth both the inside and outside of your pot. Score the top before you re-start with the coils.

5 When you have completed your pot, smooth the outside and inside for a perfect finish. Add a rim or, for extra decoration, a pair of handles. Then allow the pot to dry according to the directions on the packet.

6 Paint your pot dark red to look like terracotta from the Nile Valley. When that is dry, paint on some black geometric designs.

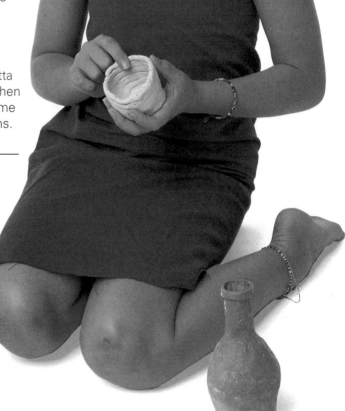

STONE VESSELS were made from the large outcrops of attractive mottled stone found in the desert and hills bordering the valley of the Nile. First, blocks of stone were cut out using a saw, and these were then shaped on the outside with chisels, **bow-drills** and **rasps**. Finally, the insides were drilled and chiselled out. Vases with narrow necks were made in two separate pieces and then cemented together.

△ *This is a replica of a wall-painting taken from the tomb of a powerful overlord from the Middle Kingdom. A grid of squares may have been used to paint the neat rows of labourers who are all in proportion to each other.*

THE BEST PRESERVED paintings were painted on to the plaster walls of the sealed tombs of the wealthy. Evidence shows that houses were painted with coloured murals and patterns too.

MAKE A TOMB PAINTING

You will need: plaster of Paris, water, bowl, polystyrene tray, pencil, ruler, paper and tracing paper, nail, paints, steel wool

1 Put the plaster into a bowl and add water gradually, stirring all the time, so that there are no dry patches of powder left. Mix the plaster with your fingers and get rid of any air bubbles.

2 When you have a smooth paste, pour the mixture into the polystyrene tray until it covers the bottom. Leave to set until it has formed into a plaque.

3 Copy or draw your own Egyptian scene on tracing paper. If you prefer you can use the ancient Egyptian method of using a grid to help you get the figure(s) in proportion.

4 When the plaque is dry, put your tracing paper over it and draw over every line, pressing hard. Scratch away the lines on the plaque with a nail to leave a clear outline.

5 Paint the plaque using earthy, natural colours. Then, using the steel wool, gently rub away small bits of the picture so that it passes for being about 3,000 years old, as shown right.

◁ *A wall-painting from the tomb of the pharaoh Horemheb which was discovered in the Valley of the Kings. The goddess Isis faces the pharaoh, and the god Harsiese is on the right.*

DRAWING, and the rules that went with it, evolved alongside writing. Artists drew and painted not what they saw, but what they knew was there. So if, for example, they were painting a chest that they knew contained a necklace in one of the drawers, they might show a side view of the chest with the necklace placed on top. And when they drew a scene, it did not simply record what they saw from their own viewpoint, but included everything and everyone that they knew to be present.

DEFINITE RULES applied to art because it had a definite purpose: to come to life in the next world. The people and objects in the afterlife had to be perfect, so tomb and temple paintings never portrayed death, disease or old age.

PEOPLE AND OBJECTS were drawn flat, from whatever angle made them instantly recognizable. People were nearly always drawn with their faces, arms and legs in profile (because they are easier to identify), but the eye and shoulders faced the front. Men were often shown as having dark skin, as they worked in the sun, whereas women were fair-skinned as they spent more time indoors.

PROPORTIONS were laid down so that people could be recognized by the gods in the afterlife, and to provide guidelines for apprentice artists. Most apprentices used a squared grid as a guide. One Middle Kingdom scale measured the standing human figure as 18 squares from the ground to the hair-line, so the shoulders started in square 16, the waist in square 12 and the knees between 6 and 7.

PAINT COLOURS were made from powdered minerals and other natural materials. These are just some examples:

Black	charcoal
Red	ochre
White	powdered limestone
Blue	copper/cobalt
Green	malachite
Yellow	iron oxide

▷ *Malachite, an oxide of copper, was ground and used as soft green eyeshadow.*

◁ *Copper was mined in Nubia, Sinai and the Eastern Desert. It was used to make tools as well as pigment.*

Reading and writing

One reason we know so much about the ancient Egyptians is because they had a written language and recorded everything. All legal and business agreements were documented, so the few who could read and write were in great demand. They were called **scribes**. Instead of an alphabet, they used **hieroglyphs**, or signs, to represent sounds. There were over 700 in all which could be used in various combinations to give particular meanings, or else to represent groups of two or three consonants.

ANCIENT EGYPTIAN belongs to a family of languages that spread across northern Africa and western Asia. Some languages in that family, such as Arabic, are still spoken today. But ancient Egyptian is a dead language, except where it survives in a form within the Coptic Church.

THE ROSETTA STONE was the key to deciphering hieroglyphs. This black stone is inscribed with text in three different languages: Greek, **demotic** script and hieroglyphs. It was discovered in 1799, near Rosetta in the Nile Delta and later decoded by the French scholar Jean-François Champollion in 1822.

△ The top section of the Rosetta Stone is in hieroglyphs, the middle in demotic and the bottom in Greek.

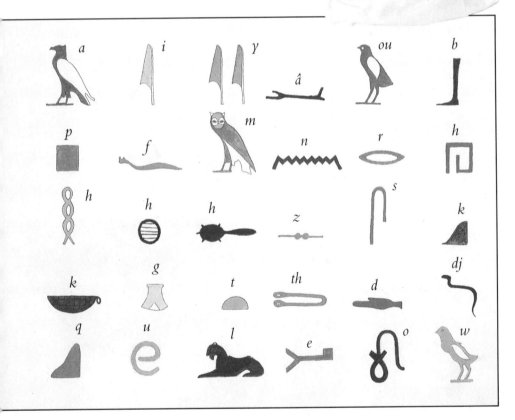

△ The use of hieroglyphs made writing complex and difficult to learn.

HIEROGLYPHS were carved into stone on monuments, painted on walls of burial tombs and used for making up a **cartouche**, or personal seal, which could be used as a signature.

hieroglyphs   demotic   Greek

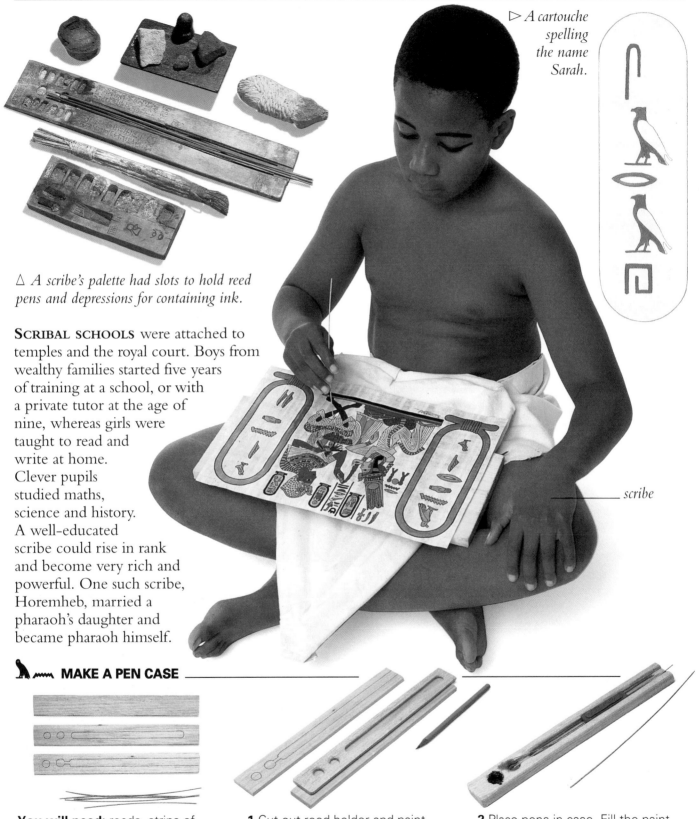

▷ *A cartouche spelling the name Sarah.*

△ *A scribe's palette had slots to hold reed pens and depressions for containing ink.*

SCRIBAL SCHOOLS were attached to temples and the royal court. Boys from wealthy families started five years of training at a school, or with a private tutor at the age of nine, whereas girls were taught to read and write at home. Clever pupils studied maths, science and history. A well-educated scribe could rise in rank and become very rich and powerful. One such scribe, Horemheb, married a pharaoh's daughter and became pharaoh himself.

scribe

⏚ ⌇⌇⌇ MAKE A PEN CASE

You will need: reeds, strips of balsa wood, marked as shown above, PVA glue, powder paints, craft knife

1 Cut out reed holder and paint wells as shown and sandwich together the layers of wood. Glue into place. Leave to dry.

2 Place pens in case. Fill the paint wells with powder paint to look like ground-up minerals. Now your scribe's palette is complete.

Egyptian inventions

The Egyptians were a clever, curious people who invented many things we recognize today. In addition to their complicated form of picture-writing (see page 40), they had advanced ideas about medicine, measuring time, mathematics and astronomy.

THE ANCIENT EGYPTIANS were the first people to organize the year into 365 days and the days into 24 hours. The Egyptian year was divided like this:

10 days = 1 week   3 weeks = 1 month
4 months = 1 season   3 seasons + 5 holy days = 1 year

THE WATER CLOCK, the most common Egyptian clock, was a vessel marked with lines on the inside. Time was measured against these levels as water dripped through a hole in the base. Sun poles, ideal in the sunny climate, were used by people of learning, such as priests, to tell the time.

MAKE A WATER CLOCK

You will need: pot made from self-hardening clay, painted and varnished inside to make it waterproof, bradawl, wax crayon, water jug filled with water, cup or glass

1 Make a small hole with a bradawl in side of pot near to base as shown left. Place glass or cup under pot to catch water dripping out of the hole. Pour water into pot, filling it up.

EGYPTIAN DOCTORS were surprisingly advanced for their time. Papyrus manuals reveal that they had a detailed knowledge of bodily systems such as digestion, circulation and the nervous system. This was gained largely through centuries of **embalming** the dead. They also studied the symptoms of sick people in order to understand illness and disease, and used plants and herbs, such as garlic and juniper berries, as cures.

MAGICIANS were valued for their healing powers too. Spells were chanted as cures and to ward off injury, sickness and danger.

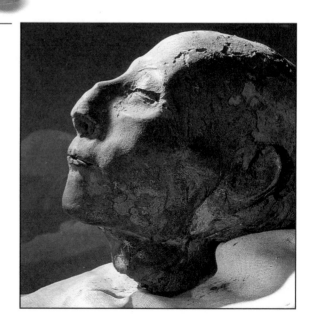

▷ *The mummified head of Nebera, chief of the royal stables of Tuthmosis III. Embalming taught doctors a lot about* **anatomy**.

MAKE A SUN POLE

7am

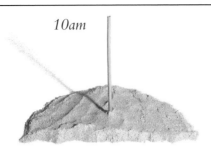
10am

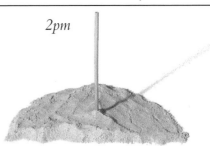
2pm

You will need: wooden post, watch

1 Find a spot in your garden that is sunny all day.

2 Push the post into the ground and mark where the shadow falls at 7am. Check the shadow's position every hour, marking it each time.

3 After a full day of sun, with a mark on the ground for every hour, your sun pole will be all set to tell you the time when the sun next appears.

2 Time the water as it drips out, using a crayon to mark the water level on inside of pot every five minutes. Once empty, refill pot and time again, checking marks for accuracy.

MEASUREMENTS were related to the human body. The main one was the cubit, equal to the distance from the elbow to the tip of the middle finger. It was further divided into palms and digits (the width of a finger).

MATHEMATICAL CALCULATIONS involving sophisticated **geometry** were used for building pyramids. The Egyptians had no signs for numbers between two and nine.

1 = | 10 = ∩   100 = ℮   1,000 = 𝕏

so 13 was written like this: ∩ | | |
146 like this: ℮ ∩ ∩ | | |
               ∩ ∩ | | |

▷ *The Egyptian measuring system worked like this:*

distance from elbow to outstretched fingertip = 1 cubit

cubit = seven palms

palm = four finger widths

elbow to fingertip = 1 cubit

Boats and chariots

The Nile was the highway of Egypt. Boats could drift downstream with the current to the north of the country, and sail upstream with the help of the northerly wind to the south. The Egyptian hieroglyph for travelling north is a boat with no sail or mast, and for travelling south it is a ship in full sail.

𓂃 **EARLY BOATS** were made from papyrus reeds, bound with string made from reed fibres. By 3200 BC timber was being imported from the Lebanon, and boatyards on the Nile were building wooden ships.

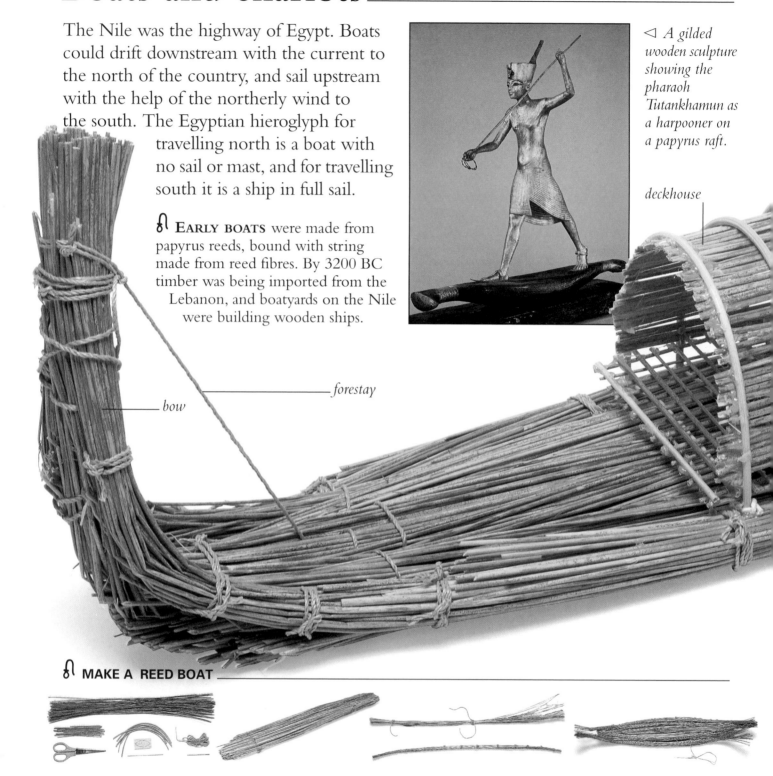

◁ *A gilded wooden sculpture showing the pharaoh Tutankhamun as a harpooner on a papyrus raft.*

deckhouse

forestay

bow

𓂃 **MAKE A REED BOAT**

You will need: bundle of thin reeds or dried grasses, scissors, thin string, bodkin, balsa wood cut as shown into handle and blade for steering oar, six lengths of basket cane for deckhouse, glue

1 Tie a small bundle of reeds with string at regular intervals. Prepare seven or eight bundles in the same way and sew them together. Trim the ends so the boat base looks like the example above left.

2 Make 2 longer bundles for the sides, as shown above left. Sew them on using the string and bodkin. Fill in the centre with more bundles if necessary and sew them to the boat base as above.

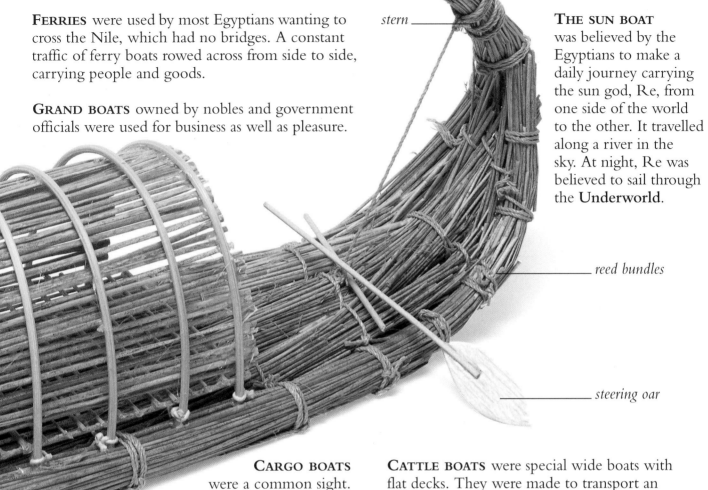

FERRIES were used by most Egyptians wanting to cross the Nile, which had no bridges. A constant traffic of ferry boats rowed across from side to side, carrying people and goods.

GRAND BOATS owned by nobles and government officials were used for business as well as pleasure.

stern

reed bundles

steering oar

THE SUN BOAT was believed by the Egyptians to make a daily journey carrying the sun god, Re, from one side of the world to the other. It travelled along a river in the sky. At night, Re was believed to sail through the **Underworld**.

CARGO BOATS were a common sight. All heavy cargo, such as slabs of stone or **obelisks**, was moved on huge river barges, towed by a fleet of small boats.

FUNERAL BARGES were used to carry bodies across the river to the embalmers' workshops. The crossing was conducted with great ceremony and dignity.

CATTLE BOATS were special wide boats with flat decks. They were made to transport an Egyptian farmer's most treasured possession – his cattle. These animals were the true measure of his wealth and worth protecting at all costs.

ROYAL BOATS ensured that the pharaoh travelled in great style and comfort. Huge, canopied boats protected royal families from the glare of the sun and the inquisitive stare of their subjects.

3 Shape the stern by tying the ends of the reeds into a tight bundle, curling them up and over and securing with string as shown (damp reeds bend more easily). Shape the bow in the same way.

4 The base of the shelter is made from a latticework of reeds glued together, and the roof from cane bent into semicircles, held in place with string. Fill in the roof from the inside with short lengths of reed.

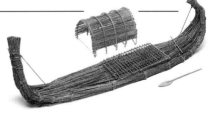

5 Glue the base of the shelter on to the boat and fix the roof on top. Glue together the oar handle and paddle. The stick at the stern is a support for the steering oar, so it can be held still. Now the boat is ready to float!

SEAGOING BOATS had to be bigger and stronger than river boats, although they did follow the same basic design. They were built of wood, mainly cedar wood, which came from the hillsides of a sea port in Lebanon called Byblos. Seagoing boats were known as 'Byblos-boats'.

ORDINARY EGYPTIANS travelled very little. Some ventured as far as the next village and, if they could afford it, made a once-in-a-lifetime pilgrimage to Abydos, a religious centre in the south. Generally, people were very suspicious of foreign places, and thought it far better to stay at home. Their greatest fear was to die in a foreign country where they would not have a proper burial, and so arrive unprepared for the afterlife

△ *A model sailing boat found in Tutankhamun's tomb, complete with oars and linen sails.*

FOREIGN TRADE was the prize that tempted Egyptians to travel. To the south lay Nubia (now Sudan), rich in gold, copper, and semiprecious stones. Strange animals such as monkeys, giraffes and panthers were also brought back.

TO THE NORTH lay the Mediterranean Sea. However, the Egyptians stuck to the more familiar north-east coastline, and traded with what are now Israel, Lebanon and Syria. Syrians travelled to Egypt too. Quite different in appearance, their colourful clothes and beards seemed strange to ancient Egyptians.

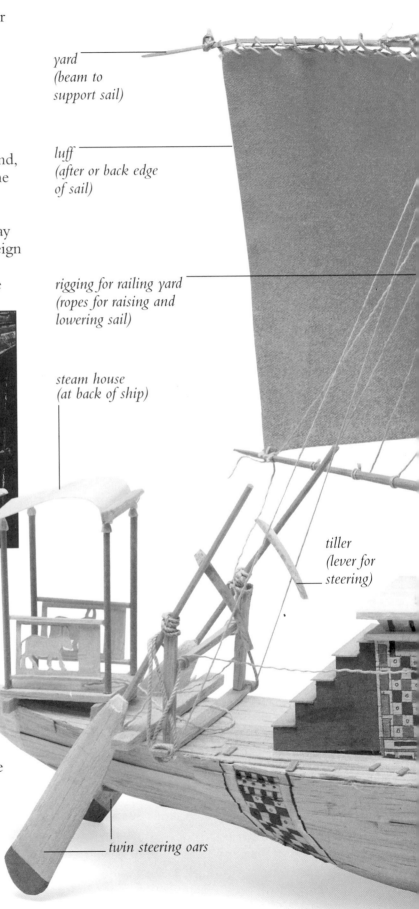

yard (beam to support sail)

luff (after or back edge of sail)

rigging for railing yard (ropes for raising and lowering sail)

steam house (at back of ship)

tiller (lever for steering)

twin steering oars

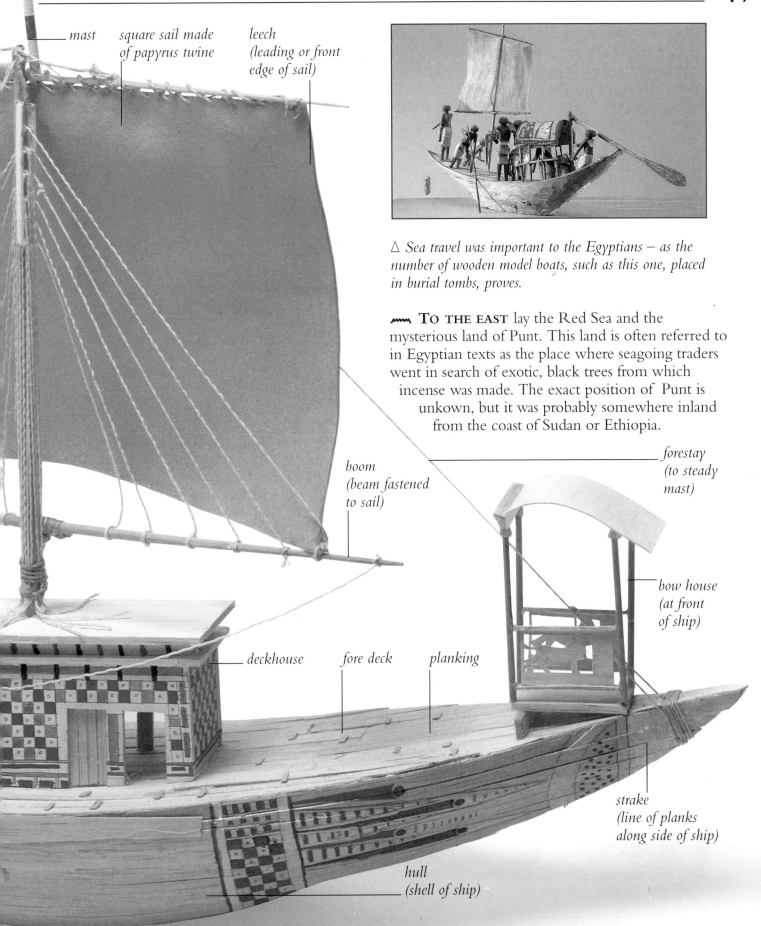

mast

square sail made
of papyrus twine

leech
(leading or front
edge of sail)

△ *Sea travel was important to the Egyptians – as the
number of wooden model boats, such as this one, placed
in burial tombs, proves.*

〰 **TO THE EAST** lay the Red Sea and the
mysterious land of Punt. This land is often referred to
in Egyptian texts as the place where seagoing traders
went in search of exotic, black trees from which
incense was made. The exact position of Punt is
unkown, but it was probably somewhere inland
from the coast of Sudan or Ethiopia.

boom
(beam fastened
to sail)

forestay
(to steady
mast)

bow house
(at front
of ship)

deckhouse

fore deck

planking

strake
(line of planks
along side of ship)

hull
(shell of ship)

THERE WERE NO PROPER ROADS in ancient Egypt. There was no point as the annual floods would have washed them away. Unless they were lucky enough to own a donkey, ordinary people had to walk everywhere. Very rich people were carried around by servants on platforms with a throne-like seat.

THE EASTERN DESERT, which lay between the east bank of the Nile and the Red Sea, provided overland routes to present day Syria and Lebanon. Trade with these countries was important as they had a wealth of metals and semiprecious stones. The Eastern Desert also yielded raw materials, such as copper and tin.

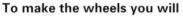

MAKE A CHARIOT

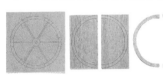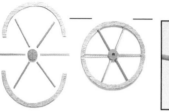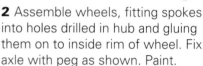

To make the wheels you will need: paper, pencil, compass, balsa wood, thin dowelling for spokes and pegs, thicker dowelling for axle, wood circles for hubs, PVA glue, craft knife

1 Draw a template for wheels as shown. Use the compass to mark two sections for each wheel on to wood. Ask an adult to help you cut them out.

2 Assemble wheels, fitting spokes into holes drilled in hub and gluing them on to inside rim of wheel. Fix axle with peg as shown. Paint.

HEAVY OBJECTS, such as stones and statues, were tied on to sledges and pulled by men with ropes. Water or oil was poured under the front of the sledge to make it slide along more easily.

horse yoke

TO THE WEST lay a desert area populated by **nomadic** tribes and known, during the years of the Old and Middle Kingdoms, as *Tjemehu*. Today it is Libya. Below *Tjemehu* was the endless stretch of the Western Desert which protected Egypt from raiding neighbours. It also provided the ancient Egyptians with limestone which they quarried from the areas close to home.

yoke pole

LONG OVERLAND journeys were made to carry out these trading operations with neighbours to the east, and for mining and quarrying operations to the west. Donkeys were laden with goods and taken on long treks across the desert. Camels, ideal animals for desert travel, were not introduced until the beginning of the Roman period in 30 BC when raiding tribesmen descended upon the fertile Nile Valley on these strange, swift-footed beasts.

◁ *This relief in the rock, from the temple of Ramses II, shows the pharaoh riding into battle on a chariot while conquering Nubia, situated to the south.*

THE CHARIOT was introduced to Egypt by the Hyksos from southern Palestine. They invaded the delta area of Egypt at the end of the Middle Kingdom period. The rich were the only people able to afford chariots. They used them for hunting and travelling around on business.

CHARIOT WHEELS were a technological marvel, given the few tools available. They were made from curved segments of wood, bound together with a leather tyre. Initially, all chariots ran on four-spoked wheels, but during the New Kingdom, an extra two spokes were added.

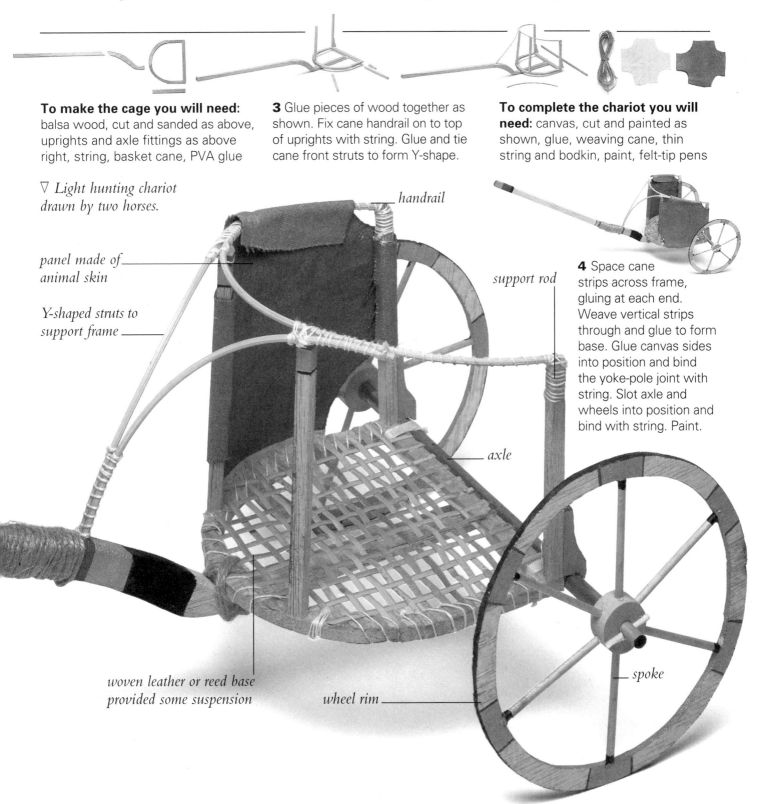

To make the cage you will need: balsa wood, cut and sanded as above, uprights and axle fittings as above right, string, basket cane, PVA glue

3 Glue pieces of wood together as shown. Fix cane handrail on to top of uprights with string. Glue and tie cane front struts to form Y-shape.

To complete the chariot you will need: canvas, cut and painted as shown, glue, weaving cane, thin string and bodkin, paint, felt-tip pens

▽ *Light hunting chariot drawn by two horses.*

handrail

panel made of animal skin

support rod

Y-shaped struts to support frame

4 Space cane strips across frame, gluing at each end. Weave vertical strips through and glue to form base. Glue canvas sides into position and bind the yoke-pole joint with string. Slot axle and wheels into position and bind with string. Paint.

axle

woven leather or reed base provided some suspension

wheel rim

spoke

Guarding the frontiers

△ *Daggers often boasted sheaths overlaid with gold.*

Ancient Egypt was the first rich and powerful civilization in history. Naturally it attracted the envy of neighbours who wanted some of Egypt's wealth for themselves. The pharaohs of Egypt would rather have conquered by influence than by war. But they were certainly prepared to push out the boundaries of Egypt, building fortresses for protection and dealing harshly with intruders if necessary.

MAKE A SHIELD

You will need: thick cardboard, scissors, canvas material, pencil, string, PVA glue, paint

1 Cut out cardboard in the shape of a shield as shown above. Then, cut out a piece of canvas, the same shape, only larger.

2 Glue canvas to card. Draw a wide border around the edge. Paint the area inside the border white with brown patches to look like cowhide.

◁ *Arrowheads were commonly made of copper and designed to kill the victim instantly.*

THE ROYAL ARMY, during the Old and Middle Kingdoms, consisted of a small group of professional soldiers and the pharaoh's bodyguards. If a campaign was being mounted, labourers would be called up from the fields. At this time, the army was made up of foot soldiers armed with either bows and arrows or axes and spears, and protected by large shields of wood or leather.

battle axe

BY THE NEW KINGDOM, warfare had become much more organized. The army was larger and better run, with horses and chariots providing extra speed. Soldiers were well-trained and were allowed to take slaves and goods from conquered armies after a successful campaign.

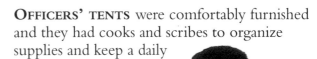

◁ *A golden fly was the pharaoh's award for bravery on the battlefield.*

〜〜 **SEVERAL DIVISIONS** existed within the royal army. Each division consisted of 4,000 foot soldiers and an elite corps of 1,000 charioteers. It was then sub-divided into 20 companies of 250 men – 200 foot soldiers (in four units of 50 men) and 50 charioteers.

〜〜 **CHARIOTEERS** fought two to a chariot and were regarded as superior to other soldiers. They had their own barracks and were only temporarily assigned to a company.

AXES AND SPEARS had wooden handles and bronze blades. Soldiers wore protective tunics with metal scales, or wrapped bands of leather around their chests.

CAMPS were set up when the army was on the move. A moat was dug around the outside and the soldiers' shields were used to make a wall.

OFFICERS' TENTS were comfortably furnished and they had cooks and scribes to organize supplies and keep a daily record of the battle.

🐊〜〜 **MAKE A BATTLE AXE**

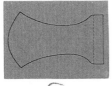

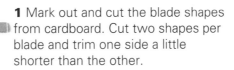

You will need: craft knife, glue, dowelling, pencil, string, silver foil, saw, cardboard

1 Mark out and cut the blade shapes from cardboard. Cut two shapes per blade and trim one side a little shorter than the other.

2 Ask an adult to help you saw down the dowelling to the depth of the blade as shown. Score a design on the blade with a pencil.

3 Glue the two sides of the blade together with the longer side underneath. Cover the blade with foil, rubbing over the design. Slot blade into the dowelling and secure with string as shown left.

Gods and the afterlife

The ancient Egyptians believed strongly in many gods who ruled everything from the sun and moon, to love, wisdom and war. Some were national gods, worshipped in grand temples all over the country, but most were local gods, worshipped in smaller temples within the towns. An Egyptian's strongest belief was that he or she would enjoy a wonderful life after death that would be a perfect version of life on earth. To be prepared, the dead were buried with all their possessions and food for the journey to the afterlife.

THE SUN GOD, RE, is central to most Egyptian legends about the creation of the world. In one version, the world is nothing but a black ocean. Then a mound of dry land emerges out of the mud and a sacred blue lotus flower grows. It opens up and out steps Re, who goes on to create all things.

▷ *An Old Kingdom group statue of the pharaoh Mycerinus between the goddess Hathor, regarded as the ideal of beauty, and Hu, the personification of a province of Upper Egypt.*

ANIMAL GODS were worshipped from the Old Kingdom onwards. The Egyptians often associated the character of an animal with that of a god. By the New Kingdom, most gods continued to be depicted with the head or body of an animal.

◁ *A solid gold statuette of Amun-Re, a New Kingdom god who was a powerful combination of the sun god Re and Amun the creator.*

Montu,
god of war

Amun,
creator god

Khons,
god of
the moon

Thoth,
god of
knowledge

Horus,
royal
protector

Hathor,
goddess
of love

Anubis,
god of the
necropolis

Osiris,
god of the
Underworld

HUNDREDS OF GODS and goddesses were worshipped by the Egyptians, and many of them were related. Shu, son of Re, was god of the air. Shu's daughter, Nut was the sky goddess whose body stretched across the horizon, held up by her father. She married Geb, her brother and god of the earth. Their heirs were Isis and Osiris (god of the Underworld) and together they ruled Egypt.

Set, brother of Osiris and Isis, and god of evil, was jealous. He murdered Osiris and cut up his body. Anubis, god of embalming and the dead, gathered the pieces and the goddess Isis restored him to life.

TEMPLES were the earthly homes of the gods and goddesses. Only priests and priestesses could enter, while ordinary people prayed at the gates.

〰 **MAKE ANUBIS**

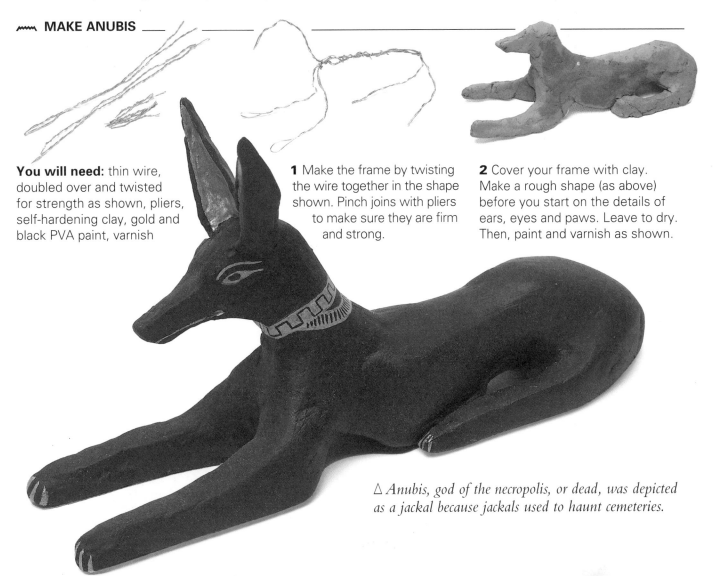

You will need: thin wire, doubled over and twisted for strength as shown, pliers, self-hardening clay, gold and black PVA paint, varnish

1 Make the frame by twisting the wire together in the shape shown. Pinch joins with pliers to make sure they are firm and strong.

2 Cover your frame with clay. Make a rough shape (as above) before you start on the details of ears, eyes and paws. Leave to dry. Then, paint and varnish as shown.

△ *Anubis, god of the necropolis, or dead, was depicted as a jackal because jackals used to haunt cemeteries.*

△ *The magnificent death mask of the young pharaoh Tutankhamun represents him as the god of the Underworld, Osiris. It is made of inlaid sheet gold and measures 54cm high and weighs over 10kg.*

THE UNDERWORLD, called Duat, was believed to be a land full of dangers, so a guidebook known as **The Book of the Dead** was buried in tombs with the dead. This book and a knowledge of all the right spells, guaranteed safe passage through the Underworld to the Hall of Two Truths.

THE AFTERLIFE, an ideal version of Egypt, was where everyone wanted to go when they died. Upon death, an Egyptian arriving in the Hall of Two Truths would be led to a set of scales by Anubis, god of the dead and of embalming. Here, after being interrogated, his or her heart was weighed against the feather of truth. If honest, the person was granted safe passage to the afterlife by Osiris. The hearts of the dishonest were devoured by a goddess known as Devourer of the Dead. Paradise was no place for spirits without a heart.

GRAVES of ordinary people have been found, and it seems they were buried in reed or wooden chests along with their possessions and food, to ensure they reached the afterlife.

THE BODIES OF THE RICH were buried with a supply of worldly goods for eternity, and models of servants to work in the fields of the gods to pay off heavenly taxes. Models of bakeries, workshops, scribes and priests were also placed in tombs, so the dead would have all the help and guidance they needed. They also believed that the dead needed a body in the afterlife, which is why corpses were preserved.

 **MAKE A DEATH MASK**

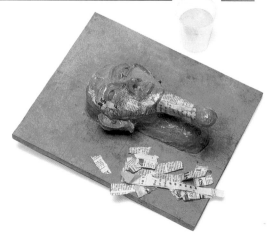

You will need: large baseboard, Plasticine modelled into a bearded face and neck as shown above, Vaseline, cardboard, newspaper torn into strips, wallpaper paste, masking tape

1 Cover the Plasticine head with a layer of Vaseline, so the paper strips do not stick to it.

2 Cut out cardboard shapes for headdress as shown.

3 Start covering the Plasticine head with the strips of newspaper and wallpaper paste. Keep the layer of paper over the face as smooth as possible, so the details of the features are not lost.

PREPARING A BODY for burial took 70 days. First the brain and internal organs (all except the heart) were removed and placed in **canopic jars**.

THE LAST CEREMONY to be performed before burial was the opening of the mouth. The priest touched the mouth of the mummy with ritual instruments so the deceased would be able to eat, speak and breathe in the afterlife.

◁ *The mummy of an adult woman which dates from around 1000 BC.*

NATRON CRYSTALS (a type of salt) were then packed around the body, which was left to dry for 40 days. There followed a period during which the body cavity was stuffed with linen and sawdust, and false eyes were put in the sockets. The body was massaged with lotions and coated with resins. Finally, 15 days were spent wrapping the body with bandages and charms to ensure its form was properly preserved.

A DEATH MASK completed the mummy. Royal masks were made of gold, while others were made of linen or papyrus and painted to look like gold.

THE COFFIN, of either wood or stone, had inscriptions and prayers carved into it and usually a pair of eyes painted on the outside so the dead could see out. A little door was painted on the inside through which the spirit could leave.

4 Slot the cardboard headdress piece flat on the board, behind the ears. Place the top of the headdress over the forehead of the model and attach to back of headdress with masking tape.

5 Cover rest of mask with paper and glue. Leave to dry. Ease the Plasticine head out from the back. The beard and ears may be difficult to remove, so be careful. Now paint.

Pyramids and burial

Pharaohs believed that they became gods in the afterlife, so their tombs had to be very grand. Pyramid tombs were built during the Old Kingdom. The shape represents the mound of earth that rose out of the dark ocean at the beginning of time, from which the creator god Re emerged (see page 52). The biggest pyramid is the Great Pyramid of Giza. It is still one of the largest man-made structures in the world.

△ *The Great Pyramid of Giza was the burial tomb of the pharaoh Cheops. It took over 20 years to build, and originally stood at 146m.*

△ *Some experts believe that a long, shallow, mud and rubble ramp was used to haul huge building blocks up to the pyramid on sledges.*

△ *As the pyramid got higher, the ramp would get longer, to keep an even gradient.*

covered causeway, nearly 1km long

valley temple

Nile

MARKING OUT the ground was the first step. It involved complex mathematics. To set out the corner blocks, the height of the pyramid and the angle of the sloping sides had to be calculated carefully. This ensured that the top would be dead centre.

TO CUT STONES the Egyptians used copper and bronze tools (iron was very scarce). Another method was to make small holes in a block of stone, along the line to be cut. Wooden wedges were forced into the holes and water was poured over the dry wood to make it swell up and crack the stone along the line.

TO SMOOTH THE SURFACE of the pyramid, great triangular facing blocks of the best quality polished limestone were cut and added to each course, from the top down. These facing stones gleamed white in the sun. The stone cutters were so skilful at cutting and fitting the blocks (they did not use cement) that even today a piece of paper cannot be slipped between two blocks.

pyramid for the queen

◁ *Pyramid complex of Sahure at Abusir.*

enclosure wall

mortuary temple

THE FIRST LAYER, or course, of stones was laid out all over the base. Side blocks were then laid out, meeting each of the corner stones. The next course was laid on the first, and so on up to 200 courses, until a single capping stone was placed on top. (In the case of the Great Pyramid of Giza, this was coated in gold.) Meanwhile, tomb chambers, ante-rooms and access tunnels inside the pyramid were beaten out of the blocks with hammers made of a hard stone called dolerite.

ARCHAEOLOGISTS have various theories on how the Egyptians heaved two-and-a-half-tonne stone blocks up a pyramid.

THE ONE RAMP THEORY suggests that a mud ramp was built and the stones dragged up it. But for the angle of the ramp to be shallow enough, it would have had to be three times as long as the pyramid, and no rubble has been found to indicate that such a structure ever existed.

THE ANGLED RAMP THEORY states that the internal core of the pyramid was built in steps and series of ramps were built, from step to step. The steps were then filled out later with smaller stones, and the facing stones set into them.

THE LEVER THEORY proposes that teams of skilled workers levered the stones up the courses.

△ *The Great Sphinx at Giza is 4,500 years old. Over 73m long and 20m high, it guards the way to the pyramid of the pharaoh Khafre.*

𓂀 **INSIDE THE PYRAMID** a series of passages snaked up and down and led to caverns and chambers, some lined with granite. Escape shafts meant the burial party could get out of the pyramid after sealing up the burial chamber and treasure stores.

△ *The coffins of royalty or noblemen were placed in a sarcophagus. By the New Kingdom, they would have the figure of a protective goddess carved into each corner.*

THE BURIAL CHAMBER was usually dug deep beneath the pyramid. Here, the coffin of the dead pharaoh was put into a stone box called a **sarcophagus**. Around the room were piled chests full of possessions, food and furniture, and models of anything an important person might need in the afterlife. On the walls, hieroglyphic spells gave the pharaoh safe passage to the afterlife.

ANTECHAMBERS were filled with treasures, so the pharaoh could enjoy a rich and comfortable afterlife. Boats were also buried with the pharaoh in case his spirit needed to travel.

AFTER THE BURIAL, the priests left the chamber, sweeping away their footprints as they backed towards the door. Then the door was sealed so that no one could enter.

THE MORTUARY TEMPLE was usually an unsealed chamber above ground. Here, priests dedicated to caring for the dead pharaoh's spirit, could leave food and offerings to the gods.

▷ *Coffins carried spells written in hieroglyphs, to protect the dead on their journey to the afterlife.*

TOMB ROBBERS have been raiding tombs for their gold, jewels and precious oils ever since they were first built. The Great Pyramid at Giza, for instance, is thought to have been robbed of almost everything when royal power collapsed at the end of the Old Kingdom.

New Kingdom pharaohs felt that pyramids were too easy to break into, so they had their burial chambers built into solid rock. Corridors and chambers were dug deep beneath the ground and the pyramid entrance was well concealed.

◁ *Inside the Great Pyramid at Giza. The burial chamber was very deep to protect it from thieves.*

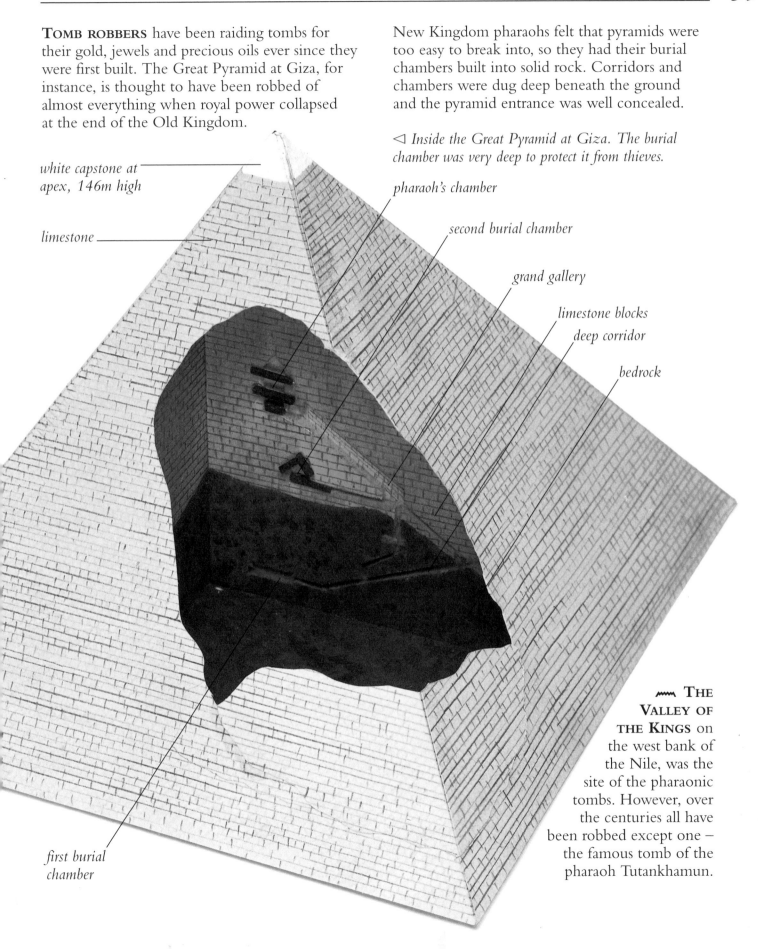

white capstone at apex, 146m high

limestone

pharaoh's chamber

second burial chamber

grand gallery

limestone blocks

deep corridor

bedrock

first burial chamber

〰 **THE VALLEY OF THE KINGS** on the west bank of the Nile, was the site of the pharaonic tombs. However, over the centuries all have been robbed except one – the famous tomb of the pharaoh Tutankhamun.

An amazing discovery

△ *The entrance to Tutankhamun's tomb in the Valley of the Kings.*

THE DISCOVERY OF TUTANKHAMUN'S tomb in the Valley of the Kings was one of the most exciting archaeological finds of the century. The tomb had lay hidden from robbers since 1327 BC.

We know a lot about the ancient Egyptians largely because they buried so many artefacts with them for use in the afterlife. As a result, their tombs reveal an enormous amount of information from which archaeologists have been able to piece together a detailed picture of their daily life. Also, Egypt's hot and dry climate is ideal for preserving these ancient sites and artefacts.

annexe – stored wine jars, oils and food

antechamber

descending corridor

sealed first doorway

FIRST EVIDENCE of the tomb was discovered in early November 1922, when an expedition, led by British archaeologists Lord Caernarvon and Howard Carter, uncovered a flight of stone steps cut into the rock face, leading downwards.

A SEALED ENTRANCE was found at the bottom of the steps, the door was plastered over and its seals were still intact. The corridor beyond the door was filled with stone rubble. Another door, the same as the entrance door, was also sealed.

stepped entrance to tomb

THE ANTECHAMBER was a stunning vision of glimmering gold. When, on 26 November 1922, Carter opened this doorway and held up his candle, he could hardly believe his eyes. The room was piled high with chests, caskets, statues, beds, chairs, chariots and weapons. Clearing the chamber and cataloguing all the objects took until February 1923.

THE PHARAOH'S BODY was brilliantly hidden. Bolted doors in the side of the shrine revealed another shrine and another. There were four in all, then a sarcophagus. Fitting inside this like Russian dolls, were three coffins. The last, made entirely of gold, was opened in October 1925. It contained the 3,000-year-old mummy of Tutankhamun, wearing a mask of solid gold inlaid with jewels and garlanded with flowers.

burial chamber

first outer shrine hood

△ *Carter chips off the hardened black ointments that had been poured over the gold coffin.*

second shrine with wooden frame and gilded surface

third and fourth shrines made of gilded wood

treasury – canopic jars containing Tutankhamun's insides, removed before embalming, were found here

THE BURIAL CHAMBER was finally entered through a blocked doorway flanked by statues of the pharaoh, in February 1923. The room was filled by a giant gold and blue shrine. The top reached to the ceiling and there was only about half a metre between the shrine and the walls.

sarcophagus

Gilded inner coffins, containing solid gold coffin and mummy of Tutankhamun

Glossary

afterlife The ancient Egyptians believed that after death they would live on in a perfect world, if they travelled safely through the Underworld.

amulet A piece of jewellery worn as a magical charm to protect the wearer against evil or illness.

anatomy The study of the way the parts of the body fit together.

anthropologist A person who studies the origins, development and behaviour of people.

archaeologist A person who studies the remains of buildings and artefacts from the past.

artefact A man-made object.

barter A system of trade where goods are exchanged instead of using money.

Book of the Dead A scroll made from papyrus reeds which was buried with the dead. It contained instructions and spells which would ensure safe passage through the Underworld.

bow-drill A simple drill made from a flint or metal-tipped stick. A bow string is wrapped around the stick and pulled back and forth. This makes the stick turn, so that the sharp end drills.

canopic jars When a body was embalmed, the internal organs were removed and stored in these jars to protect them from spells.

cartouche A royal name written in hieroglyphs and surrounded by an oval border.

civilization A developed and organized group or nation of people.

cloisonné A type of decoration made by filling an outline of metal with coloured enamel or glass.

Coptic Church The Christian Church of Egypt, established in the fourth century AD.

crook A hooked staff which looks very similar to that of a shepherd's. It was one of the pharaoh's symbols of office (along with the flail and sceptre), and it represented kingship.

culture The activities, ideas and beliefs of a group of people which form the basis of their shared way of life.

delta A place at the mouth of a river where the river splits into smaller channels, forming a triangular shape.

demotic A form of ancient Egyptian writing which replaced hieratic script around the seventh century BC. It was used by most people as it was quicker to use than hieratic.

embalming Treating a dead body using spices and ointments so as to preserve it as a mummy.

faience A glass-like substance made by heating powdered quartz or sand. The ancient Egyptians used faience to make colourful jewellery.

flail A tool used for threshing grain, which was one of the pharaoh's symbols of office. The flail represented the fertility of ancient Egypt.

flax A plant that is used to make linen cloth.

geometry The branch of mathematics that deals with lines, angles, curves and spaces. It is an important part of architecture.

henna A reddish hair dye made from a plant which was thought to ward off danger.

hieratic A shorthand form of hieroglyphs used by scribes for business, letters and stories.

hieroglyphs A form of writing which uses picture symbols to represent objects, ideas and sounds. In ancient Egyptian writing there were about 700 which were mainly used for religious inscriptions and monuments.

irrigation Supplying land with water so that crops can grow.

kiln An oven used for baking or 'firing' pottery to make it hard and waterproof.

kohl A black powder made from lead ore (known as galena) which was used as make-up for the eyes.

loom A machine used for weaving.

mummy The dead body of a person or animal which has been preserved by embalming.

natron A type of salt used to dry out bodies before they were embalmed.

necropolis A cemetery or burial ground, often near a large city. Anubis was the god of the necropolis, as well as the god of embalming and death.

nomadic Leading a wandering life with no fixed home.

obelisk A tall stone pillar with four flat sides and a pyramid-shaped top used as a monument.

ochre A red, powdery form of iron oxide that was used as a pigment, or when mixed with fat could be used as make-up for lips and cheeks.

papyrus A tall reed-like plant which grew along the banks of the Nile. The ancient Egyptians used it to make a form of paper, as well as sandals, baskets, ropes and even boats.

pharaoh A king of ancient Egypt. The word pharaoh means 'great house'.

pyramid A large burial tomb with four sloping triangular sides which was built for a pharaoh.

rasp A tool with a rough surface used to scrape and file.

sarcophagus A stone box containing a coffin.

scarab A magic symbol in the shape of a dung beetle. It was one of the most powerful symbols because it represented the sun and rebirth.

scribe A person who wrote and read for a living. Scribes often travelled around on behalf of the government, recording information on the progress of building projects and the harvest.

senet An ancient Egyptian board game.

shaduf A device used for raising water from a channel in order to irrigate the land.

shrine A place where sacred images or statues are placed and worshipped.

silt Sand, clay or other soil that is left behind by flowing water.

society People living together in an ordered community.

Stone Age The period when people used stone tools and weapons. It was during this time, in about 5000 BC, that the first settlers arrived in the Nile Valley.

Underworld A dangerous land that the Egyptians believed they would have to pass through after death, before they reached the land where they would spend the afterlife.

Index

Afterlife 5, 18, 39, 46, 52, 54, 55, 56, 58, 60
amulets 14
anthropologist 5
archaeologist 5, 57, 60–61
army 6, 16, 17, 50–51
artists and craftsmen 17, 34–35, 39
arts and crafts 34–39

Banquets 28, 31
beards 12
boats 32, 44–47
Book of the Dead 54
burial chambers 58, 59, 60-61

Caernarvon, Lord 60
canopic jars 55, 61
Carter, Howard 60, 61
cartouche 40, 41
Champollion, Jean François 40
chariots 32, 48–49, 50, 51
children 10, 12, 15, 17, 19, 24, 27, 30, 32
cloisonné 15
clothes 10–11
coffins 5, 55, 58, 61

Daily life 24
dancers 16, 31
death masks 54–55
decoration 10, 11, 14, 20, 34, 36
delta 8, 9, 32, 40, 49
demotic 40
desert 8, 18, 32, 48
drawing and painting 38–39

Embalming 55

Faience 14, 23, 28
families 19, 24, 25
farming 17, 26–27
floods 17, 18, 26, 48
food and drink 4, 28–29, 31
fun and games 30–33
furniture 22–23

Gardens 20
Giza, Great Pyramid of 5, 8, 56, 59
glass 14, 15
gods and goddesses 39, 52-53, 58; Amun 52, 53; Anubis 53, 54; Bes 22; Geb 53; Harsiese 38;

Hathor 52, 53; Horus 36, 53; Hu 52; Imhotep 22; Isis 36, 38, 53; Khons 53; Montu 53; Nekhbet 14; Nut 53, Osiris 53, 54; Re (sun god)15, 45, 52, 53, 56; Re Harakhty 15; Renenutet 27; Set 29, 53; Shu 53; Taweret 15; Thoth 35, 53
government 16, 17, 26, 27

Hair 12–13, 28
hieratic 35
hieroglyphs 35, 40, 44, 58
houses 18–23, 25
hunting 32

Inventions 42–43
irrigation 9, 26, 27

Jewellery 10, 14–15

Kitchens 19, 20
kohl 12, 13

Labourers 17, 50
law 16, 17
limestone 21, 48, 57, 59
linen 10, 11, 27, 34
looms 34–35
Lower Egypt 8, 9

Magicians 31, 42
make-up 10, 12–13
marriage 19, 24
measurements 43
medicine 42
metals 12, 15, 37, 48, 57; bronze 12, 28, 37, 57; copper 12, 37, 46, 48, 57; gold 8, 14, 15 28, 37, 46, 48, 54, 55, 57, 59 61; iron 37, 57; silver 28; tin 48
Middle Kingdom 4, 10, 11, 36, 39, 48, 49, 50, 52
mirrors 12
mummies 5, 24, 55, 61
music and musicians 16, 17, 30–31

Necropolis 54
New Kingdom 10, 11, 12, 18, 30, 31, 34, 36, 37, 49, 50, 52, 59
Nile 5, 8, 9, 11, 18, 26, 28, 29, 32, 37, 40, 44, 45, 59
nobles 12, 16, 17, 20, 31, 32

Old Kingdom 4, 10, 11, 17, 30, 48, 50, 52, 56

Papyrus 12, 17, 19, 34, 35, 42, 44, 55
pharaohs 6, 8, 16, 17, 22, 32, 50, 56, 58, 59, 60, 61; Amenemhat 6; Horemheb 38, 41; Khafre 58; Cheops 56; Mycerinus 52; Ramses II 5, 48; Sahure 57; Tutankhamun 14, 23, 37, 44, 46, 54, 59–61; Tuthmosis III 42
pottery 36–37
priests and priestesses 12, 16, 29, 53, 55, 58
pyramids 43, 56–59

Queens 6, 16

Religion 52–59
Rosetta Stone 40

Sarcophagus 58, 61
scarab 15
schools 17, 24, 41
scribes 16, 17, 35, 40, 41
seasons 26–27
senet 32–33
servants 11, 13, 20, 21, 24, 28, 50
shaduf 26
shrines 22, 61
society 16-17
sun pole 43

Taxes 16, 17, 26, 27
temples 5, 7, 16, 17, 18, 38, 52, 53, 58
tomb robbers 59, 60
tombs 5, 17, 54, 56–61
tools 37, 49; bow-drills 37; chisels 15, 37; rasps 37
towns and villages 18, 25
trade 4, 5, 6, 8, 9, 24, 46, 48
transport 44–49

Underworld 45, 54
Upper Egypt 8, 9, 14, 52

Valley of the Kings 38, 59, 60
villas 19, 20, 21

Wall-paintings 5, 31, 38–39
water clock 42–43
weapons 37, 50–51
weaving 34–35
wigs 10, 12–13, 28
writing 39, 40–41

THE ROMAN EMPIRE

Contents

The ancient Romans	4
Timeline	6
A conquering force	8
From emperor to slave	10
Togas and tunics	12
Dressing to impress	14
Life in the city	16
Gardens, mosaics and frescoes	22
Food and feasting	26
Family life	30
Education and trades	32
Gods of the Empire	34
At the games	38
Romans relaxing	42
Amazing architects	46
Feeding the Empire	48
Trade and transport	50
The Roman army	54
The fall of Rome	60
Glossary	62
Index	64

Words found in **bold** in the text can be found here

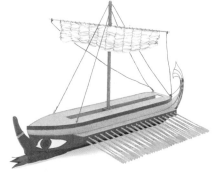

The ancient Romans

All human beings need food and shelter to survive. They also need a system of beliefs which gives shape and meaning to their lives. Throughout history, people have developed different ways of meeting these basic needs. By studying the people of the **Roman Empire**, we can learn how they used the resources around them to create a sophisticated way of life, many traces of which survive to this day.

IN THIS BOOK, we look at the **civilization** of the ancient Romans, a people of Italian origin. Two thousand years ago they conquered most of Europe, North Africa and the Middle East, creating one of the biggest empires in the world.

△ *Underwater archaeologists have explored many Roman shipwrecks in the Mediterranean Sea. By examining the cargo, they can tell what people ate, drank and traded.*

WE KNOW ABOUT THE ROMANS thanks to the many books and letters which have survived from their time. The remains of Roman cities, villas, forts and shipwrecks also help **archaeologists** to build up a picture of daily life in the Roman Empire.

THE EARLIEST ROMAN HISTORY is not known, so the Romans made up stories to fill in the gaps. They used the ancient legend of Romulus and Remus to explain how their city was founded. Legend has it that they were the twin sons of Mars, the god of war. They were abandoned at birth and rescued by a she-wolf. Romulus later became the first king of Rome and the city was named after him.

▽ *Today, statues of Romulus and Remus and the she-wolf can be seen all over Rome and other Italian cities.*

ROME was founded in 753 BC as a tiny farming settlement on the banks of the River Tiber. At the time, Italy was a land of many different peoples, speaking different languages. There were the **Etruscans** and Umbrians north of Rome, and Greek settlers in the south. The very first Romans belonged to the **Latin**-speaking peoples of central Italy.

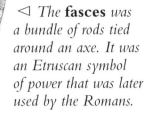

◁ *The **fasces** was a bundle of rods tied around an axe. It was an Etruscan symbol of power that was later used by the Romans.*

THE ETRUSCANS were a powerful people. In the seventh century BC, Rome came under their influence and was ruled by a series of Etruscan kings. The Etruscans were good builders and they gave Rome its first large temples.

THE GREEKS were another important influence on the Romans. They founded cities around the coast of southern Italy. The Romans copied Greek buildings and sculptures, and were influenced by Greek legends and ideas.

ROMAN CIVILIZATION lasted for many centuries. To help make sense of it, we have divided it into different periods. Each period has been given a **symbol**, to show when information relates to that time. If there are no symbols, the information covers all periods.

The Republic refers to that period in Roman history when Rome was ruled by elected officials, and the Empire started to expand. By 27 BC the Republic had collapsed and was replaced by the rule of **emperors**. Under their rule, the Empire continued to expand. Later, the Empire was divided into two parts: the Eastern and Western Empires.

KEY FOR SYMBOLS

🦅 (eagle)   **Roman Republic** 509-27 BC

🌿 (wreath)   **early imperial period** 27 BC-AD 284

☧ (**Chi-Rho**) **late imperial period** AD 284-476

THE MAKE IT WORK! way of looking at history is to ask questions about the past and to discover some of the answers by making copies of the things people made. However, you do not need to make everything in the book in order to understand the Roman way of life.

▽ *This map shows how, over many centuries, the ancient Romans were influenced by different peoples.*

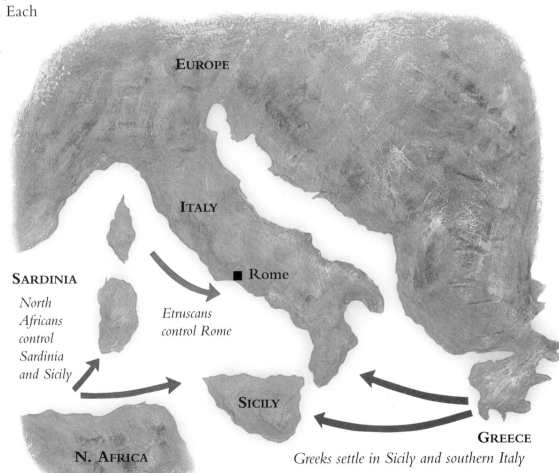

EUROPE

ITALY

■ Rome

SARDINIA

North Africans control Sardinia and Sicily

Etruscans control Rome

SICILY

N. AFRICA

GREECE

Greeks settle in Sicily and southern Italy

Timeline

Rome was ruled by kings until 509 BC. After this time, the Romans set up a new form of government called the Republic. Instead of a king, the Romans were ruled by two officials called **consuls**, elected each year from among the leading **citizens**. This system lasted for almost 500 years. During this period, Rome grew from a small city to become the capital of a huge empire.

DURING THE REPUBLIC, as the Roman Empire grew, so did the size of its armies and the influence of the generals who commanded them. In the first century BC, there were bloody wars in which rival generals fought each other for power. Eventually, only one remained: Octavian. He became the first emperor of Rome and renamed himself Augustus. He called himself the 'first citizen', rather than 'emperor' and pretended that he had saved the Republic. But although consuls were still elected, real power lay with the emperor.

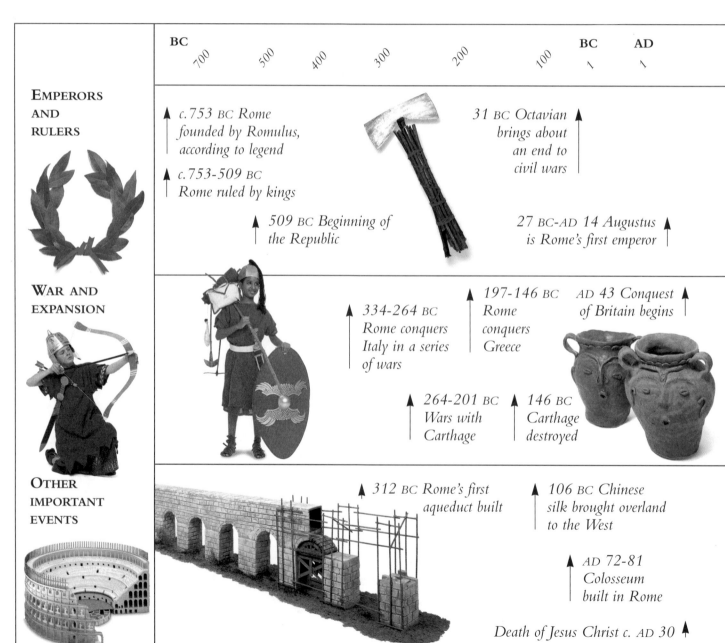

BC — 700 — 500 — 400 — 300 — 200 — 100 — BC 1 — AD 1

EMPERORS AND RULERS

c.753 BC Rome founded by Romulus, according to legend

c.753-509 BC Rome ruled by kings

509 BC Beginning of the Republic

31 BC Octavian brings about an end to civil wars

27 BC-AD 14 Augustus is Rome's first emperor

WAR AND EXPANSION

334-264 BC Rome conquers Italy in a series of wars

197-146 BC Rome conquers Greece

AD 43 Conquest of Britain begins

264-201 BC Wars with Carthage

146 BC Carthage destroyed

OTHER IMPORTANT EVENTS

312 BC Rome's first aqueduct built

106 BC Chinese silk brought overland to the West

AD 72-81 Colosseum built in Rome

Death of Jesus Christ c. AD 30

THE FIRST EMPEROR, AUGUSTUS, was a successful ruler. His reign lasted for over 40 years and the Romans got used to being ruled by just one man. When Augustus died, his adopted son, Tiberius, became emperor after him. The Empire continued to grow until, in AD 117, it reached its greatest extent. The emperor needed people he could trust to help him rule the Empire, so he appointed governors to each of the **provinces**. Most of the army's time was spent defending the borders against foreign invaders.

THE HISTORY OF ROME is not just about emperors and wars. As time passed, many changes took place in the way that people lived. Through trade, they were introduced to new goods, such as Chinese silk. Their beliefs also changed as they came across foreign religions. The Syrians introduced them to the worship of the Sun; from Egypt they learned about the goddess **Isis**. But the religion that was to have the greatest effect was Christianity. In the fourth century AD, this became the official religion of the Empire.

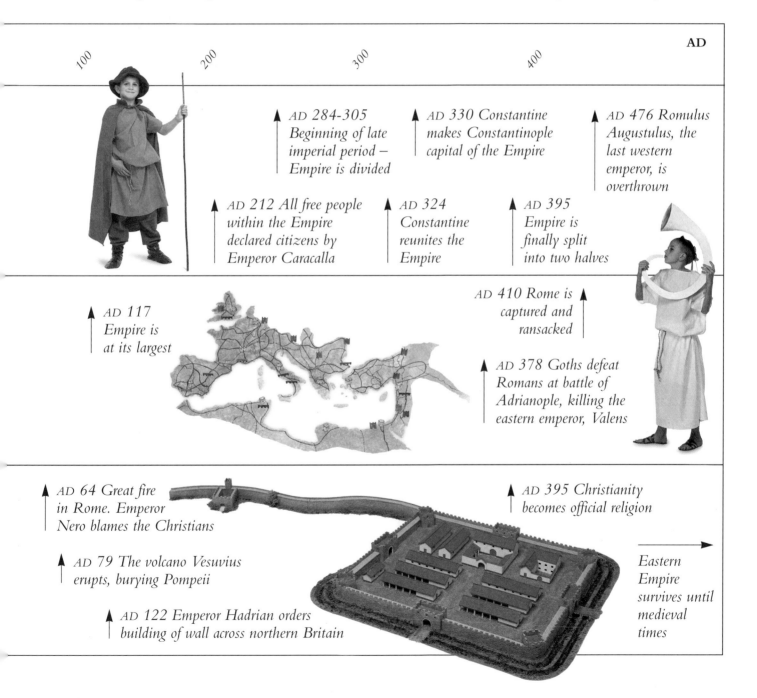

AD

100   200   300   400

AD 284-305 Beginning of late imperial period – Empire is divided

AD 330 Constantine makes Constantinople capital of the Empire

AD 476 Romulus Augustulus, the last western emperor, is overthrown

AD 212 All free people within the Empire declared citizens by Emperor Caracalla

AD 324 Constantine reunites the Empire

AD 395 Empire is finally split into two halves

AD 117 Empire is at its largest

AD 410 Rome is captured and ransacked

AD 378 Goths defeat Romans at battle of Adrianople, killing the eastern emperor, Valens

AD 64 Great fire in Rome. Emperor Nero blames the Christians

AD 395 Christianity becomes official religion

AD 79 The volcano Vesuvius erupts, burying Pompeii

AD 122 Emperor Hadrian orders building of wall across northern Britain

Eastern Empire survives until medieval times

A conquering force

In the year AD 117, the Roman Empire reached its greatest size. It stretched 4,000 kilometres from east to west, 3,700 kilometres from north to south, and had a population of over 50 million people.

🦅 ⚜ **THE WESTERN** half of the Empire was conquered as a result of rivalry between the Romans and the people of Carthage. The Carthaginians were a powerful seafaring people in North Africa who also controlled Sardinia, parts of Sicily and southern Spain. During a series of wars, Rome defeated Carthage and claimed its territory. The Romans later moved into northern Europe, conquering northern Spain, France, parts of Germany and Britain.

🦅 ⚜ **THE EAST** mostly came under Roman control during the last two centuries BC. The Romans first went east to fight a people from northern Greece who were allied with Carthage. After defeating them, more wars of conquest followed. By 30 BC most of the lands around the Mediterranean were part of the Roman Empire. Roman rule put an end to fighting between rival states and brought peace.

▷ *This is a map of the Empire during the second century AD. Some important provinces are marked in capital letters. Provincial capitals, important cities and army bases are given with their Roman names. You could compare the names to those on a modern map of Europe.*

BRITANNIA

Londinium

Isca

Colonia Agrippina

GERMANIA

Calleva

Mogontiacum

GAUL

Legio

IBERIA

Massilia

ROMA

Lugdunum

Toletum

Ostia

Mediterranean Sea

ITALIA

Emerita Augustus

Carthago

Hispalis

Thugga

MAURETANIA

AFRICA

KEY TO SYMBOLS

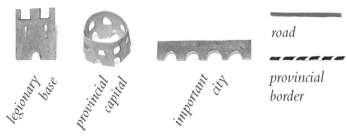

legionary base provincial capital important city

road

provincial border

TWO LANGUAGES held the Empire together. In the west, educated people learned to speak Latin; in the east, they spoke Greek. The Romans looked down on all other languages. Foreigners who could not speak Latin or Greek were called **barbarians**, because their speech sounded to Romans like a string of meaningless 'bar-bar' sounds.

ROMAN CITIZENSHIP was given to the most important people in the conquered lands. This meant that they were allowed to become Romans. Citizens had many rights denied to non-citizens. A male citizen could vote in local government, or stand for election. Becoming a citizen was like taking on a new identity: a citizen even had to take a Roman name and learn how to wear Roman clothes.

THE NUMBER OF ROMAN CITIZENS grew steadily over time. In 28 BC, there were four million: 80 years later, the figure had risen to six million. Finally in AD 212, the Emperor Caracalla allowed all free men and women, including ex-slaves, to become citizens.

Aquincum

Viminacium

Troesmia

Black Sea

Satala

ANATOLIA

Hadrianopolis

DALMATIA

Cyrrhus

Antiocha

Palmyra

Pompeii

SYRIA

Thessalonica

Ephesus

Legio

Aelia Capitolina

MACEDONIA

JUDEA

Mediterranean Sea

Alexandria

Cyrene

CYRENAICA

AEGYPTUS

Red Sea

From emperor to slave

The people of the Empire belonged to separate groups and classes, each with different rights. During the early imperial period, the most important distinction was between Roman citizens and non-citizens, or **provincials**. Citizens had more rights than provincials, and even dressed differently.

SLAVES were men, women and children who were owned as property and who were bought and sold in the market-place. Some were captured in wars, others were the children of slave parents. Household slaves could be secretaries, tutors, entertainers, cooks or servants. These slaves were far better off than those who worked on farms or down in the mines.

double pipes

▷ *A provincial farmer from northern Europe.*

▷ *A freedman could become a successful tradesman.*

△ *A household slave who is also a musician.*

ROMAN SLAVES who had been given their freedom were called **freedmen** and **freedwomen**. Many slaves saved up money and bought their freedom; others were freed by their owners as a reward for loyal service.

PROVINCIALS, or non-citizens, had different degrees of wealth and status. Unlike slaves, they could serve in the army in special support, or 'auxiliary' units. After many years of service, **auxiliaries** and their families were usually given Roman citizenship. This was one way in which the number of citizens steadily increased.

trousers were worn in the cold north

◁ *A centurion was a middle-ranking Roman citizen.*

WOMEN had fewer rights than men. They could not vote or follow careers in politics or law. Most wealthy Roman women looked after children and the home, and gave orders to slaves. However, women could own property and some ran their own businesses. Other women played important roles as priestesses in the temples (see page 35).

☙ ✶ **THE EMPEROR** had enormous power. He was the chief priest of the Roman religion and the overall commander of Rome's armies. He appointed governors to rule the different provinces of the Empire. Statues of him stood in every city and his face appeared on every coin.

laurel wreath

▷ *A noblewoman and priestess.*

purple **toga**

altar for making offerings to the gods

ROMAN CITIZENS were divided into different 'orders' or ranks, depending on their wealth and family background. At the top were the wealthy nobles who belonged to the order of **senators**. They were the generals, chief priests and governors of the most important provinces. Below them were **equestrians**, wealthy people who became civil servants, high-ranking officers or governors of smaller provinces. Lower still were ordinary citizens. They ranged from **centurions** and **legionaries**, to wealthy traders and poor farmers.

△ *The emperor was the most important person in Roman society.*

Togas and tunics

Roman men, women and children wore a simple tunic, made of wool or linen, with a belt around the waist. Some tunics had sleeves, like a T-shirt; others had armholes. It was the one item of clothing that everyone wore, rich and poor alike. Women's tunics were longer than men's, reaching to below the knees.

MALE ROMAN CITIZENS were supposed to wear a toga in public. The toga was a huge, semi-circular, woollen sheet that was wrapped around the body and arranged with folds. It took time and skill to put it on properly. Slaves and non-citizens wore the simple tunic, or *tunica*.

DIFFERENT COLOURED TOGAS were also a sign of status. Men standing for election wore a pure white toga. This has given us the word candidate, from the Latin word *candidus* (white). **Magistrates** and the young sons of wealthy families wore a *toga praetexta*, which was white with a purple border. The emperor wore a *toga picta*, which was purple with gold embroidery.

△ *This group of senators are all wearing togas. The Roman on the far right also holds the* fasces *symbol.*

WOMEN had a great variety of clothing. Some wore the *peplos* – a robe that fastened at the shoulders. Wealthy women wore clothes of brightly coloured Chinese silk and Indian cotton over their *tunica*, and decorated themselves with jewellery.

FOOTWEAR included various kinds of leather sandals. Slaves and citizens in warmer provinces wore simple sandals, like modern flip-flops. Soldiers wore stronger sandals with hobnails on the soles.

MAKE A PEPLOS

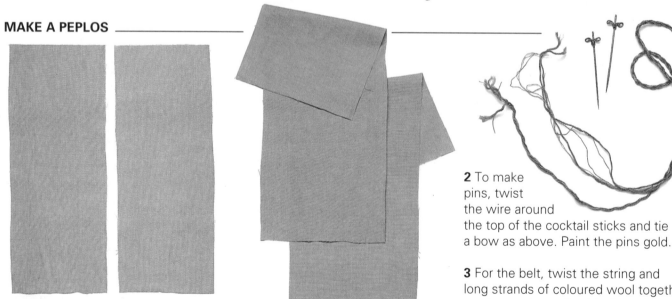

You will need: needle, thread, scissors, an old cotton sheet cut in half lengthwise, string, coloured wool, long cocktail sticks, thin wire, gold paint

1 Fold over a third of the material on each piece. You could hem the edges to prevent fraying. You will need to hold the material as shown above, up to your shoulders, in the final stage.

2 To make pins, twist the wire around the top of the cocktail sticks and tie a bow as above. Paint the pins gold.

3 For the belt, twist the string and long strands of coloured wool together as shown above. Knot both ends.

4 Ask a friend to help you put on the *peplos*. Push the pins through the folded fabric at the shoulders. Tie the belt at the waist and over the flaps of material.

MAKE A PAIR OF ROMAN SANDALS

You will need: brown felt or leather square, laces, pen, paper, scissors

1 If possible, enlarge the design above on a photocopier, so that it will fit your foot. Or, copy the design onto paper.

2 Cut out the design and draw around it on the fabric.

3 Turn the paper over and copy the design again, for your other foot. Then, cut out both shapes.

4 Stand on the centre of each piece of fabric. Use laces, or strips of the spare fabric, to lace up the loops in the sandal, as shown above.

PURPLE DYE was specially valued by the Romans. It came from a rare shellfish called the murex, found in parts of the Mediterranean.

WEAR A TOGA

▷ *This is a simple way to put on a toga. In reality togas were more difficult to put on.*

You will need: semi-circular piece of fabric with a straight edge of 4 metres

1 Hold the straight edge of the fabric behind you. Drape half over your left arm. Tuck this section into your belt.

2 Pass the right half of the toga under your right arm and around the front. Tuck a little fold in your belt.

3 Now pass the rest of the fabric over your left shoulder.

Dressing to impress

Wealthy Romans went to great lengths to keep up with changing fashions. They started each day in front of a mirror, attended by slaves who dressed their hair, applied their make-up and perfume, and plucked out unwanted hair with tweezers.

▷ *A wealthy or noble Roman woman spent a lot of time making her hair look beautiful.*

WOMEN'S HAIRSTYLES became more and more elaborate over time. They wore wigs and hairpieces curled with heated tongs and piled up high in rows of curls. Hairpins, made from bone or metal, held the curls in place. Some women wore wigs so that they could change the colour of their hair. Blond wigs were made with hair clipped from German slave girls, and black wigs were made with hair imported from India.

MEN WORE LAUREL WREATHS on their heads as a mark of rank. Victorious generals wore them on their return from successful campaigns, and Roman emperors wore them as crowns.

MAKE A LAUREL WREATH

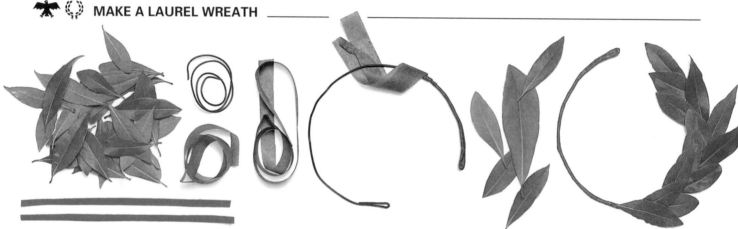

You will need: fresh bay (laurel) leaves, or leaves made from green card, strips of green tissue paper, scissors, glue, plastic-coated wire, red ribbon

1 Shape the wire into a headband. Wind and glue strips of tissue paper around the band. Starting at one end, glue the leaves to the tissue paper as shown above right.

2 When you have reached half-way around the headband, start at the other end and glue on the rest of the leaves. Finally, snip the ends of the ribbon in a V-shape, and glue as shown right.

WEARING MAKE-UP was important to noblewomen. They used paint made from chalk and white lead to whiten the face and forearms, and powdered ashes to blacken the eyebrows. Red ochre (from earth), or red wine leftovers were used as rouge for cheeks and lips. Women also used face packs made from damp bread, which they hoped would prevent wrinkles.

◁ *Many women wore beautiful metal bracelets shaped like coiling snakes.*

MAKE A ROMAN BROOCH

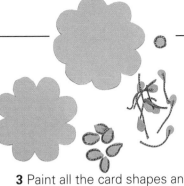

You will need: card, glue, safety pin, fine string, tape, paints, paintbrush

1 Draw two flower shapes on the card – one a little larger than the other. Draw four petal shapes, lots of little stamens and a small circle. Cut out the shapes carefully.

2 Glue bits of string around the petals and the circle. Glue lengths of string to the tips of the stamens.

3 Paint all the card shapes and pieces of string gold.

4 When dry, paint the insides of the petals different colours.

5 Glue the smaller flower on top of the larger one. Bend the edges inwards slightly. Glue the stamens onto the centre of the flower. Then glue on the petals and the circle as shown.

6 To wear your brooch, tape a safety pin onto the back, as shown above.

▽ *Brooches like these were used to fasten cloaks.*

▽ *The laurel-wreath crown was a symbol of military success and power.*

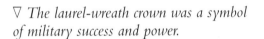

🌿 ✳ **MEN'S HAIRSTYLES** were influenced by the emperor, whose portrait was engraved on coins (see page 51). Until the second century AD, men shaved their chins, or had them plucked with tweezers by a barber. This style changed when the Emperor Hadrian, who had an ugly scar on his chin, let his beard grow to hide it. Men all over the Empire followed his example.

Some men took just as much trouble over their appearance as women. This is how the historian Suetonius described the Emperor Otho:
'He was as fussy about his appearance as a woman. His entire body had been plucked of hair and a well-made wig covered his practically bald head… He used a poultice of moist bread to slow down the growth of his beard.'

Life in the city

Many Romans lived in the large cities of the Empire. These cities were often built near rivers or close to the sea, because it was much easier to move heavy goods by water than by road. Cities were the main trading centres. There was a constant movement of wagons, pack animals and merchant ships arriving and departing.

ROMAN CITIES were often built on a grid system. Blocks of buildings called *insulae* were divided by straight streets. Each *insula* was packed with houses, shops and workshops. To save space, these buildings often joined onto each other, like a row of terraced houses.

▽ *This is a model of a typical Roman town. Most towns and cities had the same key buildings.*

△ *This is an aerial photograph of the Roman town of Timgad in Algeria. The grid system can be seen clearly.*

FRESH WATER was brought into the city by an **aqueduct**. A lot of water was needed for drinking and for the public baths, where Romans went to relax. Many cities also had sewers, and public toilets flushed by water.

split aqueduct carries water into covered reservoirs

market-place   public baths

AT THE HEART OF EVERY ROMAN CITY was the **forum**. This was a large open area, used as a market and a public meeting place. Along one side there was a long hall called a *basilica*. This was the law court and the place where merchants and wealthy Romans met to do business.

A smaller building nearby, the *curia*, was where the local council met. The council was responsible for putting on public entertainment, keeping law and order, raising taxes and looking after the roads, public buildings and the water supply.

TEMPLES for worshipping the most important gods and the Roman emperor were also built in the forum. Temples to local gods were scattered across the town. Wealthy Romans helped to pay for building temples, and in return had their names carved on them.

PUBLIC ENTERTAINMENT was an important part of city life. There were theatres for plays, and **amphitheatres** where fights between **gladiators** were held (see pages 38–39). Some of the bigger cities even had a racecourse for chariot racing.

theatre   city gates   amphitheatre   basilica   *forum*   temple   insula

curia

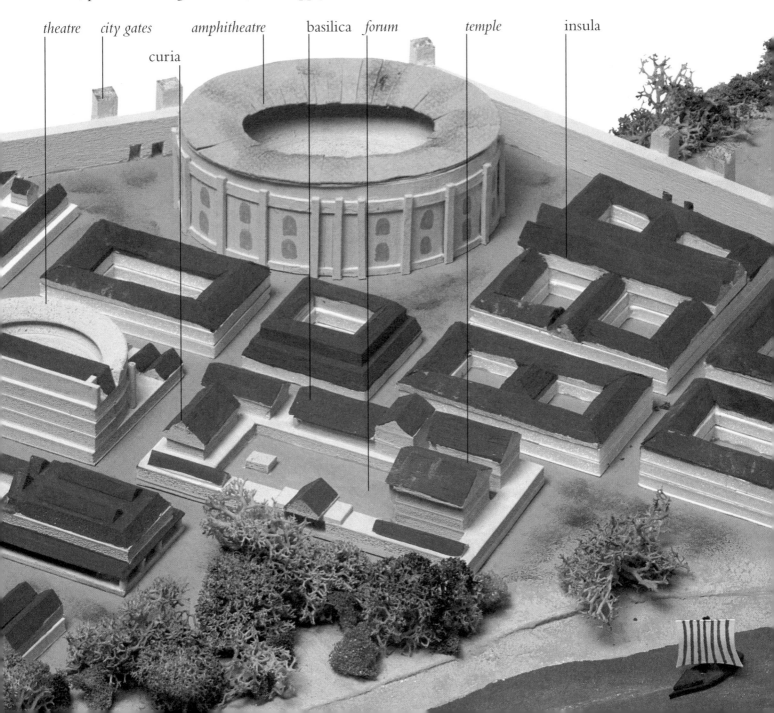

POMPEII is a town in Italy that was buried under ash when the volcano Vesuvius erupted violently in AD 79. Over the past 200 years, the houses and shops of Pompeii have been slowly uncovered. As a result, we have a picture of a whole Roman town as it was on an August day nearly 2,000 years ago.

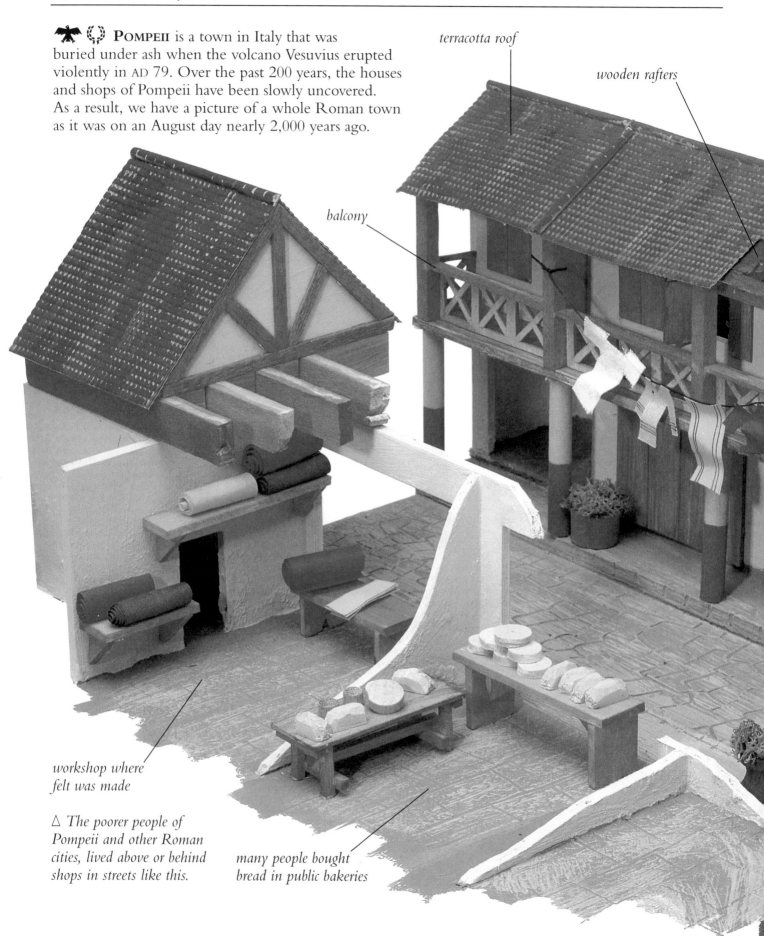

terracotta roof

wooden rafters

balcony

workshop where felt was made

△ The poorer people of Pompeii and other Roman cities, lived above or behind shops in streets like this.

many people bought bread in public bakeries

THE STREETS of Pompeii were lined with a variety of shops and bars. These were often run by freedmen who had their own slaves working for them. Each shop had a large, open front that was closed up with wooden shutters at night. There was a counter at the front where goods were displayed to customers in the street. Taverns had stone counters with jars set into them for snacks and hot drinks.

△ In this excavated street in Pompeii you can see the deep ruts in the road made by cart wheels.

THE PAVEMENTS IN POMPEII, like those of many Roman cities, were raised above the level of the road. This prevented ox-carts from knocking over pedestrians. The road sloped slightly so that rainwater and sewage ran into the gutters. Stepping-stones were laid across the road to allow people to cross without getting their sandals dirty, and also to slow down the carts.

MOST PEOPLE IN THE EMPIRE were poor, although those who were in charge were very rich. In the larger cities, the poor lived in rented rooms in blocks of flats or apartments. In smaller towns, rich and poor alike lived in the *insulae*, or blocks of housing. A rich family might own a large part of the *insula*, whereas a poor family rented perhaps only one or two rooms.

Inside the homes, furniture was very simple. The poet Martial described a typical room: 'There was a little three-legged bed and a two-legged table, with a lamp and a bucket… The neck of an **amphora** held back a little cooker covered in green rust.' Most homes did not have bathrooms. Instead, people used chamber pots which they emptied out of their windows onto the street below.

public fountain for drinking water

a one-room flat

tavern

raised pavement

gutter

stepping-stones

WEALTHY ROMANS lived in very different conditions from the poor. From the outside, the houses of wealthy Romans looked very plain. Because of the risk of burglary, most houses had only a few windows. Rooms were arranged around courtyards and gardens, and openings in the roof let in the maximum amount of light.

△ *In the evenings, homes were lit with pottery lamps. The lamps burned oil made from olives, nuts or fish.*

THE FIRST ROOM people entered in a Roman house was called the *atrium*. It was a cross between an entrance hall and a courtyard. It had a high ceiling with a skylight in the middle. Below this, in the centre of the *atrium*, was an ornamental pool to collect rainwater.

THE DINING ROOM was called a *triclinium*, meaning 'three couches'. The houses of the rich sometimes had two *triclinia*; a sheltered one for the winter, and one with a view of the garden for the summer.

THE RECEPTION ROOM was the *tablinum*. This was a cross between a living room and an office where guests were received. Important papers and valuables were kept there, safely locked in a strongbox.

A ROMAN HOUSE was often a crowded place. There were household slaves running errands, children playing with toys, and older women spinning wool together (see pages 30–31). There was also a stream of daily visitors or **clients** who came to ask advice and favours from their 'patron' – the head of the house. These were generally people who were less well off. For a wealthy Roman, the day began with a visit from his clients. The more important a Roman was, the greater the number of clients who visited him.

▷ *A wealthy Roman might have lived in a town house like this.*

bedroom (above tablinum)

peristyle garden (see page 23)

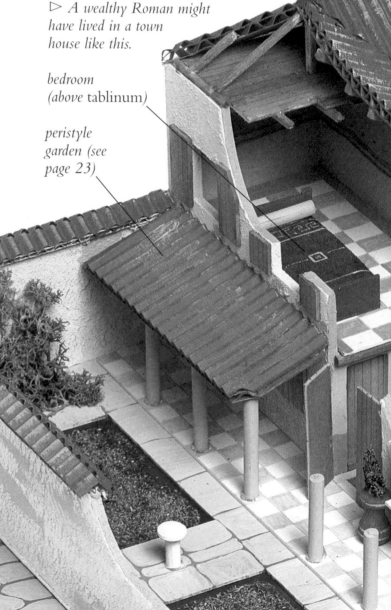

BEDROOMS were often alongside the *atrium*. Apart from the bed, there was little furniture – perhaps a chair and a table, and a pottery chamber pot kept underneath the bed.

CLIENTS were expected to arrive in a clean toga, and to call their patron 'my lord'. They would wait in the *atrium* until a slave summoned them to the *tablinum*, where the patron would receive them.

These wealthy patrons were themselves the clients of still richer men. After they had greeted their clients, they might have to visit their own patron. The only man who did not have a patron was the emperor.

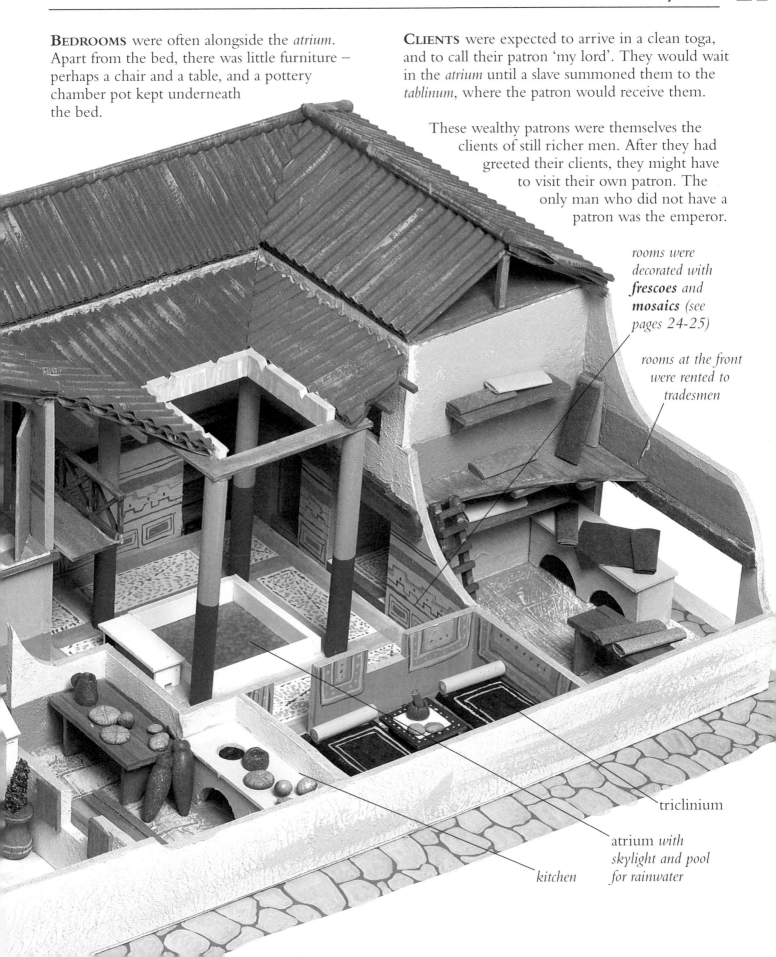

rooms were decorated with **frescoes** *and* **mosaics** *(see pages 24-25)*

rooms at the front were rented to tradesmen

triclinium

atrium *with skylight and pool for rainwater*

kitchen

Gardens, mosaics and frescoes

Wealthy Romans loved their gardens. They were neatly laid out with rows of clipped hedges and paths, and filled with fountains, pools and statues. A garden was a place to relax on a sunny day, to read or write, or just do nothing.

▷ *The gardens of a Roman town house or country villa may have been circular, like this one, or rectangular.*

small bust of a forest spirit

fountain

🏵 **MANY GARDENS** have been discovered at Pompeii. Although the plants there disappeared long ago, their roots have left spaces in the soil. Archaeologists make plaster casts of these spaces to find out what kinds of trees and bushes were planted there.

hedges trimmed to look like birds

lemon tree

FOUNTAINS and ornamental pools were carved from marble. Pliny the Younger, a writer, described the fountains of his garden: 'A fountain plays in a marble basin, watering the plane trees round it and the ground beneath them with its light spray… Another has a bowl surrounded by tiny jets which make a lovely murmuring sound.'

STATUES of gods and fighting animals were popular garden ornaments. The 'House of Stags' in Herculaneum in southern Italy, is named after two sculptures of stags being attacked by dogs. There were also statues of forest spirits such as satyrs, which were young men with the legs, ears and horns of goats.

△ Oscilla *were decorated with reliefs of gods and satyrs.*

THE PERISTYLE was a type of garden surrounded by roofed columns that gave shade. White marble or terracotta discs called *oscilla* were hung between the columns for decoration. They flashed like tiny mirrors as they caught the sun.

SLAVES who were skilled gardeners looked after the garden. They clipped bushes into the shape of animals, birds and gods. The wealthiest Romans also liked to have fish tanks in their gardens, filled with fish, eels and other seafood. They provided a fresh supply for the dinner table! Exotic birds were also popular. Peacocks were imported from India and were thought to be the sacred bird of the goddess Juno.

GARDEN WALLS were sometimes painted with pictures of trees, birds and flowers to make the gardens look bigger. If a house had no real garden, Romans painted garden scenes on a wall, to give the impression of one. Some of these still survive today. They show us what kind of plants the Romans liked to grow.

△ *This mosaic from Pompeii shows a scene from the banks of the River Nile in Egypt. The Romans hunted many of these animals and brought them back to Rome for the games (see pages 38-39).*

THE TOWN HOUSES AND COUNTRY VILLAS of wealthy Romans were full of colour. The walls of important rooms, such as the *triclinium* and *tablinum*, were covered with bright paintings called frescoes. The floors were decorated with mosaics – pictures made from thousands of tiny coloured tiles and pieces of glass.

MOSAICS were fashionable throughout the Empire. The Romans used the technique, developed by the Greeks, of making black and white patterned floors with pebbles. Later, coloured floors became popular. By cutting stones, glass, tiles and shells into little pieces known as *tesserae*, the Romans could make mosaics as detailed as paintings. There were scenes from everyday life, flowers, and different figures such as the gods, gladiators and actors. One house in Pompeii had a mosaic of a snarling dog in the doorway, with the words *'cave canem'*, 'beware of the dog', written into the mosaic.

MAKE A MOSAIC

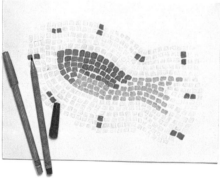
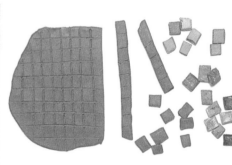

You will need: paper, felt-tip pens, scissors, self-hardening clay, paints, paintbrush, stiff card, rolling pin, tile adhesive, sponge or stiff brush, varnish (optional)

1 Draw a fish or another animal. Then cut a piece of stiff card, large enough to·cover the whole design.

2 Draw your design on a piece of paper and choose the colours you would like to use.

3 Roll out the clay with the rolling pin until it is about 3 mm thick.

4 Use a pair of scissors to mark the clay into small squares, as shown above right.

5 Cut the squares to make small tiles, or *tesserae*. Leave them to dry out.

6 Paint them in your chosen colours.

7 To create a more textured effect, you could dip a sponge in the paint and dab it gently onto the tiles. Or you could flick paint onto them, using a stiff brush.

FRESCOES were painted on a freshly plastered wall that was still damp. The colour soaked into the plaster and became fixed as it dried. The finished wall was given a protective coat of melted wax mixed with a little oil. Finally, the surface was polished to give it a glossy appearance.

THE FIRST PAINTERS only had a few colours to work with: black from soot, white from chalk, and red and yellow ochre from earth. As the Empire grew, more colours became available. The Egyptians showed the Romans how to make a rich shade of blue from copper. Vermilion, a bright scarlet, came from a mineral called cinnabar which was mined in Spain. Even more exotic and expensive colours were brought by sea from India. You could tell how wealthy Romans were simply by looking at the colours on the walls of their houses.

STYLES OF PAINTING came and went. Until about 80 BC, walls were painted to look as if they were made of coloured marble. Then, architectural scenes with columns and statues became popular. The aim was to make a room look bigger than it really was.

△ This fresco was discovered on the wall of a town house in Pompeii. The young woman is holding a writing tablet in one hand and a **stylus** in the other (see page 33).

△ Mosaics of sea creatures were sometimes used to decorate triclinium floors.

8 Cover the stiff card with a layer of tile adhesive. Press the tiles into the adhesive, following your paper design. Begin with the centre tiles and work outwards until the design is complete.

9 Leave the mosaic to dry. You could varnish it later.

Food and feasting

The staple food of most Romans was a type of stew, made from wheat, barley, beans or lentils. However, rich Romans had a more varied diet. They ate food grown on their own farms, and more expensive dishes imported from all over the Empire.

COOKING was a luxury for most people who lived in cities. Because of the risk of fire in their wooden apartments, the poor bought their meals from stalls in the street instead of cooking. Wealthy Romans had their own kitchens, and slaves who cooked for them.

food cooked on a raised hearth

amphorae

You will need: five eggs, ground pepper, 10 g butter, 75 ml milk, 5 ml honey, 25 g almonds, dash of anchovy essence or soy sauce

1 Whisk the eggs in a bowl. Then add the honey, pepper and milk.

2 Ask an adult to put the almonds on a baking tray and bake them in a hot oven 165° C (325° F) for 20 mins.

3 When cool, ask an adult to chop the nuts with a sharp knife. Now add them to the egg mixture.

4 Stir the anchovy essence or soy sauce into the egg mixture.

5 Melt the butter in a frying pan and pour in the egg mixture. Cook until the omelette is firm, turning once.

BRICK OVENS were used for baking and roasting. A fire was lit inside, heating the bricks. When the fire died, the ashes were raked out and bread or meat was pushed in. The entrance was covered and food cooked by the heat of the bricks.

◁ *A wealthy Roman would have had a kitchen like this one.*

flour

bowl for grinding spices

POTTERY JARS, or *amphorae*, leaned against the kitchen walls. They held the most commonly used ingredients – olive oil, vinegar, wine and fish sauce.

THE MOST POPULAR FOOD FLAVOURING was a spicy fish sauce called *garum*. It was made from the blood and internal parts of mackerel, an oily type of fish. The fish parts were salted, mixed with vinegar and herbs, and left in the sun until they turned into liquid. *Garum* had a powerful flavour. Only a tiny amount was needed to flavour a dish.

THE ROMANS COOKED their food rather differently to how we cook today. They used honey to sweeten food, because they did not have sugar. They also loved pepper, which came from India. They even sprinkled it on desserts and mixed it with wine.

MAKE GRAPE PUNCH

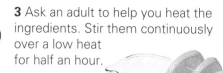

3 Ask an adult to help you heat the ingredients. Stir them continuously over a low heat for half an hour.

4 Leave to cool before serving.

You will need: four tablespoons of honey, crushed bay leaf, two dates, one litre white grape juice, pinch of: cinnamon, ground pepper, saffron and lemon for flavour and decoration

1 Chop the dates finely. Discard the stones.

2 Place all the ingredients in a saucepan.

ENTERTAINING generally took place in the evening, when wealthy Romans invited guests to dinner. They ate in the *triclinium*, or dining room, stretched out on three couches.

◁ *The Romans made beautiful glassware which they used when they entertained.*

EACH COUCH could seat three people, so the perfect number of guests at a dinner party was nine. The couches were arranged to make three sides of a square, with the fourth side left open for the slaves who brought the dishes.

THE PLACE OF HONOUR was on the right-hand side of the host who lay in the centre of the middle couch. The guests propped themselves up on their elbows and ate with their fingers. Between courses they washed their hands in finger bowls and dried them with napkins. Guests often brought their own napkins, so that they could take away any of the delicious food they had been unable to finish.

▷ *The Romans served this spiced punch cold before a meal, or warm if served during a meal.*

DORMICE were a popular dish. They were kept inside pottery jars and fattened until they were ready to cook. Then they were served sprinkled with honey and poppy seeds!

mosaics of food scraps

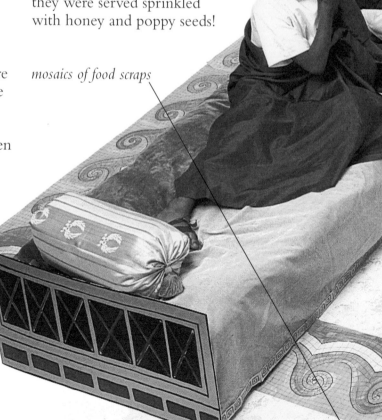

ROMANS SHOWED OFF THEIR WEALTH by serving food brought from all the corners of the Empire. Certain provinces were famous for particular delicacies. Libya, for example, was the place to find truffles, while Syria was known for its delicious pears.

UNUSUAL DISHES were especially impressive. The Emperor Vitellius, famous for his love of food, served some of the most expensive meals in history. One of his dishes, called 'Shield of Minerva', was described by the historian Suetonius: 'The recipe called for pike-livers, pheasant-brains, peacock-brains, flamingo-tongues, and lamprey-eggs [an eel-like fish]; and the ingredients, collected in every corner of the Empire… were brought to Rome in naval *triremes* [warships].'

THROUGHOUT THE MEAL, slaves who were musicians, storytellers and jugglers would entertain the guests. The type of entertainment depended on the tastes of the host. He might want to read legal speeches or extracts from his poetry. Another host might only be interested in belly-dancing!

burning lamps for light

▽ *A Roman dinner party in the* triclinium.

Family life

The word 'family' is Roman and comes from the Latin word *familia*. In Roman times, a family meant the household, which included slaves, freedmen and freedwomen.

POORER ROMANS were rarely educated. Unlike the wealthy, they did not write books and could not afford carved tombstones for their graves. Most of what we know about the daily lives of Romans comes from these sources. Because the rich were generally only interested in their own lives, not much is known about poorer Romans.

▷ *Young children played with terracotta rattles shaped like animals. This jewel-studded pig probably belonged to a child with wealthy parents.*

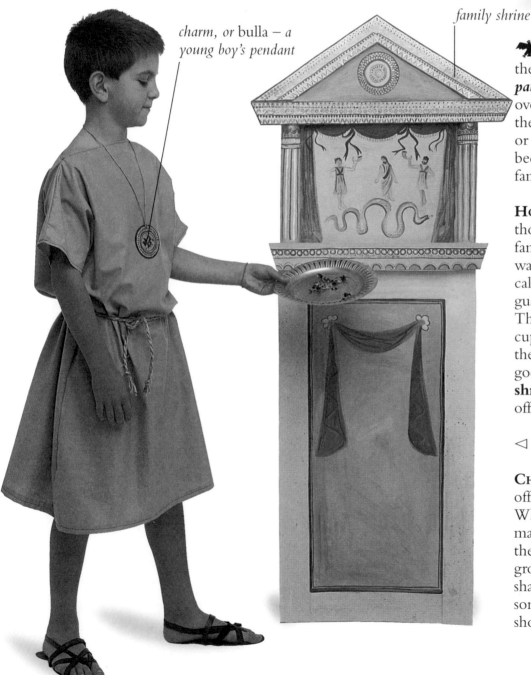

charm, or bulla *– a young boy's pendant*

family shrine

THE FAMILY HEAD was the father. He was known as the ***pater familias***. He had total power over all family members and had the right to sell them into slavery, or even to kill them. Sons only became the *pater familias* of their families when their fathers died.

HOUSEHOLD GODS were thought to watch over every family. The head of the house was protected by a guardian spirit called his *Genius*, while his wife's guardian spirit was called her *Juno*. The *Penates* looked after the food cupboards, and the *Lares* protected the home. Small statues of these gods were kept in a household **shrine** and the family made offerings to them.

◁ *A boy offers a tuft of hair to the gods.*

CHILDREN made their own offerings to the household gods. When girls became engaged to be married, they left their toy dolls at the shrine as a sign that they were grown-up. When boys were first shaved by the barber, they offered some of the hair to the gods, to show that they had become men.

MAKE A ROMAN TOY DOLL

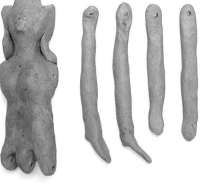

You will need: self-hardening clay, needle, string, paints, paintbrush

1 Model the clay into the parts of a doll: two arms, two legs, a body and head, as shown above right. At the base of the body, make two indents for the legs.

2 With the needle, make holes in the top of the arms and legs, through the base of the body, and right through the chest. The holes must be large enough for the string to be threaded through.

3 Leave the clay parts to dry.

4 Paint your doll as shown. Add a pattern around her neck, waist and hair for decoration. Leave to dry.

5 Thread string through the holes in the chest and arms. Knot the ends to secure. Do the same with the legs.

▷ *Roman children played with spinning tops, carved wooden animals, hoops and dolls like this one.*

🦅 🏵 MARRIAGE
had a dramatic effect on the lives of Roman women. In early times, when a young girl married, she had to leave her own *familia* and join her husband's. This meant that she had to live by the rules of a new *pater familias*. But by the end of the Republic, the Romans had invented a new system of marriage in which a wife legally remained part of her own *familia*. This gave her more freedom. She kept control of her own property and if her husband divorced her, he had to return anything belonging to her.

DIVORCE was common, especially among wealthy Romans. A husband could divorce his wife if the marriage was childless, or if he wanted to marry someone else. But wives did not have the right to divorce their husbands.

WIVES were responsible for running the household, giving orders to slaves and looking after the children. They also spent a lot of time spinning thread from wool to make clothes. In marriage ceremonies, a bride often carried a spindle for hand-spinning as a symbol of her duties as a wife.

Education and trades

Life for the sons and daughters of wealthy Romans was very different to the lives of poor children. Children of the wealthy were educated at home or at school, whereas poorer children went out to learn a trade.

POOR CHILDREN did not go to school. From an early age, they were expected to help their parents at work. A young boy of eight or nine years would either follow in his father's footsteps, or work as an apprentice in the trade of a family friend. To begin with, child workers were usually given the most unpleasant tasks, but by watching and helping, boys learned the skills of blacksmiths, bakers, launderers and goldsmiths. Girls stayed with their mothers and helped in the shop, the workshop, or the kitchen.

▷ *This is a Roman inkpot and pen from the first century AD.*

RICH CHILDREN began their education at home, where they were taught by a well-educated slave called a *pedagogue*. At the age of 11, some boys and girls went to a school run by a *grammaticus*, or grammar teacher, to study literature. They learned to speak Greek and memorized Greek and Latin poetry, taking turns to recite it. Roman noblemen and women loved quoting poetry in their conversations and letters.

PUBLIC SPEAKING was considered to be essential for all young men wishing to become politicians or lawyers. A tutor called a *rhetor* taught pupils how to arrange an argument in a logical way and how to speak persuasively. Pupils practised these skills by imagining they were taking part in law cases, either defending or accusing.

◁ *In Pompeii, young boys were employed in laundries to clean cloth in large vats, by treading it with their feet.*

MAKE A WRITING TABLET

You will need: balsa wood, red and green Plasticine, craft knife, ruler, glue, string, paint, bradawl, twig

1 For both frames cut a flat piece of wood 18 cm x 14 cm, four thick strips of wood: two measuring 18 cm x 1 cm, and two measuring 14 cm x 1 cm. Glue together as shown above right.

2 Paint the frames a rich, woody colour. With the bradawl, make two holes in one side of each frame. Thread string through the holes and tie the frames together.

3 Make seals to decorate. Cut three 20 cm lengths of string. Press the string into three red Plasticine discs. Glue to the back of the tablet.

4 Roll out two flat pieces of green Plasticine and glue inside each frame as shown.

5 To make a *stylus*, ask an adult to help you sharpen the end of a twig. Use it to write on the tablet. Smooth over the Plasticine to use again.

ROMAN NUMERALS

				40	XL
1	I	7	VII	50	L
2	II	8	VIII	60	LX
3	III	9	IX	90	XC
4	IV	10	X	100	C
5	V	20	XX	500	D
6	VI	30	XXX	1,000	M

▷ *A noblewoman reads a letter written on a wax writing tablet.*

ROMANS used letters to stand for numbers, and they are still used today on clocks and watches. Each letter had a different value and could be combined with other letters to make bigger numbers. They used I for 1, X for 10 and C for 100, so for example 1,326 was shown as MCCCXXVI. This made it quite tricky to do calculations with large numbers, especially multiplication and long division.

PUPILS wrote on thin sheets of wood using pens made from reeds or brass. They also wrote on beeswax tablets using a pen called a *stylus* to scratch letters into the tablet. One end of the *stylus* was flat, so that the wax could be smoothed over and reused.

IN SOME ROMAN TOWNS walls were covered with advertisements, so it is likely that many of the poor could read. Despite the lack of formal teaching, many poorer Romans learned to read and write a little – enough to sign their names and write a few simple documents.

Gods of the Empire

The Romans believed in many gods and goddesses who were thought to watch over different aspects of their lives. From very early times the Romans adopted Greek myths, linking the legends of the Greek gods with their own. They told the same stories about Jupiter that the Greeks told of their god, Zeus.

THE MOST IMPORTANT GODS were Jupiter, ruler of gods and men, and king of heaven; his wife Juno, queen of heaven and goddess of women and marriage; and Jupiter's daughter Minerva, goddess of wisdom and art. Together, they shared the Temple of Jupiter Capitolinus in Rome. Temples were places to worship statues of the gods. They were also places to leave valuables for safe-keeping, like banks today. It was thought that thieves would not dare to rob the house of a god.

▽ *Musicians herald the arrival of the procession.*

long, curved horn called a cornu

double pipes

▽ *The* victimarius *(sacrificing priest) carries an axe.*

a sheep is led to the altar as an offering to the gods

RELIGIOUS CEREMONIES were conducted by a priest or priestess, in front of the temple building. Processions of people brought gifts as offerings to a particular god. In return they hoped to win the god's favour. Bulls, sheep and pigs were decorated with flowers and led to the temple. The priest or priestess sacrificed the animal on an altar in front of the temple, and then burned some of the meat. The rising smoke was supposed to carry the offering up to the god.

TELLING THE FUTURE was an important part of religion. The Romans believed that the gods sent messages to warn of coming disasters, or as a sign of good luck. There were different ways of reading these messages. **Augurs** were priests who told the future by studying birds. **Haruspices** were men who examined the inner organs of a sacrificed animal to find out if the god had accepted the offering.

▽ *On festival days processions of people made their way to the temple and made sacrifices to the gods.*

◁ *A **standard bearer** leads the procession.*

sacrifices are made on the altar

◁ *The priestess stands behind the altar, in front of the temple.*

ROMAN EMPERORS had temples built in their own honour where people could make offerings to their statues. Few people believed that the emperors really were gods, but they had to honour them as gods because it was a way of showing loyalty and respect. To refuse to do so was considered treason.

△ *This statue depicts Mithras slaying a legendary bull. The bull's blood was believed to be the source of all life.*

⟨⟩ **AS THE EMPIRE EXPANDED,** the Romans came into contact with people who worshipped different gods. Some of these foreign gods were just like their own. Other gods, like **Mithras** and Isis, seemed very different, partly because they offered the promise of life after death.

⟨⟩ **THE CULTS OF MITHRAS AND ISIS** were spread throughout the Empire by merchants, traders, soldiers and slaves. These gods were worshipped at secret ceremonies, unlike Roman gods who were worshipped in public. Mithras was the god of light from Persia (ancient Iran). He was worshipped by men who met by torchlight in underground rooms.

Isis was an Egyptian mother goddess and the special protector of seafarers. Followers of Isis were persecuted until Emperor Caligula built a temple to her and allowed people freedom of worship.

MAKE A VOTIVE OFFERING

You will need: thin card, strips of newspaper, flour, water, salt, wire, large needle, ribbon, bronze paint, paintbrush

1 Draw a leg or hand and 'sweet' shape on the card as shown, then cut them out.

2 Make a runny paste from flour and water. Add a pinch of salt. Cover the card with a few layers of newspaper strips dipped in the paste. Leave to dry.

3 Paint the card shapes bronze.

4 You could write your name in Roman capital letters with a needle as shown right.

5 Coil pieces of wire into rings. Make a hole at the top and bottom of the sweet shape and thread the rings through.

6 Make a hole in the leg shape and attach to the bottom ring. Tie the ribbon to the top ring.

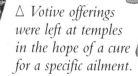

△ *Votive offerings were left at temples in the hope of a cure for a specific ailment.*

VOTIVES, or dedicated offerings, were used in temples throughout the Empire. Romans believed that the gods had the power to cause and cure illness, so people who were sick went to the temple to pray. As an offering to the gods, they left a small model of the part of the body that needed healing, with a few words inscribed on it.

SOME RELIGIOUS PRACTICES are shrouded in mystery. Face pots, some containing ashes of the dead, have been found at Roman sites in Britain and Germany. They were discovered in graves, under buildings and in streams. No one knows what the faces mean: they may represent a dead person, a god or a mask.

MAKE A FACE POT

You will need: self-hardening clay, poster paints, paintbrush

1 Take a lump of clay and roll it out into several long sausage shapes. Coil a length of clay into a round base shape as shown above.

2 Carefully join on another coil of clay and build up your pot in this way. Use your thumbs to smooth the outside of the pot and merge the coils.

3 Make little clay petal shapes for the rim of the pot. Then make a mouth, eyes, eyebrows, nose and ears.

4 Carefully add the details to the pot and smooth the joins. Leave the pot to dry completely. Then paint it brown.

CHRISTIANITY spread from Palestine in the Eastern Empire during the first century AD. Like Mithras and Isis, Christ was seen as a god who promised eternal life. Unlike those gods however, his religion was open to everyone, including slaves and the poor. At first, Rome's rulers tried to stamp out this new religion because Christians refused to pay respect to the Roman gods, or worship the emperor.

ATTITUDES TO CHRISTIANITY CHANGED when the Emperor Constantine came to power. He became a Christian, and in AD 313 he gave Christians the freedom of worship and encouraged Romans to convert.

△ *Face pots, or funerary urns, were used in burial rituals.*

At the games

The Romans had very bloodthirsty tastes in entertainment. They loved watching people and animals killing each other in the amphitheatre. There were many amphitheatres in the Empire, but the greatest was the Colosseum in Rome.

THE COLOSSEUM in Rome opened in AD 80 and held up to 50,000 people. The games usually began with bloody battles between wild beasts. Then the gladiatorial contests followed. To celebrate the opening of the Colosseum, 5,000 animals were slaughtered on the first day.

▽ *The Colosseum in Rome.*

△ *Romans hunting animals in North Africa for the games.*

DURING THE FIRST HALF OF THE GAMES, wild animals, such as rhinoceros, lions, elephants and bulls were pitted against gladiators, and each other, or let loose on criminals.

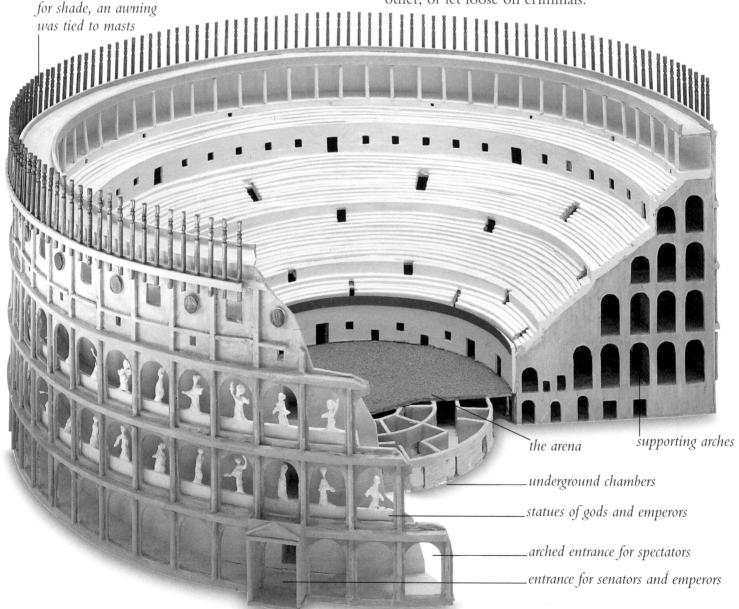

for shade, an awning was tied to masts

the arena

supporting arches

underground chambers

statues of gods and emperors

arched entrance for spectators

entrance for senators and emperors

GLADIATORS were usually slaves or criminals, although some freedmen also earned their living this way. A gladiator's life was short and hard; the majority survived only a few fights.

SUCCESSFUL GLADIATORS were treated rather like the film stars of today. They were well-trained champions who were taught combat techniques at special schools. There were different types of gladiator: the *retiarius* was armed as a fisherman, with a net and a trident – he was often pitted against a *murmillo*, the fishman. Each type of gladiator had its own group of devoted fans.

A CONTEST LASTED until one gladiator was killed or badly wounded. The wounded man threw away his weapons and begged for mercy. The crowd would shout out a verdict. If the gladiator had fought well, the emperor would give a 'thumbs-up' sign and spare his life. If he had not fought well, the emperor gave the 'thumbs-down' sign. Then, the victorious gladiator would kill the loser. An attendant dressed as a demon clubbed the loser on the head and dragged his body out through the 'gate of death'.

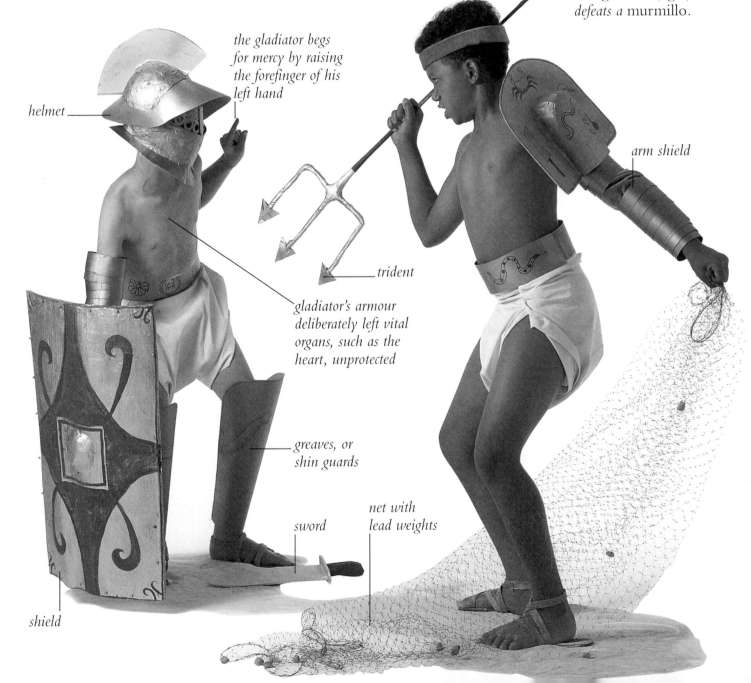

▽ *A* retiarius *gladiator (right) defeats a* murmillo.

helmet

the gladiator begs for mercy by raising the forefinger of his left hand

trident

gladiator's armour deliberately left vital organs, such as the heart, unprotected

arm shield

greaves, or shin guards

sword

net with lead weights

shield

CHARIOT RACING was the most popular entertainment in the larger cities of the Empire. The Romans may have taken the sport from the Greeks who had been racing horses for over a thousand years.

RACES TOOK PLACE on a long track called a **circus**. The biggest of all, Rome's Circus Maximus, could hold 250,000 spectators. The circus was a place to meet friends, to gamble on the horses and to enjoy a dangerous and spectacular show.

▷ *Chariots were made from lightweight pieces of wood, lashed together with thongs. This bronze statue was once a two-horse chariot.*

▽ *Watching chariot racing at the Circus Maximus in Rome was a favourite pastime for many Romans.*

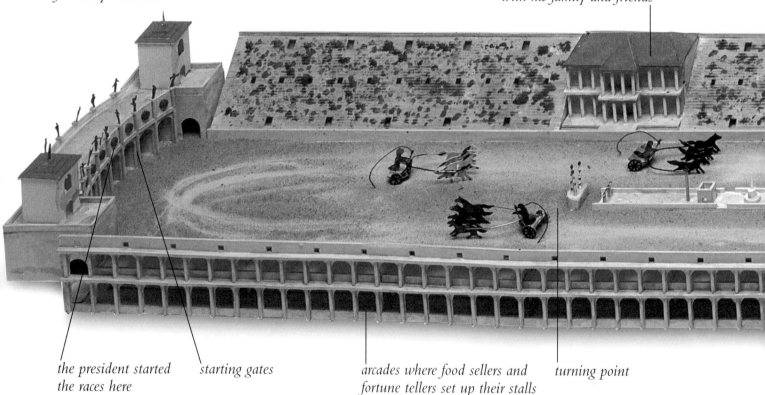

the emperor sat in the imperial box with his family and friends

the president started the races here

starting gates

arcades where food sellers and fortune tellers set up their stalls

turning point

THERE WERE FOUR TEAMS – the Whites, Reds, Blues and the Greens. Each team had its own horses, riders and stables, staffed with trainers, vets and slaves. Like football fans of today, race-goers supported one particular team. They gambled money on their team and wore its colours. The Blues and the Greens had the most supporters. Their rival fans hated each other so much that the races sometimes ended in riots.

THE RACETRACK was the only public place where men and women could sit together. According to the poet Ovid, the circus was a good place to find a girlfriend: 'Sit as close as you like; no one will stop you at all. In fact, you have to sit close – that's one of the rules at the racetrack... Ask her, "Whose colours are those?" – that's good for an opening. Put your bet down, fast, on whatever she plays... Girls, as everyone knows, adore these little attentions.'

THE PRESIDENT OF THE RACES sat at one end of the circus and it was his responsibility to get the race underway. At the blast of a trumpet, he stood up and held out a white napkin, which he dropped onto the track. At this signal, the starting gates flew open and the chariots came racing out.

The starting gates were situated at one end of the circus. Two or four chariots raced seven times around a long, narrow structure called a *spina* which had turning points at each end. The race finished opposite the judges' boxes about half-way along one side.

THE MOST DANGEROUS MOMENT was turning the chariots at the end of the track. If they were too close to the turning posts, they might crash into each other, or overturn. If they were too far away, the charioteers could lose their position.

CHARIOTEERS were mostly slaves. If they won races they could buy their freedom and grow very rich. The teams paid their stars huge salaries to stop them from joining a rival team. The fans admired their skill and courage so much that they kept busts and portraits of the charioteers in their homes. However, many charioteers died young, crushed under the hooves of the galloping horses.

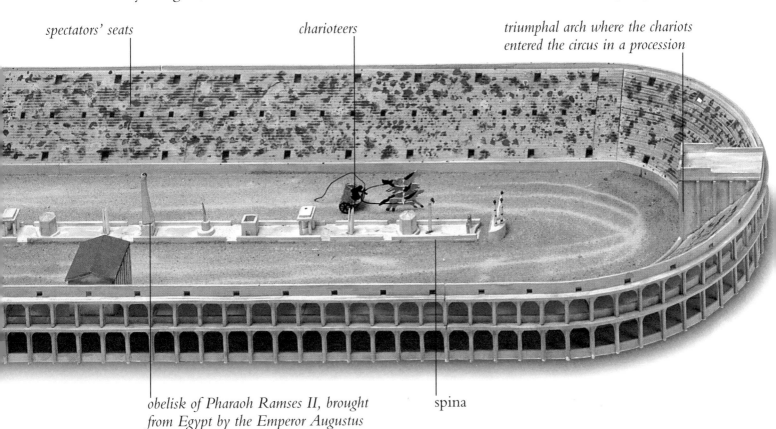

spectators' seats

charioteers

triumphal arch where the chariots entered the circus in a procession

obelisk of Pharaoh Ramses II, brought from Egypt by the Emperor Augustus

spina

THE CENTRAL 'BACKBONE', or *spina*, of the circus, was decorated with statues of the gods and goddesses who were thought to watch over sport. There were also seven large wooden eggs and seven bronze dolphins on the *spina*. At the end of every lap, an egg was removed and a dolphin was reversed to show how many laps remained. Each end of the *spina* was marked by three tall posts.

THE BEST HORSES were also treated like stars. The Emperor Caligula had a favourite horse called *Incitatus* (Speedy) which raced for the Greens. He went to great lengths to keep his horse happy. On the day before a race, troops surrounded the stable, making sure that no-one made any loud noises that might disturb *Incitatus*. Caligula even gave the horse a house complete with furniture and slaves!

Romans relaxing

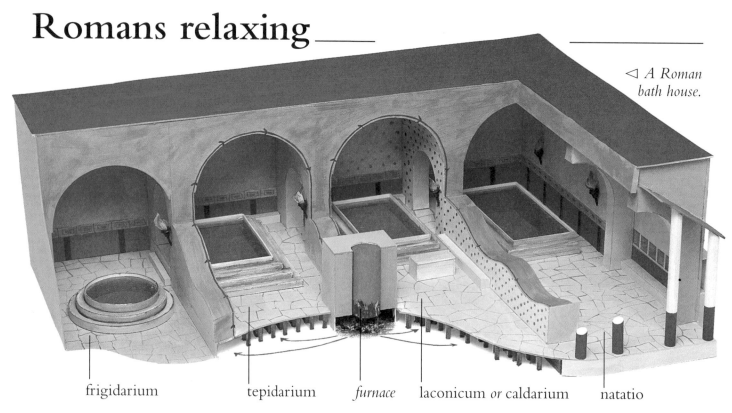

◁ *A Roman bath house.*

frigidarium   tepidarium   *furnace*   laconicum *or* caldarium   natatio

Every Roman town had at least one large public bath house. This was a place where people could go to wash the dust off, to exercise, or just to relax. Men and women visited the bath house separately, either at different times or to different areas. It cost very little to go to the baths, so only the poorest people could not afford to visit them. Many Romans went every day.

▷ *Oils were kept in the small pot, and the long, curved **strigil** was used for scraping off the oil and dirt.*

THE BATH HOUSE had a large exercise yard where people played ball games, lifted weights and wrestled. After exercising, they went to a series of heated rooms to wash and relax.

THE ROOMS and bath water were heated by a furnace stoked by slaves. Hot air from the fire passed through spaces under the floors and inside the walls. The hottest room was the one closest to the furnace.

Once inside, the bathers first went to an icy plunge pool called a *frigidarium*. From there they passed to a warmer room – the *tepidarium*. This was where oils were applied to the skin and then scraped off, so that the bather would be thoroughly clean.

INSTEAD OF SOAP, Romans used olive oil. They rubbed it all over their bodies and scraped it off with a curved metal tool called a *strigil*. Wealthy Romans had personal slave attendants to scrape them down. Poorer Romans had to rub their backs against the walls to scrape the parts they couldn't reach!

FINALLY, THE BATHERS went to a steam room, called a *caldarium*, or to the *laconicum*, or hot room. Then they were clean enough to swim in the swimming pool, or *natatio*. Around the pool there were entertainers, hairdressers and people selling food and drink. Businessmen even held meetings at the baths.

KNUCKLEBONES, or *astragali*, was a popular game at the baths. Players used the small anklebones of a sheep, which have six sides. It was an easy game to play: a player would throw the bones up into the air and try to catch them on the back of the hand. Knucklebones could also be played like dice, with each side of the bones having a different value. Wealthy Romans played with knuckle-bones made from marble, silver or precious stones.

MAKE KNUCKLEBONES

You will need: self-hardening clay, poster paints, paintbrush

1 Mould the clay into 10 knucklebone shapes with 6 sides as shown above.

▽ *Roman girls and women loved to relax at the baths by playing knucklebones.*

2 Paint the knucklebones and give five to each player.

The basic way to play knucklebones is described opposite. Each player should throw in turn. Try and catch as many on the back of your hand as possible. Add up the number of those that you manage to catch.

△ *This mosaic from Pompeii shows actors and musicians getting ready for a performance.*

THEATRE was invented by the Greeks. The Romans borrowed two main types of play from them: the first was tragedy, a serious play showing the sufferings of a great hero or heroine, usually from a Greek myth. The second was comedy, a light-hearted play about everyday life. Many Roman plays were set in Greece and performed by Greek actors.

AUDIENCES were often very noisy. People either cheered the actors, or shouted insults at them. The producer of *The Mother-in-Law*, a comedy by Terence, described his lively audience: 'I was successful in holding the audience – at least to the end of the first act. But then a rumour spread that some gladiators were going to perform – and my audience flew off in a huge crowd, pushing, shouting, fighting to get a good spot at the gladiator performance.'

MASKS were worn in most types of play. These larger-than-life masks showed the sex of the character, as well as his or her mood. Thanks to the masks, the audience could tell at once if an actor was meant to be an angry old man, a comical slave or a beautiful woman. Masks for tragedy showed an expression of horror or despair.

PANTOMIME was a performance in which a single actor mimed several parts, using a series of masks with closed mouths. It was like a solo ballet dance and demanded a great deal of skill. With their faces covered, the actors relied on movement to show their feelings. Pantomime actors were the big stars of the Roman stage.

▽ *This is a mask that a woman might have worn in a tragic play.*

MAKE A ROMAN DRUM

You will need: two lengths of coloured card 6 cm x 90 cm, paint, paintbrush, wool, glue, double-sided sticky tape, a circle of fabric 32 cm in diameter

1 Stick the ends of one of the pieces of card together to make a circle. Stretch the fabric over the circle and glue down tightly around the edges to make the drum.

2 Stick a strip of the tape along the other length of card. Wrap around the drum, sticky side to the fabric.

3 Paint your drum as shown above.

4 Tie together four tassels from your coloured wool and glue them around your drum.

△ *This kind of drum was often used in Roman theatre.*

SPECIAL EFFECTS were very popular with Roman audiences. Actors playing gods would swoop across the stage attached to wires. Even horses and carriages appeared in some plays.

MUSIC was very important in the theatre. Musicians played the pipes, trumpets, cymbals and drums, while the actors sang songs. Although we know what instruments were played, we have no way of knowing what Roman music sounded like.

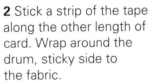

◁ *This actor is wearing a comic mask. Actors used masks and hand gestures to show different characters.*

Amazing architects

The Romans were among the best builders in history. They built things that served practical purposes, such as canals, bridges, sewers, harbours and roads. But it was perhaps in constructing aqueducts that their engineering skills were most impressive.

▽ *Rome was served by eight aqueducts, each built using wooden scaffolding such as this.*

△ *This Roman aqueduct still stands in Segovia, in central Spain.*

covered water channel

AQUEDUCTS were developed by the Romans. They are channels for carrying water that were mostly dug into the earth, following the contours of hills. Where this was not possible, the Romans built arches made of concrete and stone. It took great skill to build an aqueduct. The water channel had to slope at exactly the right angle all the way along its length, to give a steady flow of water.

AN ARCH is a curved structure which is able to support great weight. By using arches, the Romans found they could build high, strong walls using as little stone as possible.

CONCRETE was also a Roman invention. It was a mixture of volcanic sand and stone rubble, held together by mortar made from lime and water. It was strong, cheap and much easier to use than stone blocks. Concrete and arches made it possible to build structures like the Colosseum.

PLINY THE ELDER described the work involved in giving Rome its water supply: 'If we think of the abundant supply of water for public buildings, baths, settling tanks, pools, private houses, gardens and country estates close to the city; and of the distance the water travels, the height of the arches, the tunnelling through mountains, the levelling of routes across deep valleys; we can only conclude that this is a supreme wonder of the world.'

▷ *This surveyor is using a* **groma** *– a wooden cross mounted on a pole, with weighted strings at the ends which hung vertically.*

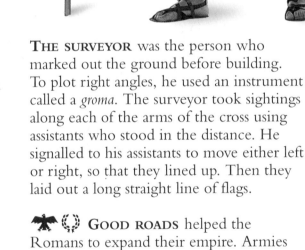

wooden scaffolding supports arches as they are being built

THE SURVEYOR was the person who marked out the ground before building. To plot right angles, he used an instrument called a *groma*. The surveyor took sightings along each of the arms of the cross using assistants who stood in the distance. He signalled to his assistants to move either left or right, so that they lined up. Then they laid out a long straight line of flags.

🦅 🏵️ **GOOD ROADS** helped the Romans to expand their empire. Armies had to be able to move from place to place as quickly as possible with all their equipment. Before the Romans, roads were muddy tracks that were almost impossible to use in wet weather, especially for wheeled transport. The Romans made paved roads that could be used almost all year round. The surface was curved so that rainwater would drain off into ditches at the edges. Roman roads were usually as straight as possible, even if this sometimes meant tunnelling through a cliff.

Feeding the Empire

Some of the best farmland in the Roman Empire was along the coast of North Africa. The soil there was good and the climate was excellent, with long, hot summers and regular rain in winter. It was the perfect place for growing wheat – in fact, North Africa produced two-thirds of the grain eaten in Rome.

△ *This fourth-century mosaic shows farm labourers gathering and treading grapes.*

ROMAN FARMS were often enormous and were owned by very wealthy people. In the first century AD, half of North Africa was said to belong to just six men. Roman landlords spent most of their time in the cities, living extravagantly. They either rented the land out to tenants, or left their farms in the hands of a bailiff who was in charge of a gang of slaves.

FARM BUILDINGS included barns for storing grain and straw, stables for the animals, and various workshops – a blacksmith's forge for making and repairing tools, and a pottery for making storage jars. There were buildings for pressing grapes and olives, and a mill for grinding wheat. The type and quality of crops grown varied throughout the Empire. Olives could be grown only in the warm south. Grapes were grown in southern Britain, but they were not as good as those from Spain or Italy.

RELIGIOUS CEREMONIES played a big part in the farmers' year. The Romans believed that ceremonies were just as important as sowing or ploughing at the right time. In May, for example, a pig, a ram and a bull were led around the boundaries of the fields and then killed as a sacrifice to the god Mars. The farmer would say, 'Father Mars, I pray that you keep disease and bad weather away from my fields and that you allow my harvest, my corn and my vineyard to flourish.'

▷ *A Roman farm on the north coast of Africa.*

team of oxen harnessed to a mechanical harvester

beehives

wheat

OLIVE TREES were grown all over North Africa, but the olives from Tripolitania (present-day Libya) were particularly famous. They were grown on dry hillsides, above fields of wheat. The olives could either be eaten, or crushed in an oil press for their rich oil.

SLAVES did most of the farm work. A trusted slave called a *vilicus* was in charge of the field labourers. They had to work very hard, if not, they might be beaten or kept in chains. Farm work was used as a punishment for town slaves whose masters thought they were lazy.

▷ *Farmers' tools were simple but effective. These knives were used for pruning grapevines.*

stables

olive press

farmhouse or villa rustica

slaves' quarters

olive grove

livestock

Trade and transport

Wherever they went, the Roman armies built roads. Although they were for military use, Roman roads made it easier to transport goods on carts pulled by mules and oxen, no matter what the weather. Heavy goods were moved by water wherever possible, along rivers on barges pulled by oxen, or across the sea on merchant ships.

THE PEACE that was brought by Roman rule helped trade to flourish from one end of the Empire to the other. The demands of the wealthy also meant that luxury goods, such as silks and spices, were brought from distant lands.

△ *Coins were used throughout the Empire.*

WITHIN THE EMPIRE, the most important trade was in metals, luxury goods, and foods such as wine, olive oil, grain and fish sauce.

Some goods were imported from beyond the Empire. Silk came from as far away as China along an overland route called the Silk Road. Spices for cooking were brought by sea from India, and incense, which the Romans burned on the altars of the gods, came overland from southern Arabia by camel caravans, or by ships sailing up the Red Sea.

KEY TO TRADE MAP

wild animals   *wild animals*   *slaves*   *corn*   *wine*   *oil*   *gold*   *metals*

▽ *This map shows where some of the goods traded around the Empire came from.*

BRITANNIA

GERMANIA

GAUL

IBERIA

ANATOLIA

DALMATIA

Rome

ITALIA

SYRIA

MACEDONIA

Mediterranean Sea

MAURETANIA

AFRICA

CYRENAICA   AEGYPTUS   *Red Sea*

△ *Traders made healthy profits from transporting exotic animals around the Empire.*

☾ ✳ **A ROMAN COIN** was like a tiny newspaper in some ways. One side was used by the emperor to announce important events, such as a military victory. He also used coins to try to win people's support. The coin might show him speaking to his troops – giving people the impression that he was in firm command. Another coin might show the emperor as the chief priest, so that people would think that the gods were behind him.

▷ *A merchant weighs some fruit using a set of scales.*

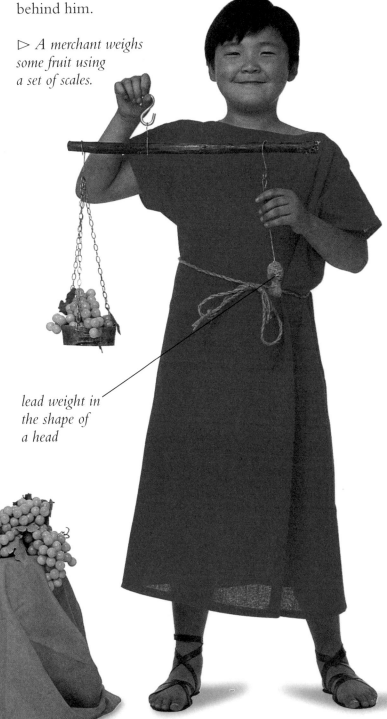

lead weight in the shape of a head

☾ ✳ **PLINY THE ELDER** thought that foreign luxury goods were costing the Empire too much: 'At the lowest reckoning, India, China and Arabia carry off one hundred million *sestertii* a year from our Empire – such is the bill for our pleasures and our ladies.'

WILD ANIMALS were brought from all parts of the Empire and from lands beyond for the games in Rome. Bears were shipped from Scotland and Ireland. Elephants came from Africa and India.

☾ ✳ **THE SAME COINS** were used throughout the Empire which made trading simple. The basic unit was a copper coin called an *as*. A larger copper coin, called the *dupondius*, was worth 2 asses; a bronze coin, the *sestertius*, was worth 4 asses; a silver *denarius* equalled 16 asses; and a gold *aureus* was worth 100 asses.

SHIPS were used to move people and goods around the Empire and beyond. As well as travelling for trade and religious reasons, some wealthy Romans went sightseeing, and some even had guidebooks.

▽ *A Roman war galley.*

sail was lowered before going into battle

underwater battering ram

up to five men manned each oar

WAR GALLEYS were slim, fast vessels. They were powered by oarsmen who sat on benches below deck, pulling in time to orders shouted by the helmsman. At the bow, or front, there was a battering ram made from wood covered in bronze. Galleys would try to ram enemy ships in the side. Then the crew of marines (naval soldiers) would jump on board the enemy ship for hand-to-hand fighting.

PIRATES were a menace in the first century BC. Fleets of pirates based in the eastern Mediterranean raided coastal towns and seized any ships they could. They stole the cargoes and held the crews for ransom, or sold them as slaves. In 67 BC, the Romans gathered a fleet of war galleys and hunted the pirates down to make the sea safe.

THE SAILING SEASON lasted from March to November. Few ships put to sea in winter because of the risk of storms, and because of shorter daylight hours. However, the city of Rome needed wheat grown abroad to feed its people, so some huge grain ships had to make the dangerous winter journey from North Africa. When grain supplies ran low in the granaries, there was panic in Rome.

IN THE SECOND CENTURY AD, the Greek writer Lucian described the *Isis*, one of the great grain ships that sailed out of Egypt: 'What a big ship! About 180 feet [55 metres] long and something over a quarter of that wide… And then the height of the mast! And how the stern rises with its gentle curve, with its golden beak, balanced at the opposite end by the long rising length of the prow, with a figure of the goddess Isis on either side!'

▽ *Merchant ships carried people, food supplies and wild animals for the games.*

yard

foresail, or steering sail

MERCHANT SHIPS were used to move goods around the Empire. These ships were large and round-bellied, to provide lots of storage space for all the sacks of grain and *amphorae*, or pottery jars, holding oil or wine. Because of their shape, these ships were stable but very slow. They had a big square sail on the mast with a smaller sail at the bow. Two large oars at the stern, or rear, were used for steering.

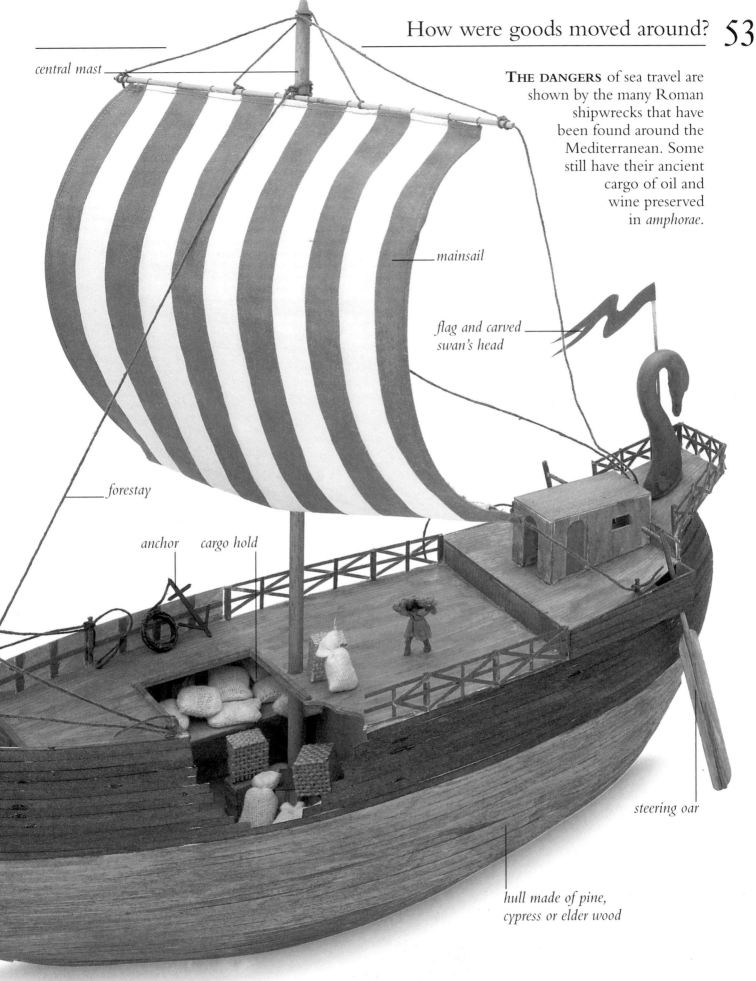

central mast

THE DANGERS of sea travel are shown by the many Roman shipwrecks that have been found around the Mediterranean. Some still have their ancient cargo of oil and wine preserved in *amphorae*.

mainsail

flag and carved swan's head

forestay

anchor   cargo hold

steering oar

hull made of pine, cypress or elder wood

The Roman army

In the first century AD, the Roman army was mostly made up of legionaries and auxiliaries. There were 28 legions, mainly stationed around the borders of the Empire. Each one had a number and a name that was either a nickname or the place where the troops were raised. For example, the sixth legion was called *Victrix*, or victorious, and the ninth legion was called *Hispana*, or Spanish.

lionskin headdress worn over a helmet

◁ *A legionary from the first century BC.*

A LEGIONARY was a Roman foot soldier. On marches, they had to carry heavy loads of weapons, tools and supplies. If they were not fighting or training, legionaries had to do building work. They cut down trees, quarried stone, and built roads, bridges and forts.

▽ *A Syrian archer of the early second century AD.*

Syrian archers wore long robes

△ *An aquilifer from the first century AD.*

AUXILIARIES were soldiers who came from the provinces and who were not Roman citizens. They were poorly paid, earning only a third of the legionaries' rate. Auxiliaries fought using the familiar weapons of their own countries. Cavalrymen came from Gaul (France) and North Africa, slingers from islands off Spain, and archers from Syria. Auxiliaries supplied the extra fighting skills that the legions lacked.

🌿 **THE AQUILIFER,** or eagle bearer, carried the standard of the legion – a golden eagle on a pole. Smaller units also had standards, such as golden hands or busts of the emperor. These were used to rally the soldiers in battle. Aquilifers had to be very brave, for they led the men into the most dangerous places on the battlefield. The lionskins on their helmets were a symbol of their rank and courage.

long spear used for stabbing from horseback

▽ *A cavalry officer from the fourth century* AD.

silver-plated helmet

▷ *A centurion from the middle of the first century* AD.

helmet with sideways crest

🦅 🌿 **EACH LEGION** had around 5,500 soldiers, including 120 horsemen who acted as messengers and scouts, keeping an eye on the enemy. The rest of the soldiers were divided into small units called centuries, each of about 80 men. Six centuries grouped together made a cohort.

silver and gold medals on chest

vine cane used to point at, or beat, the men

🌿 **A CENTURION** was an officer in charge of a century. To show his rank, he wore special armour made from silver-coloured metal scales and shiny greaves (shin guards). He also wore a helmet with a sideways crest as a sign of his status. He kept his men in order by beating them with a vine cane, either as a punishment, or to make them work harder.

✳ **CAVALRYMEN** played an even more important role during the later Empire, when large armies of soldiers on horseback fought alongside the legions, defending the Empire. By the fourth century, the cavalry carried long swords and round shields.

LEGIONARIES were full-time soldiers. They joined the army at about the age of 18, and had to serve for the next 20 to 25 years. It was a hard life, but it also offered security and regular pay to the poorest Roman citizens. Through good service, legionaries might be promoted to the rank of centurion. If they survived the battles they fought, they could retire and live a comfortable life.

New recruits had to swear an oath that they were free-born Roman citizens, not slaves. Sometimes, slaves tried to join the legions. If they were discovered, they were executed.

DRILLING AND MARCHING took up a large part of the legionaries' day. In his book *Military Service*, the author Vegetius described the type of training programme that legionaries were put through: 'Every recruit, without exception, should in the summer months learn to swim, for it is not always possible to cross rivers on bridges… They should be accustomed also to leap and strike blows at the same time, to rise up with a bound and sink down again behind the shield… They must also practise throwing their javelins at the posts from a distance to increase their skill in aiming, and the strength of the arm.'

MAKE A PAIR OF ARMOURED SHOES

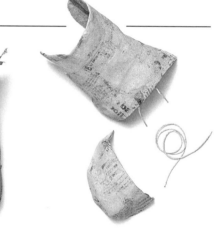

You will need: scissors, chicken wire, paper, string, flour, water, salt, paint

1 Ask an adult to help you mould the chicken wire to fit the top of your feet.

2 Make a runny paste of flour and water. Add a pinch of salt. Cover the shapes (inside and out) in layers of strips of paper dipped in the paste. Leave them to dry.

3 Cut off the tops of the toes as shown to make toe shields.

4 Cut four 8 cm lengths of string. Use paper and paste to fix the string to the underside of each foot cover and the toe shields. Paint the shields as shown.

5 Make two small holes in the sides of each shoe. Thread string through the holes and tie around your ankles.

PUNISHMENTS were harsh in the army. Soldiers who fell asleep on guard duty or who ran away in battle were stoned to death. If a whole unit showed cowardice or refused to obey orders, it could be punished with decimation, which meant that one man in every ten was killed.

However, life was not all bad for a Roman soldier. At Vindolanda, a Roman fort in northern Britain, archaeologists found many letters written on thin sheets of wood. In one letter, dating from AD 120, a soldier complains that his unit has run out of beer!

▷ *This is a copy of foot armour that was found in the south of Italy, in an early Greek settlement.*

🦅 🌀 **BAGGAGE MULES** trotted alongside the marching soldiers. There was one mule for every eight men. It carried a leather tent and a millstone for grinding corn. Other mules were loaded with dismantled catapults, used for hurling stones at the enemy.

supplies carried on a wooden cross on the legionary's back

cooking pots

🦅 🌀 **A JAVELIN,** or *pilum*, had a long metal tip that bent on impact. This meant that the enemy could not throw it back. Soldiers fought in tight formation, obeying trumpet signals. After throwing their javelins, they drew their short swords and thrust at the enemy from behind their shields.

🦅 🌀 **WHEN ATTACKING** an enemy stronghold, soldiers grouped together and covered themselves with their shields for protection. This defence was called 'the tortoise'. The men gathered into a square and those at the edges linked their curved shields together to make a wall of wood. The men in the middle held their shields above their heads to make a roof. This kept them safe from enemy missiles.

▽ *An early legionary shown with the equipment he was expected to carry on long marches.*

cloak

water pouch

turf cutter

mattock for building camp

javelin, or pilum

spear

wooden shield carried on legionary's back

ON A CAMPAIGN, Roman soldiers slept in leather tents in temporary marching camps, which they set up at the end of each day. The rest of the time, they lived in barracks in permanent forts made of wood or stone.

FRONTIER FORTS were dotted along the borders of the Empire. They were usually manned by auxiliaries recruited from the local area, so German auxiliaries defended the Empire against German invaders. Legionaries lived some way behind the frontier, providing a second line of defence. If the front line was attacked, guards in the watch-towers would light beacons to send the urgent news.

▽ *This is a typical Roman frontier fort.*

mile castle built every Roman mile (1.5 km) along frontiers

a main gateway

stables

barracks

workshop

FORTS changed over time, but they were often rectangular and surrounded by a ditch. Early forts were protected by a wall of timber and turf. Later, they were built with stone. Two main roads crossed the camp, leading to four gates, one on each wall. The fort was a permanent home for the soldiers, so it had to be as comfortable as possible. The soldiers always had their own baths, and sometimes amphitheatres for gladiator contests.

THE HOSPITAL was an important building in every fort, as the soldiers were often sick and sometimes injured. Military doctors knew how to reset broken bones, and they operated to remove splinters or arrowheads from wounds.

defensive ditch

THE COMMANDER'S HOUSE, or *praetorium*, was a lavish building with heated rooms where the commander lived with his family and their slaves. The business of running the legion took place in the headquarters, or *principia*. It had a strongroom for the legion's money, a shrine for the standards, and a platform for addressing the troops.

IN THEIR FREE TIME, soldiers could drink beer, gamble with dice and organize wrestling matches, horse races and tug-of-war contests. The commanding officers preferred hunting deer and wild boar with packs of dogs.

IN MAINLAND EUROPE there were wide rivers which also acted as frontier lines. The Romans built forts and watch-towers along the west bank of the Rhine and on the southern bank of the Danube. They used them to keep an eye on the fierce German tribes across the river.

THE EMPEROR HADRIAN ordered that a wall be built across northern Britain to defend the frontier. The Romans called the people who lived north of the wall *Picti*, or painted ones, because they covered themselves in war-paint.

▷ *The Emperor Hadrian ordered the building of a 120 km-long wall, sections of which can still be seen today.*

granary

hospital

headquarters, or principia

commander's house, or praetorium

watch-tower

The fall of Rome

In the fourth century AD, the Roman Empire was weakened by a series of invasions. German tribes poured over the Rhine and Danube rivers. To meet the threat, the Roman Empire was split into two halves. There was an emperor in the west, sometimes ruling from Rome, and another in the east ruling from Constantinople (Istanbul) in Turkey.

✠ **ROME WAS CAPTURED** and plundered in AD 410 by Alaric, king of a German people. The news of the fall of the city shocked the Roman world. Jerome, a monk in Palestine, wrote to a friend: 'Terrifying news has come to us from the West. Rome has been taken by assault… My voice is still and sobs disturb my every utterance. The city has been conquered which had once controlled the entire world.'

△ *Many tourists visit the remains of the Colosseum in Rome.*

THE GERMAN INVADERS set up their own kingdoms in Western Europe. One group, the Franks, settled in Gaul and became the French. Other German peoples, the Saxons and Angles, settled in Britain and became the English. The invaders did not usually want to destroy the Roman Empire. As a result, many aspects of the Roman way of life were kept alive in Western Europe.

▷ *The title 'Caesar' was used by the emperors, from Augustus to Hadrian, and by other powerful rulers throughout history.*

◁ *The eagle, once the symbol of the Roman Empire, is now a symbol of the USA and appears on the one-dollar bill. For the Romans, the eagle was the king of birds and represented Jupiter, the king of the gods, and god of the sky.*

ROMAN POLITICS AND LAW have had a lasting influence. The USA has modelled its system of government on the Roman Republic and adopted the eagle as a national emblem. Throughout history, many rulers have looked to the power and inspiration of the emperors and the Roman Empire. In some countries, rulers adopted the title 'Caesar': in Russia, it became 'Tzar', and in Germany it became 'Kaiser'.

THE EASTERN EMPIRE survived for another thousand years. It was only in 1453 that the last eastern emperor died defending his capital, Constantinople, against the Muslim Turks.

By the 16th century the Empire no longer existed, but its influence lived on in the lands surrounding the Mediterranean in the form of architecture, language, literature and government.

ROMAN ARCHITECTURE still influences modern buildings. Public buildings, such as banks, libraries, churches and museums, are often modelled on Roman temples, with tall, decorative columns.

THE LATIN LANGUAGE developed into French, Italian, Spanish, Portuguese and Romanian. Pure Latin was kept alive in church services and writings. It also became, with Greek, an international language for scientists who classify plants, animals and parts of the body using Latin names.

THE MONTHS OF THE YEAR are still known by their Roman names. March, for example, is named after the Roman god Mars, and August gets its name from Rome's first emperor, Augustus. The planets are also named after Roman gods.

cyclamen
Cyclamen persicum

△ *Latin is used to classify plants and species of animals.*

Glossary

amphitheatre An oval-shaped Roman building without a roof. It was used for public shows, such as fights between gladiators and wild animals.

amphora A tall pottery vase with two handles used for transporting and storing wine, olive oil, vinegar and fish sauce.

aqueduct An artificial channel, made of stone and concrete, used for carrying water from one area to another.

archaeologist Someone who searches for and studies the remains of past times, such as ancient buildings and artefacts.

atrium The entrance hall of a Roman house.

augur A religious official whose job was to find out whether the gods approved or disapproved of a course of action. The augur did this by watching the flight and behaviour of birds. No important decisions were made in Rome without consulting the sacred flock of chickens.

auxiliary Soldiers drawn from the non-citizen population of the Empire. They were paid less than citizen soldiers. On retirement, they became Roman citizens.

barbarian A word used by the Greeks and Romans to describe foreigners.

centurion A middle-ranking Roman officer in charge of a 'century' of men (80).

Chi-Rho (pronounced ky-roh) A sign used by early Christians to show their faith. It combines the Greek letters X (Chi) and P (Rho), the first two letters of the word Christ.

circus An oval track for chariot races. The most famous was the Circus Maximus in Rome.

citizen A citizen of the Roman Empire was a full member of the Roman state, and had more rights than a non-citizen.

civilization A developed and organized group of people or nation. The Romans believed that civilization was marked by town life, laws, reading and writing, and religious ceremonies.

client A person who owed loyalty to a wealthier Roman, who was their patron.

consul The most important Roman government official. Two consuls were elected each year.

early imperial period The period of Roman history from 27 BC to AD 284. For most of this time, the Empire was ruled by the emperor.

emperor The ruler of the Roman Empire. The rule of the emperors was known as imperial rule.

equestrian A member of a class of wealthy Roman citizens. Each equestrian owned a personal fortune of at least 400,000 sestertii.

Etruscans The people who lived in north-west Italy in ancient times. The Etruscans were an important influence on the Romans.

fasces A bundle of rods, tied around an axe, and an Etruscan symbol of power, adopted by the Romans.

forum The central market-place and public meeting area in every Roman town.

freedmen and freedwomen Slaves who bought or were given their freedom. If their former owners were Roman citizens, they became citizens too. However, they did not have as many rights as free-born citizens.

fresco A type of wall painting in which paint is applied to damp plaster.

gladiator A man who fought in the arena, either against another gladiator, or an animal. Gladiators were mostly slaves, although those that were successful were able to buy their freedom.

groma A tool used by Roman surveyors to plot straight lines, right-angles and grids.

haruspice A religious official whose job was to predict the future or to find out the wishes of the gods. He did this by inspecting the inner organs of sacrificed animals. He also interpreted lightning and unusual events in nature, such as earthquakes.

insula A block of housing in a Roman town.

Isis An important Egyptian goddess worshipped by the Romans. She was seen by her followers as the queen of the whole universe. Isis also had specific roles as a goddess of wheat and barley, childbirth, and seafarers.

late imperial period The period of Roman history from AD 284 to 476. For most of this period, the Empire was divided into two halves. It also became a Christian empire.

Latin The language spoken by the Romans and the other peoples of Latium, an area in central Italy. The ancient people of Latium were called Latins.

legionary A Roman citizen who served as an infantry soldier in a legion.

magistrate An elected official who governed the Roman state. Under the Republic, the most powerful officials were the two consuls. There were also the praetors, who were in charge of justice, and the quaestors, who looked after state money.

Mithras A god of light, first worshipped in Persia, and later, in secret, by men throughout the Roman Empire.

mosaic A picture made from hundreds of tiny pieces of pottery, stone or glass tiles, pressed into cement.

pater familias The father and head of a Roman family.

province A large area of the Roman Empire ruled by its own governor.

provincial A native of one of the provinces of the Roman Empire. Provincials had fewer rights than citizens, but were much better off than slaves.

Roman Empire The different lands and peoples ruled by the Romans. 'The Empire' also means the period when Rome was ruled by emperors, rather than by elected officials.

Roman Republic A period when Rome and the Empire were ruled by elected officials.

senators A member of the senate, a council of leading nobles who advised the consuls and the Emperor. In the Empire, senators commanded the armies and governed provinces. To be a senator, you had to be elected as a member of the magistrates, and have a huge personal fortune of at least a million sestertii.

shrine A place where holy objects, such as statues of gods, were placed and worshipped. Many Romans had shrines in their homes.

standard bearer Someone who carried a pole with a flag, metal eagle or a placard on the top. Standards were used in religious processions, and as rallying points for soldiers in battle.

strigil A curved metal tool that was used at the Roman baths for scraping oil and dirt off skin.

stylus A pen-like instrument used for writing on wax tablets.

symbol A sign, or an object that stands for something else, is said to be a symbol. For example, a cross is a symbol of Christianity; a lionskin headdress is a symbol of bravery.

tablinum A Roman reception room.

toga A gown worn by Roman citizens. It was made of a single woollen sheet and wrapped around the body.

triclinium A Roman dining room with three couches in an open square for guests to lie upon.

Index

Amphitheatre 17, 38, 58
amphorae 19, 26, 27, 52, 53
animals 16, 19, 24, 34, 36, 38,
  40-41, 45, 48, 51, 52, 61
aqueduct 6, 16, 46-47
archaeology 4, 18-19, 22, 56
architecture 46-47, 60, 61
armour 38, 54-57
army 6, 7, 11, 47, 50, 54-57
auxiliaries 10, 54, 58

Barbarians 9
baths, the 16, 42-43

Carthage 6, 8
cavalry 54, 55
centurions 11, 55, 56
chariot racing 17, 40-41
children 10, 30-31, 32, 33
Circus Maximus 40-41
cities 4, 16-17, 49, 48
citizen 6, 7, 9, 10, 11, 12, 56
clients 20, 21
clothes 9, 12-15; toga 11, 12,
  13, 21; tunica 12, 13
coins 15, 50, 51, 60
Colosseum 6, 38, 46, 60
commanders 58, 59
consul 6

Education 30, 32-33
emperor 5, 11, 14, 17, 21, 35,
  37, 39, 40, 51, 55, 60, 61;
  Augustus 6, 7, 41, 61; Romulus
  Augustulus 7; Caligula 36, 41;
  Caracalla 7, 9; Constantine 7,
  37; Hadrian 7, 15, 59; Nero 7;
  Tiberius 7; Valens 7; Vitellius 29
entertainment 17, 28-29, 38-41
equestrians 11
Etruscans 4, 5

Face pots 37
fall of Rome 60-61

family life 20, 30-31
farms 26, 48-49
fasces 5, 12
food 19, 26-29, 48-49,
  50-53; grape punch 28
  honey omelette 27;
forts 56, 58-59
freedmen/women 10, 12, 19,
  39, 30, 39, 56
frescoes 21, 23, 24-25
furniture 19, 20, 21, 28, 41

Games, the 24, 38-41
gardens 20, 22-23, 47, 61
generals 11, 14
gladiators 17, 38-39, 44, 58
gods 7, 17, 23, 30, 34-37, 41,
  45, 48, 51; Isis 7, 36, 37, 52;
  Juno 23, 34; Jupiter 34, 61;
  Mars 48, 61; Minerva 34;
  Mithras 36, 37
governors 7, 11
Greeks 4, 5, 8, 9, 24, 44

Hairstyles 14-15
Herculaneum 23
homes 20-21, 26

Jewellery 14-15

Knucklebones 43

Language 4, 9, 32, 60
Latin 4, 9, 32, 60, 61
law and order 17, 61
legionaries 11, 54, 56, 57, 58

Magistrates 12
make-up 14
marriage 31
masks 37, 44, 45
mosaics 21, 24-25, 28, 44, 48
music 10, 34, 41, 44, 45;
  Roman drum 45

Pantomine 44
patrons 20, 21
Pompeii 7, 18-19, 22, 24, 25,
  32, 44
priest/priestess 11, 34-35
province 7, 8-9, 11
provincial/non-citizen 9, 10,
  12, 54

Religion 5, 11, 17, 23, 24, 30,
  31, 34-37, 48, 50, 51, 52
  Christianity 6, 7
roads 19, 46, 47, 50, 58
Roman numerals 33
Romulus and Remus 4, 6

Senators 11, 12
ships 4, 29, 50, 51, 52-53
slaves 10, 12, 14, 19, 20, 21, 23,
  26, 28, 29, 30, 31, 36, 39, 40,
  41, 42, 48, 49, 52, 56, 58
society 10-11
standard-bearer 35, 55

Temples 5, 11, 17, 34, 35, 36,
  37, 61
theatre 17, 44-45
tools 5, 49, 54-57
toys 30-31
trade 6, 10, 16, 36, 50-53
trade (apprenticeship) 32
transport 29, 47, 50-53

Vesuvius 7, 18, 19
votives (offerings) 36-37

War 6-7, 8-9, 39, 52, 54-59
weapons 39, 54-57
writers: Jerome 60; Lucian 52;
  Martial 19; Ovid 40; Pliny the
  Younger 23; Pliny the Elder
  47, 51; Seutonius 15, 29;
  Terence 44; Vegetius 56
writing tools 25, 32-33

NORTH AMERICAN INDIANS

Contents

Studying Indian life	4
Across the sea	6
Furs and feathers	8
Homes and shelters	14
Tribes and families	22
A healthy diet	26
Sport and leisure	30
Arts and crafts	34
Getting around	40
Why make war?	46
Language differences	48
A spiritual life	52
Give and take	56
Looking back	58
Post-contact times	60
Glossary	62

Words marked in **bold** in the text can be found here

Index	64

Studying Indian life

All human beings need food and shelter to survive. They also need things to look forward to that give their lives hope and meaning. Throughout history, different groups of people around the world have come up with their own ways of meeting these basic needs. Studying past **civilizations** can tell us how people used the resources around them to build shelters, how they farmed or found food, and how they met their spiritual needs and hopes for a better future.

△ *This Crow Indian in Montana is decorating buffalo hides which were used for making dwellings (see page 17).*

△ *Shoshoni Indians of the Great Basin lived in fertile regions near the Grand Teton mountains.*

THE INDIANS were scattered over a vast country. It had a wide range of climates and **terrains**, from parched deserts in the Southwest to the frozen wastes of the North to the dense forests in the East. Those who lived in the Canadian Subarctic region had to deal with an even more extreme climate. We look at their lives, along with those of the people who lived even further north, in *Arctic Peoples*, another title in the Make it Work! History series.

TO HELP YOU study this vast area, with its wide range of different peoples, North America has been divided into seven climate regions. Each has a symbol which is used purely as a guide, when information relates to a group of people from a particular part of the country.

KEY TO THE SYMBOLS AND AREAS

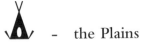 - the Plains

 - the Northeast

 - the Northwest

 - the Southwest

 - California

 - the Southeast

 - the Great Basin and Plateau

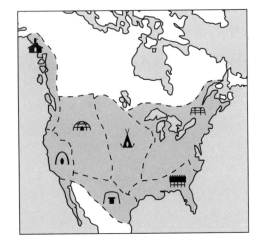

IN THIS BOOK we look at how the North American Indians lived from five hundred years ago, just before their traditional way of life was changed by the arrival of European settlers, to the present day. We can build up a picture of what this life was like from the tales told by the explorers and traders. These people were among the first from other parts of the world to have any contact with North American Indians. We can also learn a great deal from the stories that have been passed down from generation to generation by the Indians themselves. The studies of **archaeologists** and **anthropologists** are another source of information (see page 58).

THE TRADITIONS AND LIFESTYLES of North American Indians are a vital and living part of the country's history. They are kept alive by many of today's Indians who have chosen to live as their ancestors did. Other Indians prefer to live in a style that has different cultural roots.

▽ *These Plains Indians continue to live according to the traditions of their ancestors.*

△ *This Blackfoot Indian chief is painting pictures showing experiences in his life (see pages 50-51).*

THE MAKE IT WORK! way of looking at history is to ask questions of the past and find answers by making replicas of the things people made. However, you do not have to make everything in the book to understand the Indians' way of life. You should also realise that some of the objects included are based on sacred or ceremonial traditions. Therefore, they deserve the same respect as you would give to objects that are special to your own culture or beliefs.

▽ *The Iroquois Indians believed that these sacred masks gave the wearer the power to cure illnesses.*

Across the sea

Scientists believe that, over 50,000 years ago, the first people arrived in the continent that is now North America. They were **Ice Age** hunters from Siberia. They followed mammoth and giant bison south, as they searched the icy landscape for food. At that time, a huge area of ice formed a kind of bridge between Siberia and Alaska, so the hunters and their prey gradually moved from one continent to another. About 11,000 years ago, the world warmed up, this ice bridge sank and the countries were separated by what is now the Bering Strait.

NORTHWEST COAST

(warm, wet summers; cool, wet winters)

Haida
Tlingit
Chinook
Nootka
Kwakiutl

CALIFORNIA

(hot and dry all year round)

Chumash
Miwok
Pomo
Yahi

SOUTHWEST

(hot and dry all year round)

Pueblo Indians
Apache
Navajo
Yuma
Hopi
Zuni

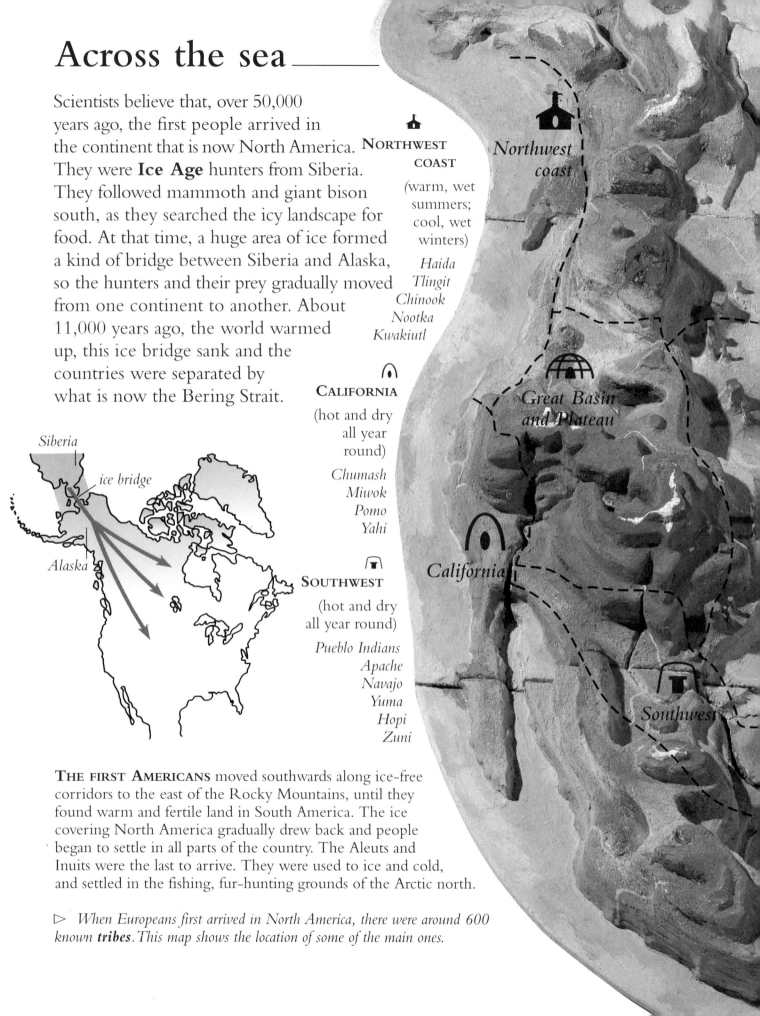

THE FIRST AMERICANS moved southwards along ice-free corridors to the east of the Rocky Mountains, until they found warm and fertile land in South America. The ice covering North America gradually drew back and people began to settle in all parts of the country. The Aleuts and Inuits were the last to arrive. They were used to ice and cold, and settled in the fishing, fur-hunting grounds of the Arctic north.

▷ *When Europeans first arrived in North America, there were around 600 known **tribes**. This map shows the location of some of the main ones.*

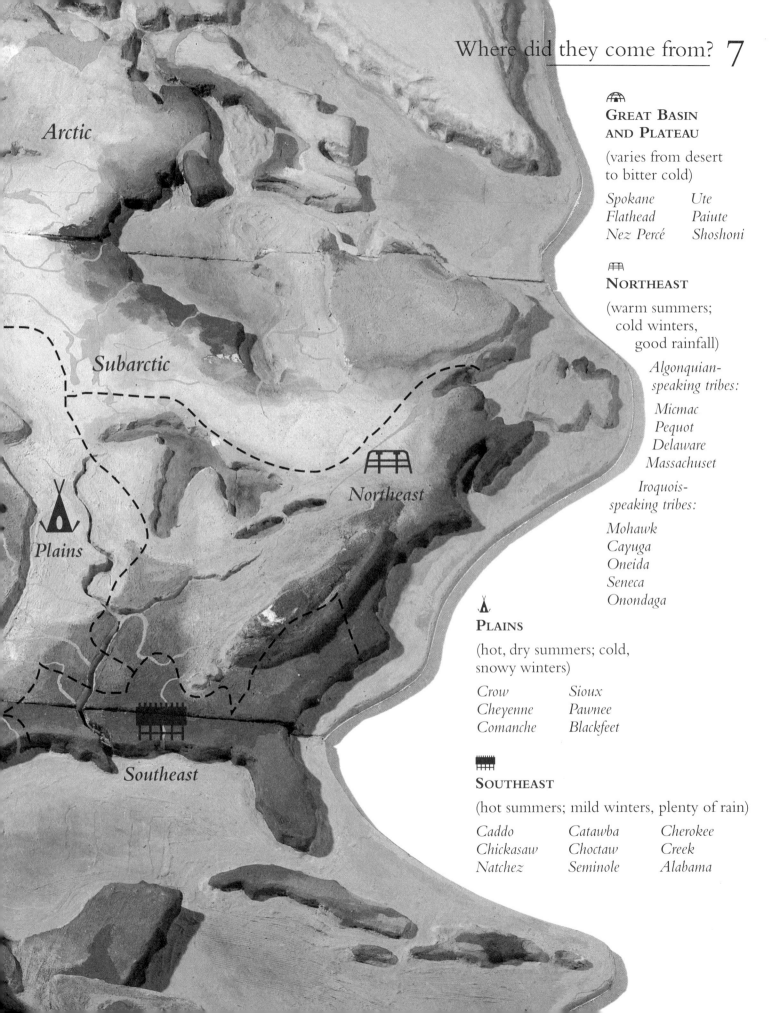

Arctic

Subarctic

Plains

Northeast

Southeast

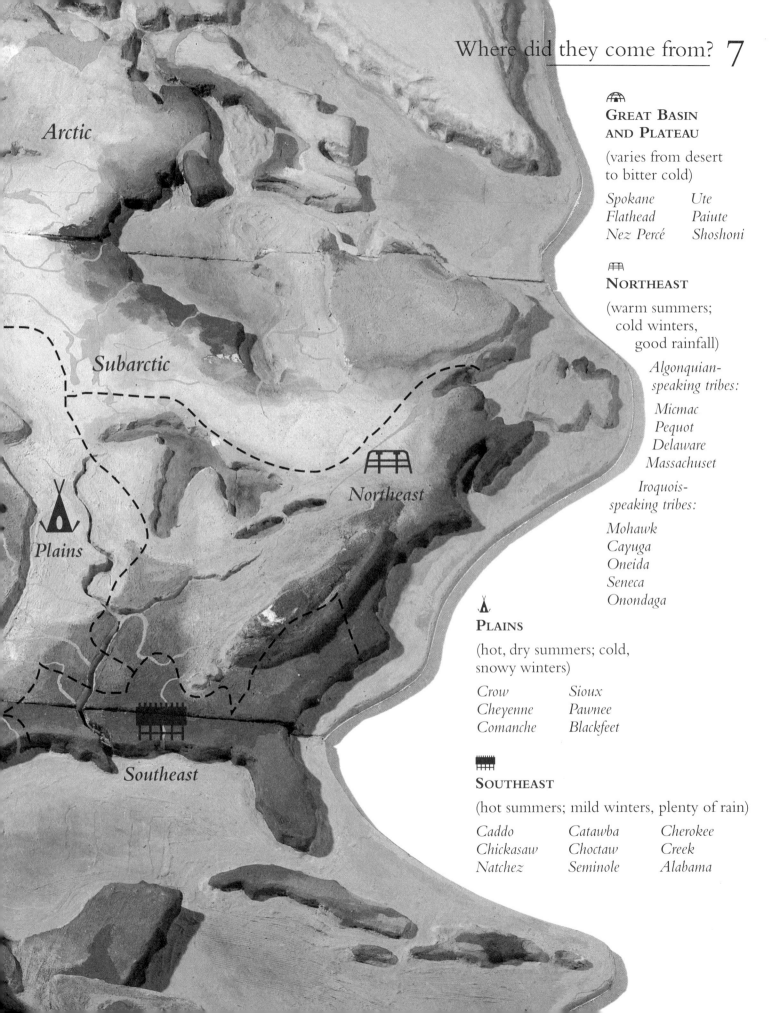
GREAT BASIN AND PLATEAU

(varies from desert to bitter cold)

Spokane	Ute
Flathead	Paiute
Nez Percé	Shoshoni

NORTHEAST

(warm summers; cold winters, good rainfall)

Algonquian-speaking tribes:

Micmac
Pequot
Delaware
Massachuset

Iroquois-speaking tribes:

Mohawk
Cayuga
Oneida
Seneca
Onondaga

PLAINS

(hot, dry summers; cold, snowy winters)

Crow	Sioux
Cheyenne	Pawnee
Comanche	Blackfeet

SOUTHEAST

(hot summers; mild winters, plenty of rain)

Caddo	Catawba	Cherokee
Chickasaw	Choctaw	Creek
Natchez	Seminole	Alabama

Furs and feathers

Although many people think of traditional North American Indian dress as fringed tunics, feather headdresses and braided hair, this is not what everyone wore. It is the summer dress of some Plains tribes. The clothes people wore depended on where and how they lived, as with everything in American Indian life. Tribes in northern and eastern areas needed warm clothing. Many western and southern tribes wore very little, some decorating their bodies with tattoos. Hunting tribes made clothing from animal hides and fur, while gatherers and farmers used plant fibres.

△ The first North American settlers were tall, well-built Siberian people, with broad faces, high cheekbones, straight black hair and brown skin.

⚐ WARBONNETS were headdresses made from golden eagle feathers. Warriors proved their bravery by collecting feathers from the fierce, powerful birds. They cut and coloured them in different ways to let others know about their fighting skills (see page 46).

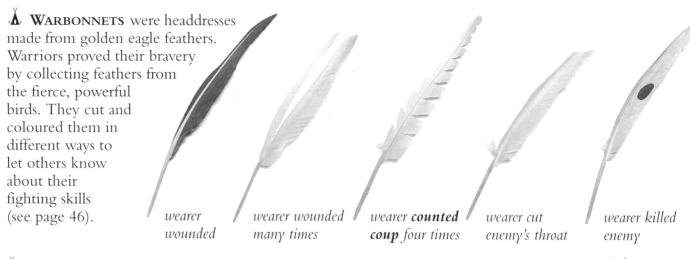

wearer wounded *wearer wounded many times* *wearer counted coup four times* *wearer cut enemy's throat* *wearer killed enemy*

⚐ MAKE A SIOUX HEADDRESS

You will need: canvas or other plain fabric, 12-15 feathers, coloured sticky tape, coloured ribbons, paint, paintbrush, scissors, Velcro, glue

1 Paint the tips of the feathers and wrap sticky tape around the quills.

2 Cut a canvas strip long enough to fit around your head with a good overlap and twice as wide as the headband will be. Turn in and glue the edges, then fold the strip in half lengthways. Mark and paint a design on it, as shown.

3 Glue inside the folded strip, leaving small, evenly-spaced pockets for the feathers. Glue a feather into each pocket. Decorate the headdress with coloured streamers made from the ribbons.

BODY PAINT made from reddish-brown mud called ochre, mixed with animal fat, was used by woodland tribes to paint their bodies. The designs and colours showed that people belonged to a special group, or told of their brave deeds or dreams. Body paint had a practical use, too. The grease in the paint protected skin from the sun, wind, cold, and from stinging and biting insects.

TATTOOS were worn by people in the hot, sunny Southeast and in California. They wore few clothes, and used tattoos to decorate and express themselves. They used needles made from cactus pins or slivers of bone to prick patterns on their skin.

HAIRSTYLES AND HEADGEAR were an important way to look different but still fit in with tribal traditions. Some groups smeared their hair with mud and sculpted it into elaborate shapes. Many warriors shaved their heads so they looked fierce and threatening. They sometimes tied a stiff tuft of animal hair, known as a **roach**, in the centre.

TWEEZERS made from shells, wood or bone were used by men to pluck hairs from their face. They rarely grew beards or moustaches.

HATS were made by many tribes, using the materials that came to hand. California Indians wove sun hats from reeds and decorated them with poppies. On the Northwest coast, hats were woven from cedar bark. Woodland tribes wore headbands made from fur or hide, or turban-like sashes woven from plant fibres.

4 Stick strips of Velcro on to the ends of the headband so you can fasten it around your head.

THE MEN OF THE GREAT PLAINS wore only a piece of soft **buckskin** passed between their legs and tied with a belt. In winter, when the weather was fiercely cold, the men added fitted, thigh-length leggings and a knee-length tunic.

WOMEN'S LEGGINGS were held up with garters just below the knee. Dresses were often made of two deerskins sewn together, with the animals' legs making natural sleeves. In the chillier north, both men and women wore robes made from softened buffalo skin with the hair left on.

CHILDREN wore nothing in the summer, and child-sized versions of adult clothes in winter. Tunics, leggings and dresses were often decorated with quill-work or beaded embroidery.

△ *Ute warriors from the Great Basin and Plateau area wore magnificent breastplates of bone, porcupine quills and shells, and decorated themselves with body paint.*

MAKE A PLAINS OUTFIT

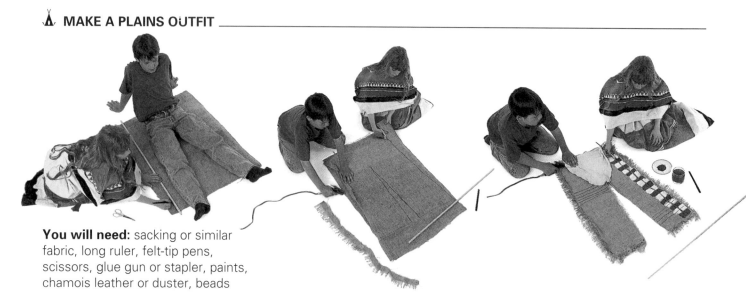

You will need: sacking or similar fabric, long ruler, felt-tip pens, scissors, glue gun or stapler, paints, chamois leather or duster, beads

1 To make the leggings, fold fabric in two and to make a rectangle. Measure and mark the trouser shape, as shown, using a long ruler or a straight piece of wood.

2 Cut through the two thicknesses of fabric. Glue or staple the seams (or sew them), adding strips of frayed fabric to the outer seams to look like fringes.

3 Paint designs directly on to the fabric, then glue or sew on a triangular duster, chamois leather or scrap of leftover fabric. This represents the buckskin loincloth.

△ *Clothes with a lot of beadwork were very heavy and were usually just worn for special occasions.*

ANIMAL SKINS used for clothes had to be softened. This skilled work was done by women, who rubbed the skin with a mixture of animal brains, liver, ashes and fat. They soaked it in water and pulled, stretched or even chewed the leather until it became soft buckskin. Clothes made from skins were dry-cleaned by rubbing in clay and chalk to absorb the dirt.

△ MAKE A PAIR OF MOCCASINS

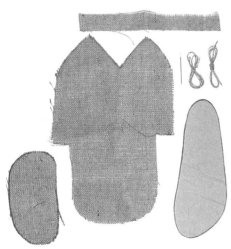

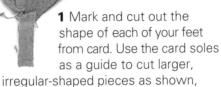
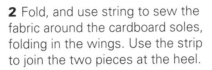

You will need: sacking or similar fabric, card, felt-tip pens, paints, thin string, a darning needle or bodkin

1 Mark and cut out the shape of each of your feet from card. Use the card soles as a guide to cut larger, irregular-shaped pieces as shown, then cut a toe piece and a thin strip.

2 Fold, and use string to sew the fabric around the cardboard soles, folding in the wings. Use the strip to join the two pieces at the heel.

3 Decorate the toe piece with paint or felt-tip pens.

4 Sew the toe-piece into position with string, as shown. Finish off your moccasins by stitching around the top edge, starting and finishing at the heel end. Then you can adjust the fit by tightening the string.

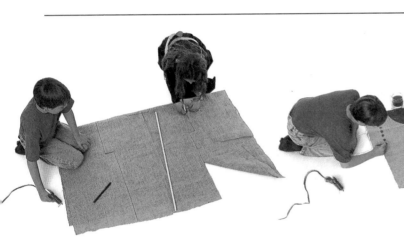

4 To make the tunic, fold a long piece of fabric into a rectangle, with the fold at the top. Measure and mark the shape, as shown, then cut it out through the two thicknesses of fabric. Cut a neck hole at the top. Glue, staple or sew the seams, as before.

5 Decorate your tunic with patterns, using paints or felt-tip pens. Add fringes, beads or feathers. You will find suggestions for designs and colours on page 37.

6 To make a woman's outfit, just make a long tunic (see page 13).

△ **MOCCASINS** were made in various styles for different uses. Some were low cut and others came almost to the knee. Work shoes had hard **rawhide** soles, while shoes worn at home were soft–soled. Moccasins helped protect people's feet from sharp stones, spiky plants, poisonous snakes and stinging insects.

▷ *Plains warriors carried spears and hide shields (see page 47) and wore elaborate headdresses (see pages 8-9).*

JEWELLERY AND ORNAMENTS were made from many different materials. Coastal tribes used shells, while Plains people used quills from birds' feathers and from porcupine spines coloured with vegetable and mineral dyes. Northern people had long been making copper necklaces, and once southern tribes had learned how to work silver, they made beautiful ornaments with bold tribal designs.

buffalo-horn helmet

ceremonial headdress

shell decoration

deerskin apron

GLASS AND CERAMIC BEADS brought by Europeans were very popular because cutting, drilling and polishing stones and shells to make beads was hard work. The most important beads were **wampum**, made in the Northeast from ground, polished shells. They were used for decoration, keeping records, sending messages, making medicine and as money.

decorated goat-hair blanket

woollen tunic

Nez Percé   Chumash   Tlingit   Navajo

THE NEZ PERCE lived in high Plateau country to the west of the Rocky Mountains. The weather was cold and no crops grew. People relied on gathering roots, berries and nuts, and on fishing and hunting. Nez Percé warriors wore ermine-tail and buffalo-horn helmets, and buckskin war shirts with porcupine-quill decoration and horsehair tassels.

THE TLINGIT, like other Northwestern tribes, were wealthy and led comfortable lives. The winter months were a time of festivals and fun. Party outfits included blankets woven from goat hair and plant fibre tunics. It rained often, so people wore waterproof hats, tightly woven from spruce roots. Their tunics were good rainwear, too, drying out more quickly than a soggy deerskin ever could.

THE CHUMASH lived near the Californian coast, in an area with plenty of food and a warm climate all year round. Women wore two deerskin apron-type garments around their waists. The back skirts were painted and decorated with shells, and the front aprons were fringed. Shoes were made of plant fibre. Women decorated their faces to show which family they came from.

MOHAWK WARRIORS wore fringed animal hide cloths around their waists, with leggings and moccasins. They had tattoos on their foreheads that declared their bravery in battle, and sometimes wore fan-shaped roaches made of animal hair. Their war clubs were carved from a wood so hard that it was known as ironwood.

feather decoration

bead necklace

hide cloth

leggings

fringed tunic

Plains

Mohawk

Seminole

THE NAVAJO herded sheep, introduced by Spanish settlers, and therefore had access to wool. They wove blankets, often boldly striped and decorated with patterns unique to them. Women wore simple tunic dresses made from two pieces of blanket, tied at the waist with a woven sash. Leggings, soft moccasins, and beads and buckles of silver completed their traditional outfits.

THE SEMINOLE were a group formed by Creek Indians and other people from different areas. They gradually came together in the Southeast after Europeans began to settle in North America. Their clothes were influenced by early European styles of dress, which they decorated with their own elaborate patchwork and beadwork.

Homes and shelters

The climate of the vast North American landmass varies between year-round snow and ice in the frozen North and scorching heat in the deserts of the Southwest. As the Indians settled into their homelands, they built houses and shelters that were suited to the climate and natural features of their particular region. They used whatever materials came to hand.

A LEAN-TO was a temporary shelter built by Subarctic peoples from sticks, leaves or bark.

A PLANK HOUSE was a winter home for the tribes of the Northwest. It was made from hand-split planks fixed on to a frame made from logs, and it was usually rectangular.

TEPEES were perfect homes for the **nomadic** buffalo-hunting Plains Indians. They were portable and were made of buffalo skins and wooden poles.

HOGANS were typical Navajo homes. They were hexagonal or octagonal in shape and were usually built facing east. They had a log and stick framework, plastered with mud and more wood or stones.

CLIFF DWELLINGS, or **pueblos**, were the homes of tribal groups in the Southwest, where humans have lived for at least 6,000 years and a settled farming culture thrived. Houses made of mud, rubble and blocks of stone built into rocky cliffs were called pueblos (meaning villages) by the Spanish, who arrived in the 16th century.

REED HOUSES were made from reed mats covering a wooden pole frame. Inside, there was often a central pit for a fire, with a smoke hole in the roof. These conical houses were often found in the Southwest and California.

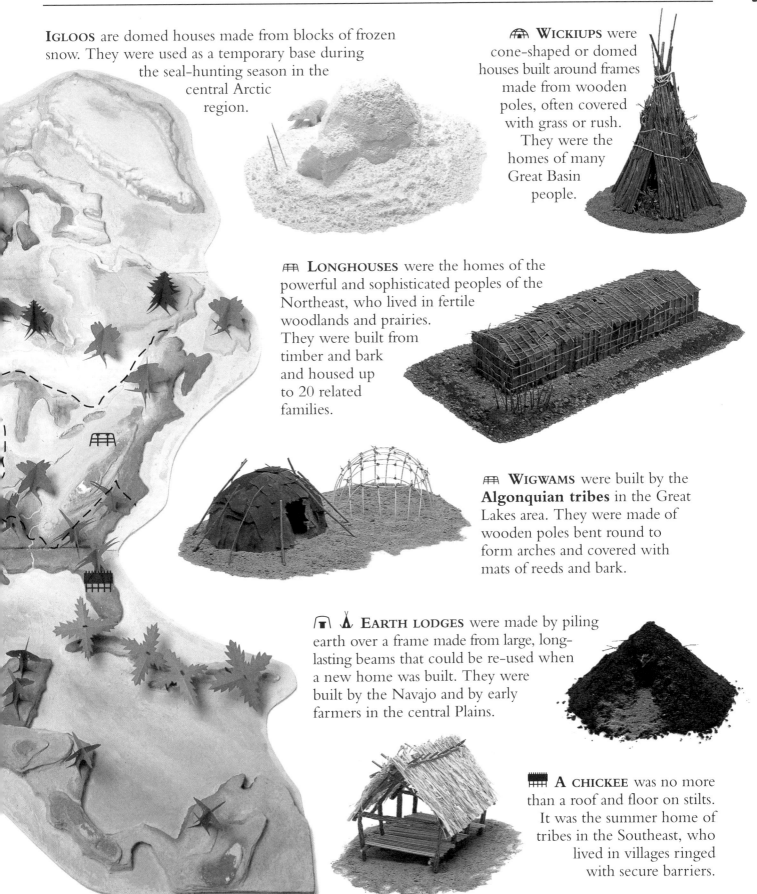

IGLOOS are domed houses made from blocks of frozen snow. They were used as a temporary base during the seal-hunting season in the central Arctic region.

WICKIUPS were cone-shaped or domed houses built around frames made from wooden poles, often covered with grass or rush. They were the homes of many Great Basin people.

LONGHOUSES were the homes of the powerful and sophisticated peoples of the Northeast, who lived in fertile woodlands and prairies. They were built from timber and bark and housed up to 20 related families.

WIGWAMS were built by the **Algonquian tribes** in the Great Lakes area. They were made of wooden poles bent round to form arches and covered with mats of reeds and bark.

EARTH LODGES were made by piling earth over a frame made from large, long-lasting beams that could be re-used when a new home was built. They were built by the Navajo and by early farmers in the central Plains.

A CHICKEE was no more than a roof and floor on stilts. It was the summer home of tribes in the Southeast, who lived in villages ringed with secure barriers.

▲ **NOMADIC TRIBES** such as the Cheyenne and the Sioux spent much of their lives on the move across the central Plains following the buffalo, which were their main source of food. They were resourceful and clever people. Their tepees were pleasant, practical homes that were cool in summer, warm in winter, strong enough to stand up to fierce winds and big enough for the family and all their belongings.

▲ **TEPEES** were made from up to fourteen buffalo hides sewn together with buffalo sinews (the tough, stringy fibres that attach muscle to bone). Needles were carved from buffalo bone.

△ *These Comanche women, photographed in 1890, have pegged out buffalo skins so they can scrape them clean.*

▲ **MAKE A TEPEE**

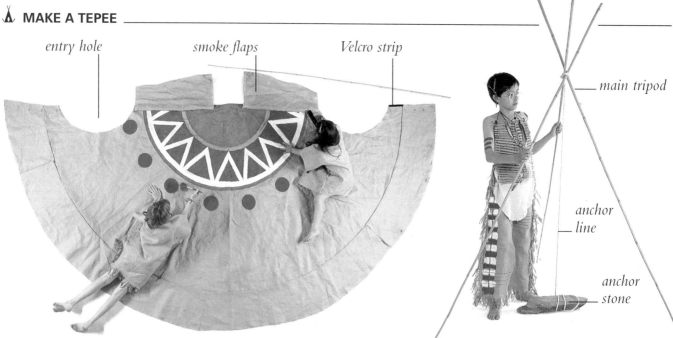

entry hole   *smoke flaps*   *Velcro strip*

main tripod

anchor line

anchor stone

You will need: hessian sacking 4.5 m wide and 2 m long, or old double sheets or blankets, drawing pin, string, scissors, garden canes, stapler or needle and thread, rope or washing line, paints, brushes, PVA glue, Velcro strip, short sticks

1 Cut a piece of string 50 cm shorter than your canes and use it like a compass to draw a semi-circle on the fabric. Pin one end to the centre of the long side of the fabric and tie a pencil to the other end. Swing the string round and mark an arc.

2 Cut small, matching semi-circular openings for the entry hole, as shown. Stick or staple strips of Velcro on either side of the hole for fastening the tepee over the canes.

3 Cut out the smoke flaps as shown and staple or sew them in place. Make a small triangular pocket in the top inside corner of each flap of the tepee cover (see step 7).

4 Paint the cover, adding PVA glue to the paint to make it waterproof. Use the scissors carefully to make holes for the tent pegs around the base.

5 Make the tepee frame using 3 canes. Tie them together, with the thicker ends at the top. Use a heavy object as a weight to secure the other end of the rope, as shown.

6 Wrap the cover carefully around the cane tripod and secure it by sticking the Velcro strips together. Plains Indians used tepee pins to hold the covers of their tepees in place. You can make your own pins using short sticks. Make holes in both layers of the tepee cover, where it overlaps, and thread the pins through the holes, as shown.

🔺 **THE MAIN TRIPOD** was tied together on the ground, then heaved upright using an anchor line made from rawhide. A family tepee was usually five metres high and just under five metres in diameter, which is about as big as a medium-sized room.

🔺 **SPECIAL PATTERNS AND COLOURS** were used by each tribe to paint their tepees. Families would adapt the tribal pattern for their own family. The number of dots, for instance, may have represented the number of lakes in the area. Women did the painting, using coloured soil mixed with buffalo blood and ground-up rock.

7 Slide more poles inside the tepee cover to make the frame stronger. Fix the base, using short sticks as tent pegs. Push one end of a cane into each smoke flap pocket to prop the flaps open. Finally, cut out and pin on a door flap to fit the entry hole.

🔺 **ON RAINY DAYS** a tepee's smoke flaps were closed and fastened with tepee pins.

🔺 **MEN AND WOMEN** had their own particular responsibilities. Women made and put up tepees, while men kept look-out. Two women would take about an hour to erect one tepee.

🔺 **BLACK ELK**, a Sioux Indian, said: *"Our tepees were round like the nests of birds and these were always set in a circle, the nation's hoop, a nest of many nests where the Great Spirit meant for us to hatch our children."*

smoke flaps

entry hole

tepee cover

tepee pin

INSIDE THE TEPEE people slept on piles of warm, furry buffalo skins. When they gathered around the fire, they had comfortable wooden backrests to lean against. They stored their food, medicines and clothes in soft hide bags, embroidered with elaborate tribal patterns. A typical Plains Indian family had many horses but owned few possessions apart from the things they really needed.

TO PROVIDE EXTRA INSULATION against wind and cold, tepees often had decorative inner linings which trapped a pocket of warm air between the two layers to keep the inside temperature comfortable.

THE FIREPLACE, sometimes raised on a slab of stone, was the main source of light and heat. The supply of firewood was never allowed to run low.

WARNING: DO NOT LIGHT FIRES IN A MODEL TEPEE

△ *This soft buffalo-hide tepee liner belonged to a Cheyenne family. Tepee liners were not hung all around the tent, but were attached at the points where the wind whistled through, positioned at waist height to protect people from draughts as they sat around the fire or lay in bed.*

VENTILATION was provided during warm summer weather by rolling up the sides of the tepee to let the air in.

BACKRESTS were used only by the men of the family. The firm but springy supports were made of wooden slats lashed together with leather strips.

EVERYTHING HAD ITS OWN PLACE inside the tepee. The beds were placed on either side of the fire. The fire itself was set in front of the central anchor rope. Backrests were positioned against the sides and a supply of firewood was kept just inside the door.

A **STRICT CODE** of manners meant that a Plains Indian could not just walk into a friend's tepee. There were rules to follow:

- If the door flap was open, visitors could enter, but if it was closed, they had to wait to be invited in.

- Male visitors went in first, moved around to the right and waited for the host to offer them a seat on his left. Women could then enter, and they turned left.

- Men were allowed to sit cross-legged, but women were not.

- Guests invited to a meal had to bring their own spoons and bowls and eat everything their host provided for them.

- No one was allowed to walk between the fire and another person.

- When the host lit his pipe, it was the signal for the guests to go home.

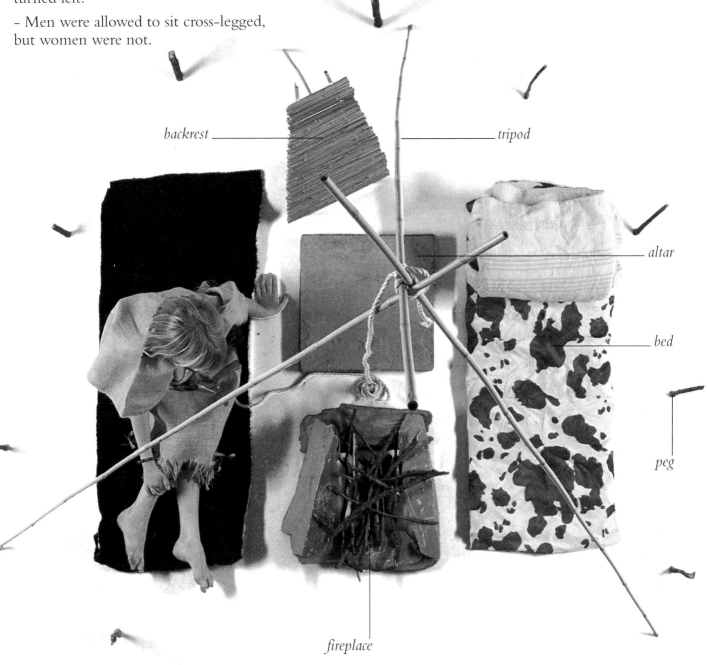

backrest

tripod

altar

bed

peg

fireplace

🏠 **THE IROQUOIS PEOPLES** settled on the east coast, in what is now southern Ontario, Quebec and New York State. They built villages and farmed the rich land, where there was plenty of firewood and clear, clean water from the many rivers and springs. They lived in close-knit groups and their villages were collections of enormous longhouses, surrounded by high, protective fences, or palisades, made of sharp stakes. But these villages were not really permanent. Early farming methods exhausted the land after about 20 years. When the crops would no longer grow, it was time to move on and rebuild in a more fertile place.

🏠 **LONGHOUSES** were as high as they were wide, and in some cases as long as a football field. One house was home to a group of related fireside families. Each family had its own space along the side of the house, and shared a fire in the central corridor with the family opposite. There was a door at each end, but no windows. Smoke from the fires eventually found its way out through a series of ventilation holes in the roof, but the inside was very smoky. As a result, many longhouse people suffered from eye trouble and became blind as they grew old.

🏠 **MAKE A LONGHOUSE**

fire corridor   *sleeping platform*

You will need: base board, three lengths of wood (two thick, one thin), thick and thin twigs, DIY filler, soil, glue, scraps of fabric or leather

1 Make sleeping platforms and a fire corridor by laying the strips of wood parallel to one another, with the thinner one in the middle.

2 Cut some thick twigs to the same length and glue them upright, spacing them equally on the board.

3 Mix the filler with water to make a paste and spread it over the board and platforms. Sprinkle the soil over the wet filler so that it sticks.

4 Cut beams from thick twigs to make the roof frame. Stick pairs of beams together to make the roof shape, as shown, and glue them in place on the top of each pair of upright posts. Make a framework of thin twigs over the walls and roof to form a support for the bark tiles.

5 Cut the fabric or leather roughly into squares. Glue them on to the framework in overlapping layers, starting at the bottom so that there are no cracks for rain to seep in. Glue a lattice of thin twigs over the top of the tiles.

6 Make a palisade from sharpened twigs. Stick them to the base board, sharp ends up and pointing outwards, to form a defensive wall around the longhouse.

☊ MAKE AN EARTH LODGE

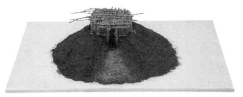

You will need: base board, thick and thin twigs, moss or leaves, soil, glue

1 Cut all the thick twigs to the same length and glue upright to the base board in a square. Leave a small gap in one side for the doorway.

2 Lay a lattice of thinner twigs over the top and cover with moss or leaves. Pile soil over the frame to form a cone, leaving a clear pathway to the door.

When Navajo people built their earth lodges, they hammered the frame posts into the ground, with each post touching the next, to form a solid wall of timber. They made the doorway the width of a man's shoulders, so the house was easier to defend against intruders.

bark tiles

upright beam

roof beam

framework of thin poles to hold tiles down in high winds

palisade to defend the longhouse village

⌂ LONGHOUSE BUILDING MATERIALS were mainly wood and bark. The outer frame was made from thick posts, firmly driven into the ground. Horizontal beams were lashed in place with strong bark fibres. The roof frame was made from thinner poles and the whole house was covered with overlapping tiles of ash or elm tree bark.

⌂ THE PALISADE was made from stakes which were spaced so that the distance between them was just the width of a man's shoulders. Villagers could come and go freely but attacking warriors had to thread their way through with their arms pinned to their sides, making it very difficult to use their weapons.

Tribes and families

A Plains Indian village was made up of groups of families, or **clans**, who often traced their relationship to one another through the women of the family. There could be 50 or more loosely-related clans in a tribe, which occupied an area of land, or territory. The most important ties were not to the tribe but to the immediate family. The mother, father and children who shared a home and a fireside are sometimes called a fireside family.

ʌ **TEPEES** were set up with their entrances facing east, to keep out the winds that usually blew across the open Plains from the west. They were grouped according to family relationships.

▽ *Tepee villages were built on carefully chosen sites, close to a river or stream and sheltered from the wind wherever possible.*

strips of buffalo meat curing in the sun

door flap

tepee frame

buffalo chips for making a fire

ʌ **LIFE ON THE MOVE** meant a tough routine for the Indians who hunted buffalo in the vast, dry, windy central Plains. They spent their lives packing up camp, dragging or carrying their possessions, and setting up camp all over again. But their efforts were repaid by a constant supply of food, clothing and shelter from the buffalo.

ʌ **VILLAGES** were run by chiefs and elders, who were chosen by their fellow villagers to offer wise advice, rather than to tell people what to do. Most people could do as they chose, as long as they worked for the general good. Men usually hunted and fought, while most women cleaned skins, made clothes, put up tepees and cooked.

coloured streamers for
sending messages to
the spirit world

wooden tepee
pins holding
the cover in place

smoke
flap

cooking pot made
from a buffalo
stomach

prepared buffalo
skins pegged out
to dry

▲ **Marriage** was not always a relationship between one man and one woman. The women had so much work to do that they would often welcome the idea of their husband finding another wife to share their chores. There were usually more women than men in a clan anyway, because war and hunting caused so many casualties among the men.

tepee cover with painted
symbols telling of the
spirits, or of battles
fought by the owner

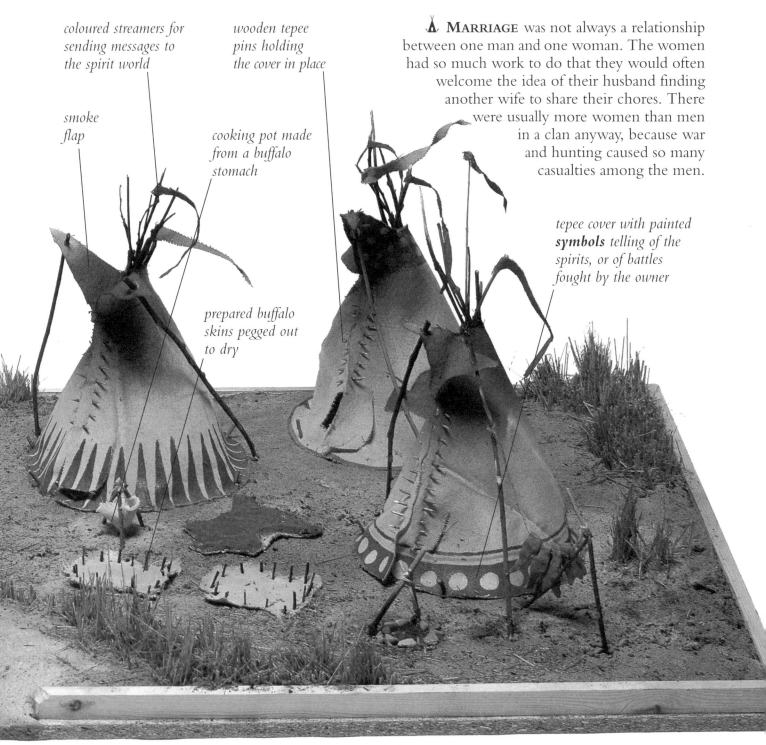

▲ **Children** had a carefree time, playing with toy bows, tepees or dolls and learning about the life they would lead as adults. They were always expected to behave in a way that would bring no danger or dishonour to their clan or group. They learned very quickly not to cry or make a fuss if an enemy was near.

▲ **Warriors** were usually men, but some women also fought and hunted. Men thought so highly of one Crow warrior woman, known as Woman Chief, that they were scared to ask to marry her. She 'married' four women so she would have someone to look after her tepee. If a man preferred to work in the home, no one minded.

The Northwestern tribes lived in fishing villages on the strip of land between the mountains and the sea. There were nearly 50 tribes there, leading well-ordered, comfortable lives. They had a flourishing trade in dried and smoked fish and finely woven basketware, making them the richest of the North American Indians. These were the tribes most concerned with showing their social rank and wealth.

Wooden houses were strung out in villages along the coastline, with all the houses facing the sea. Each plank house was home to several related families and the carved **totem poles** outside let everyone know the histories of the families living there.

△ *Totem poles were made by skilled carvers of the Northwestern tribes. Their main function was to record family crests and glorious moments of family history.*

MAKE A PLANK HOUSE AND TOTEM POLE

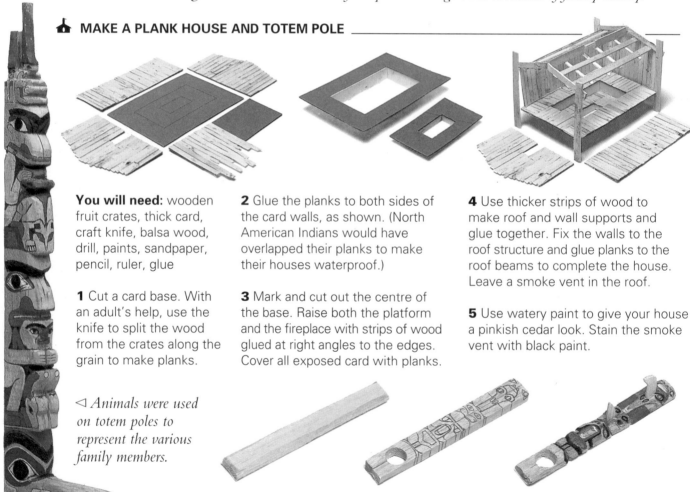

◁ *Animals were used on totem poles to represent the various family members.*

You will need: wooden fruit crates, thick card, craft knife, balsa wood, drill, paints, sandpaper, pencil, ruler, glue

1 Cut a card base. With an adult's help, use the knife to split the wood from the crates along the grain to make planks.

2 Glue the planks to both sides of the card walls, as shown. (North American Indians would have overlapped their planks to make their houses waterproof.)

3 Mark and cut out the centre of the base. Raise both the platform and the fireplace with strips of wood glued at right angles to the edges. Cover all exposed card with planks.

4 Use thicker strips of wood to make roof and wall supports and glue together. Fix the walls to the roof structure and glue planks to the roof beams to complete the house. Leave a smoke vent in the roof.

5 Use watery paint to give your house a pinkish cedar look. Stain the smoke vent with black paint.

6 To make a totem pole, cut a piece of balsa wood a little taller than your house. Sand it to make a flattened cylinder shape and drill a hole for the doorway as shown.

7 Draw out your design and carve the lines with a craft knife. Glue on extra pieces for wings or beaks. Sand and paint your totem pole and glue to the front of your plank house.

🏠 **CEDAR WOOD** was easy to carve and hollow out to make **canoes**. The stringy bark gave fibre for making baskets, ropes and clothes. Northwestern Indians believed that these trees must be on Earth to help humans.

🏠 **RAINFALL** is high on the Northwest Coast, and the winters are cold. Plank houses were made of overlapping cedar planks so that the rain ran off. They had no windows, just a hole in the roof which could be closed with a wooden shutter.

🏠 **A PLANK HOUSE** was home for up to six families, related through the women. Their shared living space was about 15 metres square, with a sunken area in the centre where children played and women cooked. A sleeping platform around the edge was divided into family spaces, with the most important family at the back and the lowliest near the draughty door.

🏠 **A POTLATCH** was organized by a Northwestern family to celebrate a special event, such as a wedding. They put on a lavish feast and gave their guests many valuable gifts, including canoes, slaves, furs and blankets. The more gifts a host gave, the higher his status rose. The guests who received the most then had to throw an even greater potlatch. Among Northwestern tribes, being wealthy meant being more important. People used potlatches to show how rich they were, and to settle old rivalries. Through potlatching, they could force their rivals to give away everything they owned.

smoke hole
in roof

totem
pole

A healthy diet

North American Indians lived on a healthy diet of meat or fish, grain, nuts, fruit and other food plants. Most tribes had learned how to preserve meat and fish by drying or smoking, so there were always emergency supplies if the hunters came back empty-handed.

⚑ **BUFFALO HUNTING** was exhausting and lonely, but was seen as very noble. A hunter would spend most of his time tracking and killing buffalo, a dangerous task done on foot before Europeans brought horses to North America. To succeed, men had to be in tune with nature and the animals they hunted. They sometimes dressed in a buffalo skin and moved amongst the herd. They only took what they needed and never killed just for the sake of it.

△ *Ishi, a Californian Yahi Indian, photographed in 1914 making a leister, a harpoon for spearing salmon.*

▦ **ANIMALS** that provided food for the Indians were treated with great respect. A ceremony was held for the first salmon caught in each run. It was taken to a special altar, welcomed with speeches and cooked with great care. They believed that there were people living in the sea who took the form of salmon each year. If they were not treated properly, they might never come again.

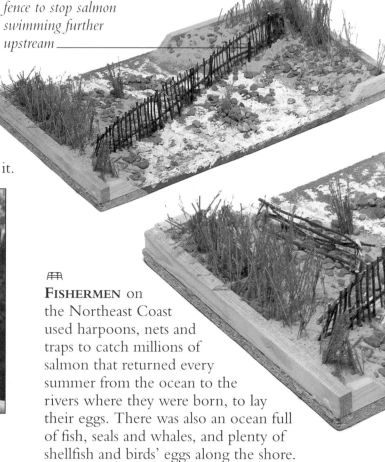

fence to stop salmon swimming further upstream

▦ **FISHERMEN** on the Northeast Coast used harpoons, nets and traps to catch millions of salmon that returned every summer from the ocean to the rivers where they were born, to lay their eggs. There was also an ocean full of fish, seals and whales, and plenty of shellfish and birds' eggs along the shore.

▦ MAKE A SALMON TRAP

You will need: base board, paint, dried grasses, stones, twigs, sand, craft knife, glue

1 Paint a river on the board. Make sand banks either side, dotted with dried grasses and pebbles.

2 Build a fence across the river. Glue the crosspieces to the supports.

(Northeastern Indians would have pushed the supports into the ground and tied the sticks with sinew.)

The fence stops the salmon from swimming further upstream. As they will never turn back, they struggle and leap against the fence, while more fish keep coming up behind them.

3 Make trapping gates in the same way as the fence. Bend twigs to make the rounded ends of the tunnel-shaped pens. Add to the fence.

Men with spears would have waded into the killing pen. Any fish not harpooned at once were swept back by the current into the trapping gates and collected in the pens.

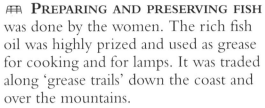 **PREPARING AND PRESERVING FISH** was done by the women. The rich fish oil was highly prized and used as grease for cooking and for lamps. It was traded along 'grease trails' down the coast and over the mountains.

▷ *Fish traps were made to much the same design all over the Northeast and Subarctic.*

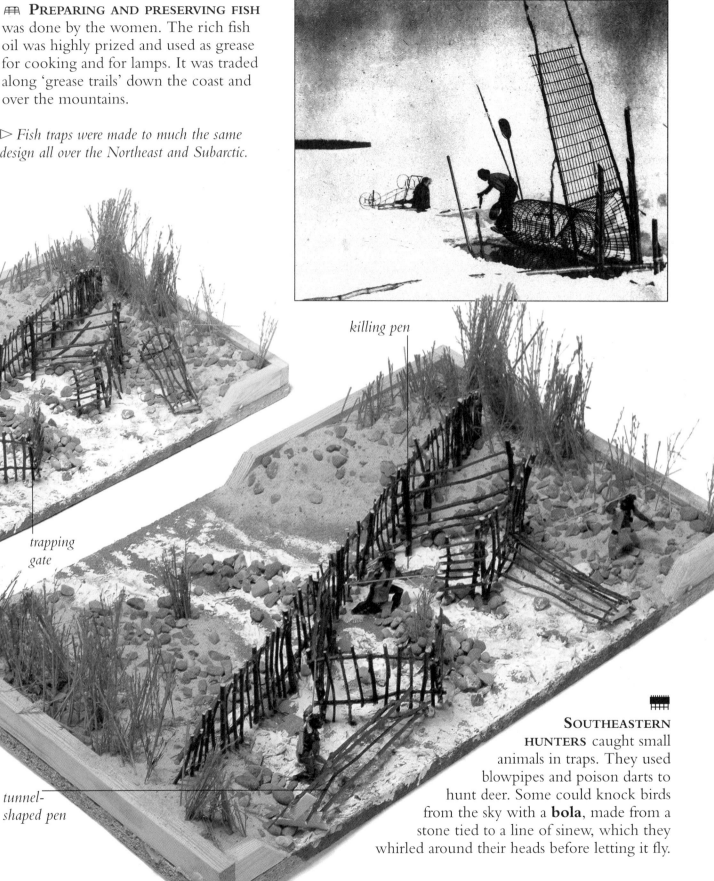

killing pen

trapping gate

tunnel-shaped pen

SOUTHEASTERN HUNTERS caught small animals in traps. They used blowpipes and poison darts to hunt deer. Some could knock birds from the sky with a **bola**, made from a stone tied to a line of sinew, which they whirled around their heads before letting it fly.

THE THREE MAIN FOOD CROPS grown by North American Indians were corn, beans and squash. Farmers used tools made of wood or bone. Men turned the earth and women planted the seeds.

RUBBING STICKS TOGETHER to make fire took so long that fires were often left smouldering all day. Many huntsmen travelled with a slow-burning rope so they had a quick way of lighting fire when they set up camp.

RICH SOIL meant good crops, and Indian farmers believed in putting something back into the earth in thanks for what came out. The Iroquois, for example, put herrings into the ground before they sowed corn. The goodness in the fish made the soil much richer.

A TYPICAL IROQUOIS MEAL included roasted meat, raw salad, baked pumpkin and corn dumplings. Families ate just once a day, before noon. Meals were eaten in silence, standing or squatting on the ground. Men ate first, and women and children ate what was left. Children were told that if they did not thank their parents for each meal, they would be punished with a stomach ache.

MAKE HOPI BOILED CORN CAKES

You will need: 3 cornhusks (the outer part of a corn cob), 1 cup of cornmeal flour, half a cup of honey, blue food colouring (optional)

1 Boil the cornhusks until they are soft. Drain them and let them cool.

2 Put the cornmeal in a bowl and gradually add about a cup of boiling water, until the mixture is like thick custard.

3 Stir the honey into the mixture and add blue colouring if you like. (The Hopi grew blue corn, so their corn cakes had a bluish tinge.)

4 Open out the cornhusks and drop 2 spoonfuls of corn mixture into the centre of about 20 of them. Fold them neatly into parcels. Shred the remaining husks and use the shreds to tie up the parcels.

5 Ask an adult to help you bring water to the boil in a large saucepan, then carefully put in the corn cake parcels.

6 Boil the parcels for 15 to 20 minutes, then take them out with a slotted spoon. Let them cool before you unwrap and eat them.

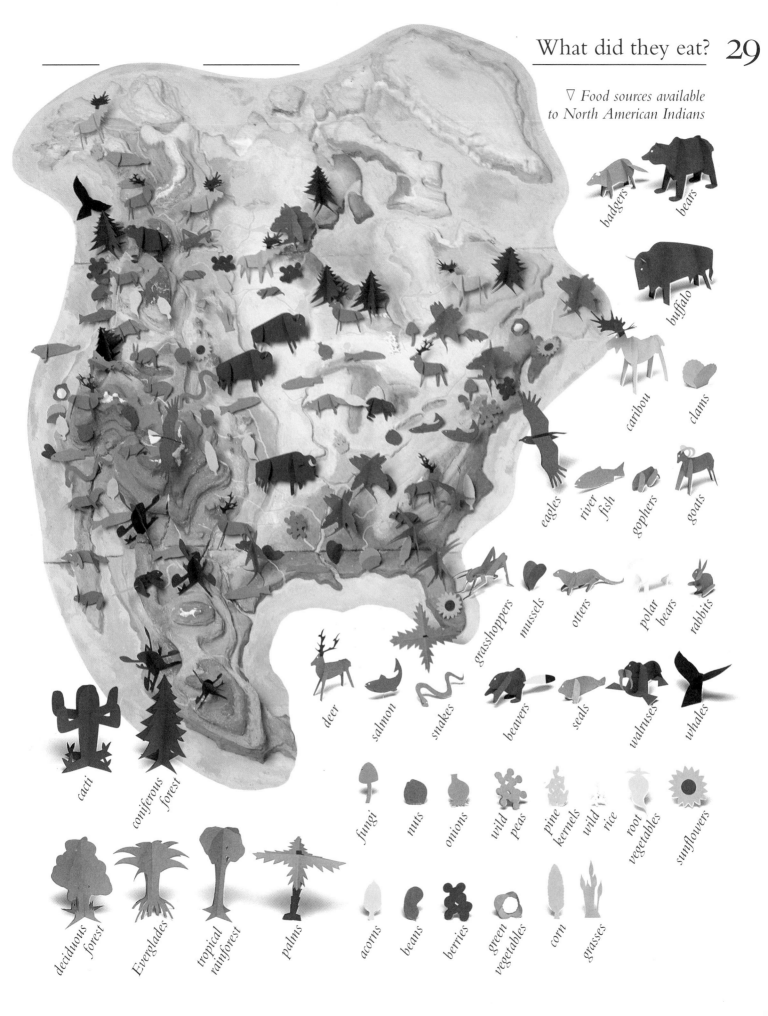

▽ *Food sources available to North American Indians*

badgers

bears

buffalo

caribou

clams

eagles

river fish

gophers

goats

grasshoppers

mussels

otters

polar bears

rabbits

deer

salmon

snakes

beavers

seals

walruses

whales

cacti

coniferous forest

fungi

nuts

onions

wild peas

pine kernels

wild rice

root vegetables

sunflowers

deciduous forest

Everglades

tropical rainforest

palms

acorns

beans

berries

green vegetables

corn

grasses

Sport and leisure

Most North American Indian games and sports were a preparation for life. Men played vigorous team games to help prepare themselves for war, and hunting games to sharpen their skills. Women played games of skill and chance, using their everyday work tools. Both men and women also liked to sing as they placed bets in games of chance. They made music to summon up good spirits and good luck.

△ **Lacrosse** players were allowed two sticks each.

MAKE A LACROSSE STICK

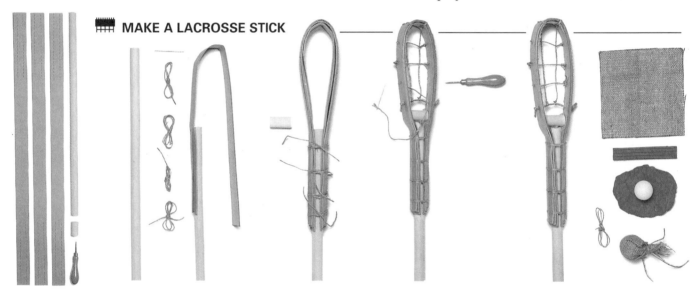

You will need: broomstick or thick dowelling, strong card, string, glue, bradawl, saw, ping-pong ball, square of sacking or other fabric, Plasticine

1 Ask an adult to help you cut three strips of card, and to cut the handle and spacer bar from the dowelling. Bend one strip of card around and carefully glue both ends to the handle, as shown.

2 Repeat with the other two strips, until you have a loop made of three thicknesses of card. (The North American Indians would have used strips of hide.) Use string to tie the loop securely in place.

3 Push in the spacer bar at the top of the handle and glue it into place. Use the bradawl very carefully to make holes around the loop.

4 Thread string through the holes to make the net, as shown. Knot the ends on the outside of the loop to hold the net in place.

5 To make the ball, flatten the Plasticine and wrap it tightly around the ping-pong ball. Cover with the square of fabric and tie tightly with string. (North American Indians used a ball of animal hair, covered with hide.)

GAMBLING GAMES were very popular with women, who sometimes played for very high stakes, such as offering to become a slave to the other player. Games were more often played for furs, skins, household goods, moccasins or horses.

POST BALL was played just for fun by both men and women. They set up a post in the village square and the object was to hit the post with a ball. The women could use their hands, but the men could use only sticks.

throwing the ball

picking up the ball

tackling, or checking, to get the ball from another player's net

players jumping to catch the ball in their nets

WAR'S LITTLE BROTHER was a fearsome game. It is still played today in a much more controlled form, known as lacrosse. Then, up to 100 people could play in each team. The pitch had no boundaries and the huge goals could be up to 100 metres wide. Players had to hurl a ball through the goal posts, and the game was won by the first team to score 12 goals. It often lasted for hours. There were no rules of fair play so it was a bloody battle, with many casualties. Players were pushed, beaten with sticks, often badly injured and sometimes killed.

THE AWL GAME was a game of chance. The board was marked out on a blanket. Each player pinned an awl (a tool used for piercing hides) through the blanket in various places. They moved their awls around the blanket in opposite directions.

FOUR STICKS were thrown at the central stone to decide each move. One carried a special mark. If a stick fell flat side up, it counted for one move. If the mark came up, it meant an extra throw. The board showed dry and flowing rivers. Dry rivers were safe, but players who fell in flowing rivers or on an opponent's position had to go back to the start.

MUSIC AND DANCE were central to the Indian way of life and everybody took part. People believed that music was the language of the spirits. Mothers sang lullabies to their children, warriors sang to call upon their guardian spirits, hunters made magic animal music and farmers chanted to their crops. There were ceremonial songs for births, marriages, deaths and funerals.

▷*These Ute musicians and dancers in the Great Basin and Plateau area were photographed in 1900.*

RATTLES, RASPS AND DRUMS were used to create rhythms. Turtle shells, coconuts, gourds, and buffalo horns were natural percussion instruments. People made other instruments from wood or hide. A gourd rattle's sound could be improved by putting pebbles or beans inside, along with a few of the original seeds to help the rattle keep its spiritual powers.

rattle

MAKE A RATTLE

You will need: a tennis ball, dried beans or peas, dowelling, glue, paper, paint, thick string, coloured raffia

1 Make holes on either side of the tennis ball, put the beans inside and push the dowelling through, as shown.

2 Tear the paper into pieces and glue them on to the ball in a smooth papier-mâché layer. When the glue has dried, wind the string round the handle and ball, sticking it in place as you go. Leave a gap around the middle of the ball.

3 Decorate the rattle by painting a pattern on the plain part of the ball and adding a raffia tail.

MAKE A DRUM AND DRUM STICK

You will need: a flower pot, canvas or other fabric, glue, thin string, paints, felt-tip pens, two thin sticks or dowels, Plasticine, string, raffia

1 Cut a curved piece of fabric to fit around the pot and glue it on. Cut another piece to fit over the top and reach well down the sides.

2 Plait the string to make a decorative cord. Stretch the fabric over the pot and use the cord to tie it firmly in place just below the rim.

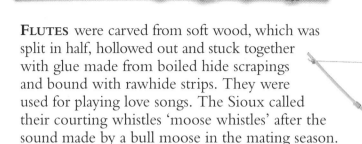

flute

FLUTES were carved from soft wood, which was split in half, hollowed out and stuck together with glue made from boiled hide scrapings and bound with rawhide strips. They were used for playing love songs. The Sioux called their courting whistles 'moose whistles' after the sound made by a bull moose in the mating season.

WHISTLES made music for war. Warriors rode into battle blowing whistles made from eagle bones. Eagles were a symbol for courage.

INDIAN SONGS were not complicated. They had a simple tune, usually going down the scale from high notes to low notes. Songs and chants were owned by the person who had made them up. If the singer had enjoyed a long and happy life, the right to sing the song would be passed on to their family or even sold for a high price.

△ *A group of Californian Indians called the Maidu made a simple musical bow. The player plucked the single string, changing the pitch of the note by opening and closing his or her mouth.*

drum

THROBBING DRUMS were like a heartbeat to the Indians. Their sound was sacred, particularly that of the water drum, which could only be played by those thought worthy, such as distinguished warriors.

4 Stick blobs of Plasticine to the end of each stick and cover with fabric tied with string. Decorate with raffia and paint patterns on the sticks.

3 Finish off with a loop of cord for a handle. Paint the drum to make the cloth look like buffalo hide. Wetting the fabric with paint will shrink it and improve the tone of the drum. Use felt-tips to decorate the drum.

drumstick

Arts and crafts

In some **cultures**, art is a way of showing things as they are. For North American Indians, art was more than that. It was a way of expressing their hopes and fears, of thanking the Creator for nature's gifts and pleasing the Creator with prayers and promises. Because of this, their art was symbolic. They used symbols and signs to represent their ideas, beliefs, dreams and visions. When Indian artists drew an animal or person, they were trying to show the inner spirit, not the outer appearance.

△ *This Californian Karok basket-maker was photographed in 1896. She is using the twining method, rather than the coiling technique shown below.*

BASKETS were made by almost all Indians, but the tribes of the Southwest were particularly skilful basket-weavers. They used them for everything from cradles, storage chests and sieves to bird and fish traps, backpacks, hats and mats. Some were so tightly woven that they were waterproof, and could even be used for brewing beer. Materials included rushes, bear grass, yucca leaves and willow, steamed until the fibres were supple. Symbolic designs were woven into the baskets using fibres that had been coloured with mineral or vegetable dyes.

🞄 MAKE A BASKET

You will need: thick twine or plaited string, raffia, darning needle

1 Thread the needle with a length of raffia. You will need several lengths to make the basket.

2 Begin the basket base by coiling the twine or plaited string tightly. Work outwards from the centre. Sew each layer to the last one, as you build up the coils.

3 Once you have a flat base, about five coils deep, begin to build up the sides of the basket. Finish off by sewing down the end of the twine securely.

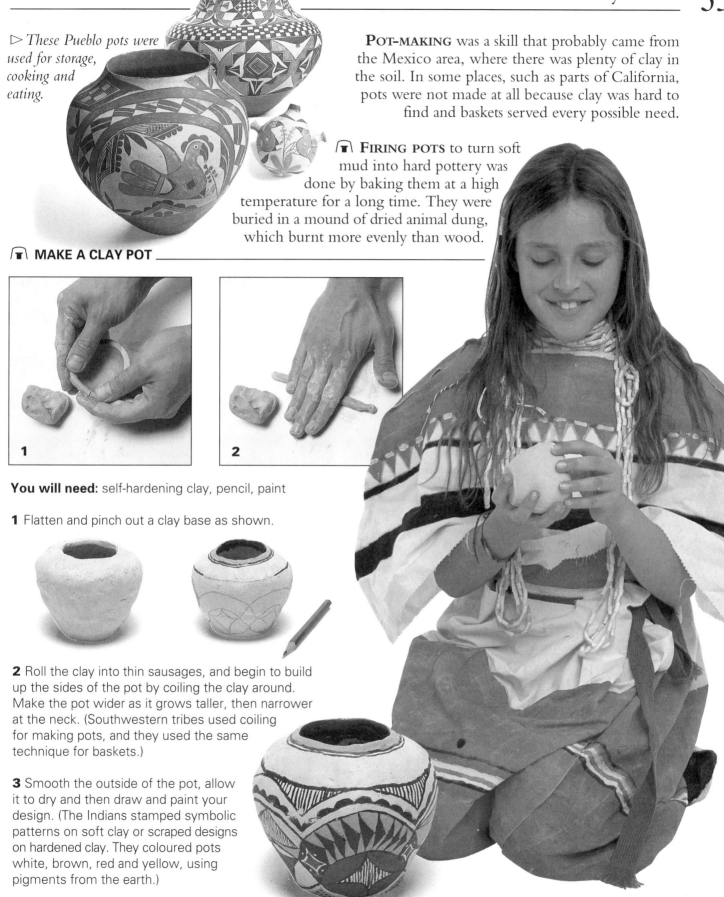

▷ *These Pueblo pots were used for storage, cooking and eating.*

POT-MAKING was a skill that probably came from the Mexico area, where there was plenty of clay in the soil. In some places, such as parts of California, pots were not made at all because clay was hard to find and baskets served every possible need.

⊤ **FIRING POTS** to turn soft mud into hard pottery was done by baking them at a high temperature for a long time. They were buried in a mound of dried animal dung, which burnt more evenly than wood.

⊤ **MAKE A CLAY POT**

1

2

You will need: self-hardening clay, pencil, paint

1 Flatten and pinch out a clay base as shown.

2 Roll the clay into thin sausages, and begin to build up the sides of the pot by coiling the clay around. Make the pot wider as it grows taller, then narrower at the neck. (Southwestern tribes used coiling for making pots, and they used the same technique for baskets.)

3 Smooth the outside of the pot, allow it to dry and then draw and paint your design. (The Indians stamped symbolic patterns on soft clay or scraped designs on hardened clay. They coloured pots white, brown, red and yellow, using pigments from the earth.)

TEXTILES have been woven in North America for 2,000 years. Very early cloth was not woven on a loom. The threads were made by spinning fibres from plants and animal hair, and woven together by knitting, crochet, plaiting and twining in many different ways.

THE DYES AND PAINTS used by North American Indians were made from minerals and plants. Minerals are found in different coloured soils. Iron in soil gives a range of reds, yellows and browns. Soil with copper makes greens and blues. Graphite makes black, and clay, limestone and gypsum make white. Colour can also be taken from plants, berries, roots, moss and bark. Boiling or soaking the materials with the plant changes their colour.

DESIGNS AND COLOURS had different meanings for different tribes, and even for individual artists. Sometimes the artist had a dream that showed him or her what designs and colours to use. Although it is difficult to say exactly what particular colours meant, there were some general uses:

Blue	Female, moon, sky, water, thunder, sadness
Black	Male, cold, night, disease, death, underworld
Green	Earth, summer, rain, plants
Red	War, day, blood, wounds, sunset
White	Winter, death, snow
Yellow	Day, dawn, sunshine

DYEING FABRIC

 turmeric makes bright yellow

 onion skin makes yellowy brown

 blueberries make mauve

 *avocado pear skin makes pink*

You will need: white cotton fabric, piece of muslin, string, ingredients for colour (see left), cutting board, knife, old pan, wooden spoon, jug or bowl, strainer

1 Choose which colours you want to dye your fabric and prepare the ingredients. Place them on the muslin and tie into a bundle with the string.

2 Put the fabric and muslin bundle into the pan. Cover with water and ask an adult to help you boil it.

3 When the fabric has changed colour, let the dye cool and strain it into the jug so you can re-use it.

4 Let the fabric dry out naturally. Remember that the colour will fade and run if you wash it.

▷ *Chilkat dance blankets were worn by Northwestern Tlingit people for ceremonies (see p38). They were decorated with stylized symbols representing animals.*

tail and wing shape of a bird

human face to symbolize a bird's body

frog's head

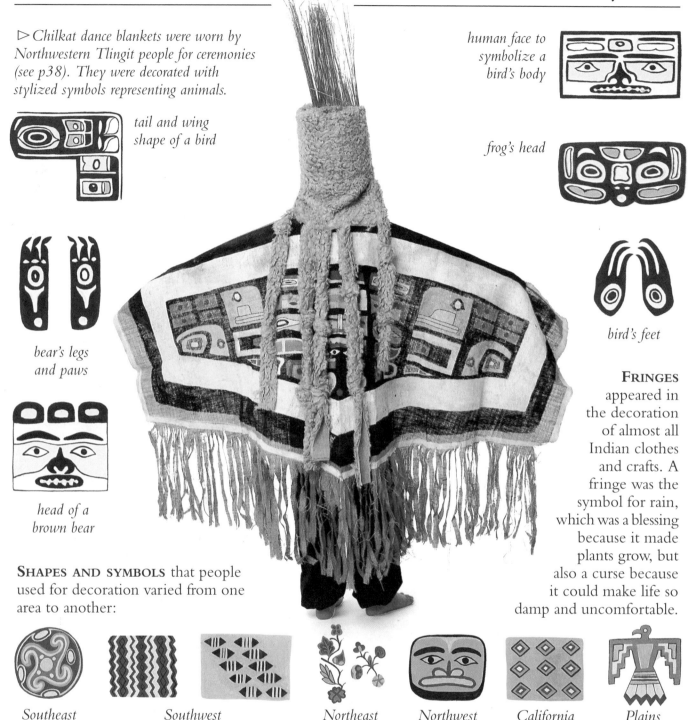

bear's legs and paws

head of a brown bear

bird's feet

FRINGES appeared in the decoration of almost all Indian clothes and crafts. A fringe was the symbol for rain, which was a blessing because it made plants grow, but also a curse because it could make life so damp and uncomfortable.

SHAPES AND SYMBOLS that people used for decoration varied from one area to another:

Southeast *Southwest* *Northeast* *Northwest* *California* *Plains*

CURVES AND SPIRALS were popular in the Southeast, where bird and animal shapes were often used.

PARALLEL LINES as well as curves feature in the culture of the Southwest.

THE FLOWING LINES of plant and flower shapes were used by woodlanders in the Northeast.

BIRDS, FISH AND HUMAN FACES featured in the Northwest, often within a curved shape.

TRIANGLES, RECTANGLES AND SQUARES were used in many designs in California, especially for basket work.

GEOMETRIC SHAPES, particularly triangles, were popular with the Plains Indians.

SIMPLE LOOMS with a fixed warp (the vertical threads) were used in ancient times in the Southwest. Later, people in this area developed the true loom. It had a pair of horizontal sticks separating every other thread of the warp. The weft (the horizontal threads) could then be pushed through from side to side with a shuttle, making weaving much easier and quicker.

THE CHILKAT, a branch of the Tlingit tribe, were expert weavers. In their homelands, there were no flocks of fleecy sheep and no wild cotton, just mountains and cedar trees. People wove with the hair of wild mountain goats and shredded fibres from the soft inner bark of cedar trees. A blanket took up to a year to make.

MAKE A SIMPLE WEAVING FRAME

You will need: strips of wood, glue, pencil, ruler, small nails, hammer, large bodkin, coloured wool

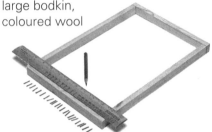

1 Glue and nail the strips of wood to make the frame, as shown. Measure and mark positions for the nails at each end. Make them close together and evenly spaced. Ask an adult to help you hammer the nails in.

2 To make the warp, tie a piece of wool to the first nail at one corner. Stretch it back and forth across the frame, looping it around the nails. Tie it off on the last nail.

3 To make the weft, thread a length of coloured wool through the bodkin and wind it around as shown.

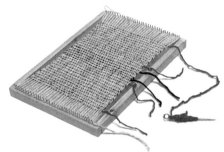

4 Tie the loose end of the wool to the outside warp thread, then weave the bodkin in and out from side to side.

5 When you want to change colour, tie the new wool to the outside warp thread as before.

6 When you have filled the frame, tie the end of your last weft row to the outside warp thread and carefully lift your finished piece off the nails. Tie together the two loops at each corner.

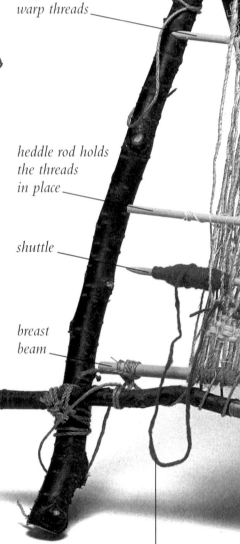

shed rod makes the shed, or space, between the warp threads

heddle rod holds the threads in place

shuttle

breast beam

weft or horizontal thread

▣ **THE SPIDERWOMAN** was a spirit who wove webs to catch rain clouds, and had taught the first people on Earth how to weave. Weavers in the Southwest used the symbol of the spiderwoman in their designs as a way of thanking her for the knowledge which she had passed on to them.

warp beam

batten

cloth being woven

shuttle with the weft thread wound around it

△ *Present-day Navajo Indians weave using the traditional methods and designs.*

warp or vertical thread

weaving frame

shed, or space where the shuttle passes through

▣ **THE NAVAJO** are perhaps best known for their beautifully woven blankets with strong, geometric designs. The ideas for the designs, it is said, came directly from the weaver's inner spirit. The women who made them boasted that their blankets were so closely woven, they could hold water. They always made a tiny mistake in the weaving, as they believed if they were ever to make one perfect thing, their lives would be complete and their time on Earth would be over.

Getting around

Walking was the main way of getting around on land until horses were brought to North America by Europeans. The Indians developed all kinds of backpacks and baskets to help them carry things more easily. When they travelled by water, they found that every lake, river or sea presented different problems, so each kind of water had its own type of boat.

🔺 **SEAWORTHY BOATS** were built by tribes living along the Northwest Coast. Plenty of large, strong, straight cedar trees grew there, and could be cut down, dug out, and shaped to suit both deep ocean waters and the shallows off the coast. Large dugouts, with high, curved ends to stop inshore waves splashing aboard, were used for trading runs up and down the coast. For fishing and whaling trips in the open sea, people built bigger, stronger boats with straighter sides.

🔺 **BUFFALO-HIDE CANOES** were circular river craft made of hide stretched over a wooden frame. They were found on the edge of the Plains, where there were few trees for boat-building.

TRADING was the main reason for travelling. Apart from the nomadic Plains Indians, who followed herds of buffalo, people usually stayed close to the territory in which they were born. Some did move between summer and winter villages, some travelled to wage war on neighbouring tribes, and some journeys were made to attend tribal gatherings and ceremonies.

platform from which hunters could spear fish

high bow to keep waves out

🔺 **CANOE-MAKING TOOLS** included stone and bone axes, adzes, gouges and wedges that were used to hollow out the cedar logs. To soften the wood for final shaping, the logs were sometimes filled with water and hot stones, or a carefully controlled fire would be lit to burn away the inside.

carved or painted decoration, often representing animals, to show the owner's importance

△ *Sea-going canoes were dug out from a single tree. Some could carry up to 60 warriors.*

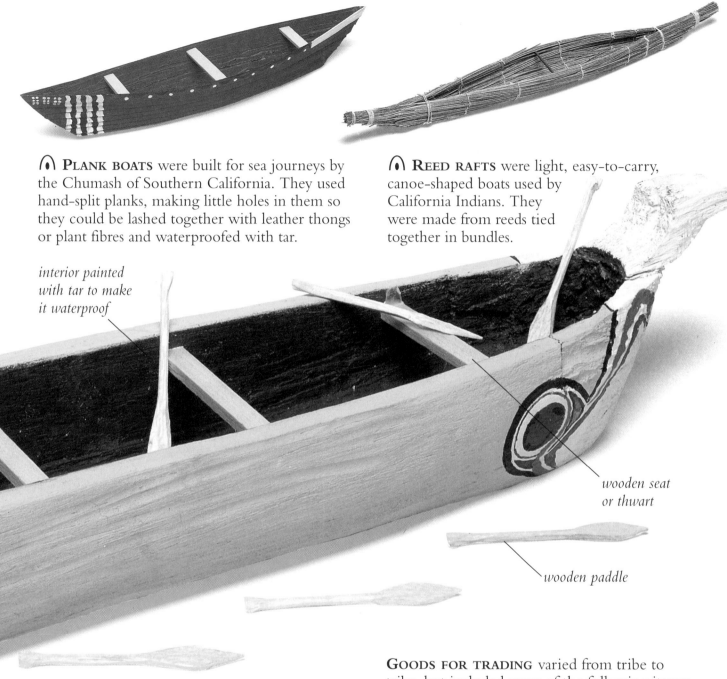

PLANK BOATS were built for sea journeys by the Chumash of Southern California. They used hand-split planks, making little holes in them so they could be lashed together with leather thongs or plant fibres and waterproofed with tar.

REED RAFTS were light, easy-to-carry, canoe-shaped boats used by California Indians. They were made from reeds tied together in bundles.

interior painted with tar to make it waterproof

wooden seat or thwart

wooden paddle

THE PRICE OF GOODS traded by North American Indians went up and down according to supply and demand. When something is plentiful, it is worth less, and when there is little available, the price goes up. These values applied when there were few horses and many buffalo:

8 buffalo robes	=	1 ordinary horse
5 buffalo robes	=	1 bear-claw necklace
1 buffalo robe	=	36 iron arrowheads

GOODS FOR TRADING varied from tribe to tribe, but included some of the following items:

- Baskets, acorns, seaweed, dried fish, shells
- Dried fish and fish oil, salt, boats and dugouts, copper and silver jewellery
- Hides, horses, eagle feathers
- Blankets, wool, dyes, jewellery
- Shells, wampum, furs, copper and copper tools, pearls
- Tobacco, shells, pearls

BOATS OF DIFFERENT SHAPES were built for different conditions. Tribes living by lakes and riversides needed light, easy-to-steer canoes that they could take out of the water and carry when it became too dangerous or shallow. Small canoes were perfect for shooting over waterfalls, but larger boats were needed for carrying goods for trading. A boat with a low bow and stern is good in calm waters. A high bow and stern give protection from rough waters but slow the boat down because of greater wind resistance.

gunwale   *decorative stitching*

wooden paddle

BIRCH TREES were plentiful in the Northeast and the Great Lakes area. These tall, thin, straight trees are wrapped in up to nine layers of bark which come off in sheets when carefully peeled. The outer skin is thick and white, the inner skins thinner, browner and softer.

CANOE BARK was peeled from a cut tree in the spring, when the outer layer is at its thickest. It was used, brown side out and white side in, to cover a frame of cedar wood. The bark sheets were sewn together with spruce roots. The seams were then made waterproof with a covering of gummy sap from the pine tree, heated until it became a thick, gooey syrup.

PADDLES were shaped from wood, anchors made from stones, bailers from shells and ropes from plant fibre or strips of hide. North American Indians saw no need for sails on their boats. They did not particularly want to go where the wind blew them, so paddles were all they needed for their short fishing and trading trips.

MAKE A BIRCH BARK CANOE

You will need: thick and thin balsa wood strips, bulldog clips, craft knife, pencil, needle, thread, paints, glue

1 Take the thick strip of balsa, mark out the gunwale (the top part) of the canoe as shown, and cut it out carefully, using a craft knife.

2 Soak the thin strips of balsa in hot water for half an hour. Lay the gunwale over the strips and fold them upwards to make the sides of the canoe. Lift the gunwale into position and glue it to the top of the sides, using clips to hold it in place.

3 When dry, cut off any balsa sticking out above the gunwale. Glue on a thin finishing strip and sew it in place as shown.

4 Sew thin strips of balsa wood together to make ends of the canoe.

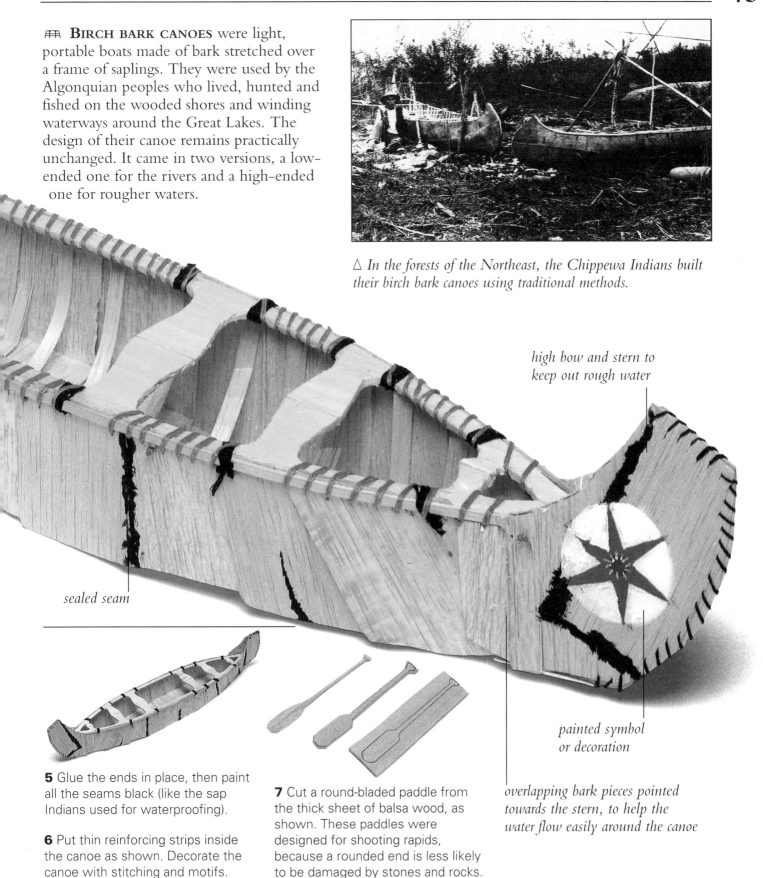

⊞ **BIRCH BARK CANOES** were light, portable boats made of bark stretched over a frame of saplings. They were used by the Algonquian peoples who lived, hunted and fished on the wooded shores and winding waterways around the Great Lakes. The design of their canoe remains practically unchanged. It came in two versions, a low-ended one for the rivers and a high-ended one for rougher waters.

△ *In the forests of the Northeast, the Chippewa Indians built their birch bark canoes using traditional methods.*

high bow and stern to keep out rough water

sealed seam

painted symbol or decoration

5 Glue the ends in place, then paint all the seams black (like the sap Indians used for waterproofing).

6 Put thin reinforcing strips inside the canoe as shown. Decorate the canoe with stitching and motifs.

7 Cut a round-bladed paddle from the thick sheet of balsa wood, as shown. These paddles were designed for shooting rapids, because a rounded end is less likely to be damaged by stones and rocks.

overlapping bark pieces pointed towards the stern, to help the water flow easily around the canoe

⚐ BEFORE THE HORSE was introduced to North America about 400 years ago, all land journeys were made on foot. Anything that needed to be carried was hauled along by women, or by dogs pulling a **travois** made from two dragging poles attached to a harness. Nomadic Indians following a buffalo herd on foot covered only about ten kilometres a day. They had few possessions, and kept their tepees small so they were easy to carry.

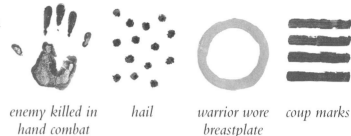

enemy killed in hand combat   *hail*   *warrior wore breastplate*   *coup marks*

△ *Plains warriors decorated their horses with painted symbols.*

⚐ MAKE A TRAVOIS

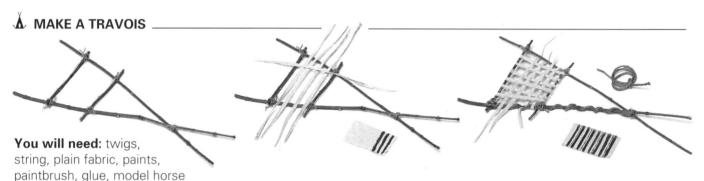

You will need: twigs, string, plain fabric, paints, paintbrush, glue, model horse

1 Use two long twigs and two short cross-pieces to make the basic shape, as shown. Tie them securely.

2 Cut thin strips of fabric and weave them to make a carrying platform. Glue to the frame. (Indians tied a travois with strips of buffalo hide.)

3 Wind string around the length of the poles and glue it. (Plains Indians used strips of hide for this, to protect the horse's skin from chafing.)

⚐ AFTER THE HORSE was brought to the **New World** by Spanish settlers, life for Plains Indians was transformed. They used horses to move swiftly in battle, to outrun buffalo and to pull the travois. A camp could now move 50 kilometres in one day. Tepees became bigger and more spacious. Women no longer had to carry heavy loads, and had more time for leisure and for making things. People owned more and could transport things more easily.

⚐ A SIOUX SONG tells of the respect and honour with which Plains warriors treated their horses:
My horse be swift in flight
Even like a bird:
My horse be swift in flight.
Bear me now in safety
Far from the enemy's arrows
And you shall be rewarded
With streamers and ribbons red.

4 Bend and glue thin twigs to form a cage on the platform. Cut and paint a piece of fabric for the horse blanket. Paint symbols on the horse. Tie the poles and blanket to its back.

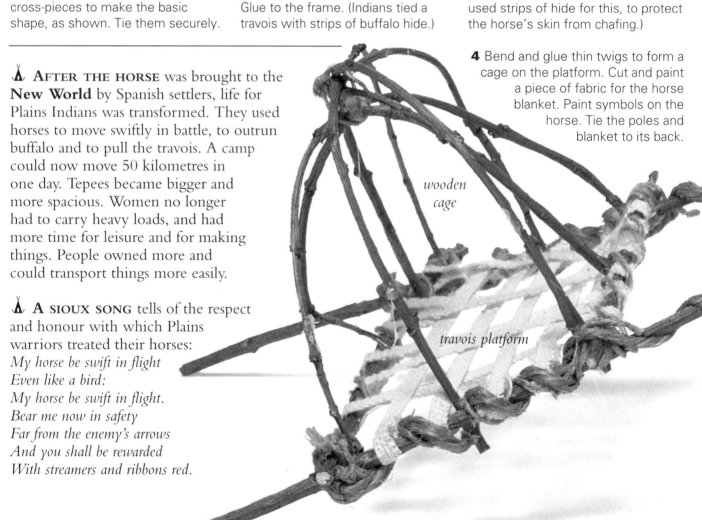

wooden cage

travois platform

△ *Young children often rode on a travois. Sometimes a wooden cage was put over the platform to keep passengers and possessions from falling off.*

BABIES were carried on cradleboards by their mothers. They were tightly wrapped up and strapped on with leather thongs, so that they could not wriggle about and were kept warm and safe.

SADDLES AND BRIDLES were made from buffalo hide and hair. A braided buffalo-hair rope or a thin strip of rawhide looped around the horse's lower jaw was all Plains horsemen needed to control their horses. While out hunting or fighting they rode bareback or used a simple hide saddle stuffed with buffalo hair. Women had wooden saddles padded with hide. Stirrups were made from wood, steamed into shape and covered in rawhide. Wealthy horse owners often had their tack decorated with paint and beads.

TRAVOIS were made by women. They were proud of their craftsmanship and were thought to be bad wives if their hide straps were cut unevenly or, worse still, had hair on them.

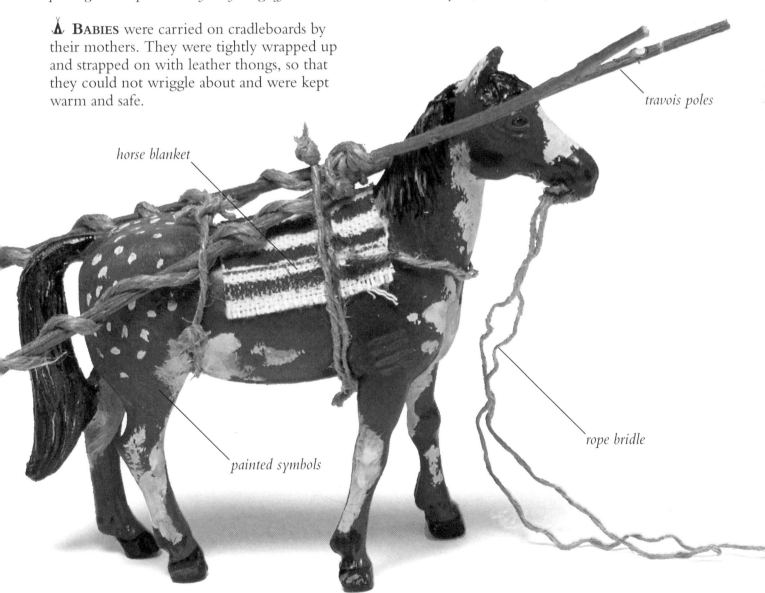

travois poles

horse blanket

painted symbols

rope bridle

Why make war?

It started with the hunt. A hunter needed to be brave, confident and skilful, and was rewarded with glory and praise if he was successful. For North American Indians, the respect given to successful hunters was perhaps the most important thing in life. War was seen as the greatest hunt of all, offering men the chance to come home heroes. Raids for horses and arguments over hunting grounds were among the many reasons why they set out on the warpath.

△ *This Plains warrior was an Arapaho chief in 1870.*

war club

INDIAN WARRIORS crept up on the enemy quickly and quietly, attacked fiercely, then turned and ran for it. There was no shame in retreat.

coup stick

△ BRAVERY was measured by how close warriors got to their enemy. Riding in close to touch the enemy with a coup stick was called counting coup. It was seen as more courageous than killing at 50 metres with a bow and arrow.

△ A BOW WITH ARROWS was an Indian warrior's main weapon. The Sioux made their bows from ash wood, with a bow string made of two twisted sinews. A war bow could be fired more quickly than a gun and be deadly accurate over 100 metres.

△ MAKE A BOW AND ARROW

You will need: thin strip of wood, string, feather, piece of foam sponge, cotton thread, kebab stick, glue, paints, craft knife

1 Mark the bow as shown and shape and nick the ends as shown, using the craft knife carefully.

2 Make a loop in the string, thread into the nick at one end and tie to the other end, bending the bow a little as shown.

3 Wrap and glue two lengths of string around the bow to make a handgrip as shown.

4 Make flights for the arrow by splitting the spine of the feather and cutting out 3 small sections as shown above.

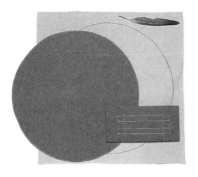
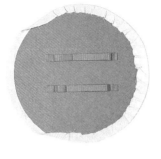

You will need: strong card, plain fabric, feathers, raffia, paint, pencil, bradawl

1 Cut a large card circle and a slightly larger fabric circle. Glue the fabric to the card, sticking it down around the edge, as shown. Cut two card strips as handles and glue to the back of the shield.

2 Draw your design on the front of the shield and paint it. Make small holes in the shield with the bradawl, thread raffia through them and tie on feathers as decoration.

⚔ **RAWHIDE SHIELDS** were painted with magic signs and kept wrapped up before battle so the magic could not leak away.

war axe

▦ **TOMAHAWKS** were curved, weighted clubs used for hitting enemies. They could also be thrown with fearsome force and accuracy.

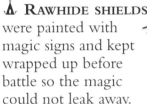
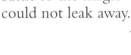

spear

▦ **A CHEROKEE WARRIOR** said:
"We cannot live without war. Should we make peace with our present enemy, we must at once look out for some other people with whom we can indulge in our beloved occupation."

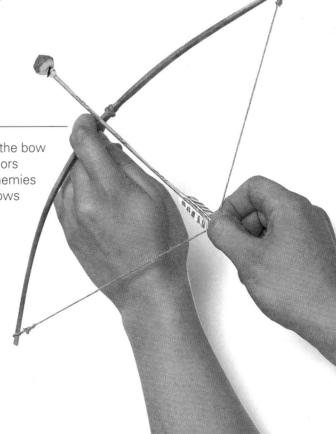

6 Paint and decorate both the bow and the arrow. Indian warriors painted pictures of their enemies on their arrows, so the arrows would know where to go. You can dip the arrow tips into paint and fire them at a target.

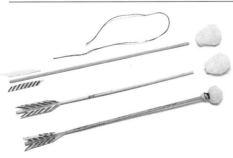

5 Glue the flights onto the kebab stick as shown. Cut the arrow down to half the length of the bow. Stick a small ball of foam onto the cut end of the arrow and secure with thread.

NEVER FIRE AN ARROW AT ANYONE. EVEN A TOY ARROW CAN CAUSE AN ACCIDENT.

Language differences

As recently as 200 years ago, there were over 300 languages spoken in North America. None of these had any links to languages that were spoken in the **Old World**. Groups belonging to the same tribe did not necessarily speak the same language, and people who did share a language were often spread over a wide area, because of trade and nomadic ways of life. So Indians developed sign language to help them communicate with their neighbours. It allowed them to express emotions and feelings, as well as warnings and signals.

SIGN LANGUAGE used by North American Indians was made up of a mixture of mime and signalling, based on actions and shapes of things rather than on sounds. When Plains Indians visited Europe in the last century, they found they could communicate easily and naturally with deaf people.

EARLY EUROPEAN EXPLORERS and settlers tried to write down the sounds of Indian words, but some just could not be accurately conveyed using our alphabet. Some Indian words have turned into familiar place names:

Place	Pronunciation	Meaning
Alabama	alba-amo	plant reapers
Dakota	dak-hota	the friendly ones
Canada	kanata	cabin
Illinois	ili-ni-wak	men
Idaho	ee-dah-how	behold! the sun coming down the mountain
Iowa	aayahooweewa	sleepy
Kentucky	ken-tah-teh	land of tomorrow
Minnesota	minne-sota	cloudy water
Texas	tiesha	friend

PLAINS SIGN LANGUAGE

Indian - rub back of hand twice

Cheyenne - chop at left index finger

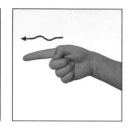
Comanche - imitate motion of snake

Crow - hold fist to forehead, palm out

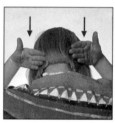
Osage - move hands down back of head

Pawnee - make V sign and extend hand

Nez Percé - move finger under nose

Sioux - hand across neck as if cutting

alone - right hand to the right

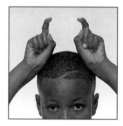
buffalo

cannot - move finger along palm and down

horse

bad - make fist then open downwards

moon

opposite

| Caught the Enemy | Eagle Horse | He Dog | Kills by the Camp | Spotted Face | Stabber |

△ *Indian names were very meaningful. People were often named after an animal or a special event in their lives (see page 54). These* **pictographs** *of names were used as signatures by the Sioux.*

SMOKE SIGNALS
were sent by hunters and warriors in the flat, open Plains country, on clear days when no wind blew. By flapping a blanket across the column of smoke from a fire, they made combinations of long and short puffs to tell of the presence of buffalo or the approach of enemies. The system was far from reliable.

▷ *A Plains Indian girl and a Nez Percé boy would have been able to speak to one another using sign language.*

LANGUAGE WAS SPOKEN, not written. For centuries, North American Indians saw no need for alphabets, or for writing down the many stories and traditions they carried around in their heads. Since they did not put their thoughts on paper, they developed fantastic memories and were good at telling stories and making speeches. They used their spoken language in a beautiful, moving way.

THE MAIN REASON why we know today about the Indians' rich spoken tradition is through the powerful speeches that were made by their chiefs and leaders in **post-contact** times. These speeches were usually about their sadness at losing their lands and at the white man's wasteful ways with nature.

CHIEF SEATTLE made a speech when the city of Seattle was founded on his homelands in 1855. He said:
"There was a time when our people covered the whole land as the waves of the wind-ruffled sea cover its shell-paved floor...Every hillside, every valley, every plain and grove, has been hallowed by some sad or happy event in days long vanished. Even the rocks, which seem to be dumb and dead as they swelter in the sun along the silent shore, thrill with memories of events connected with the lives of my people, and the very dust upon which you now stand... is rich with the blood of our ancestors."

SEQUOYA'S CHEROKEE ALPHABET was the only written form of an Indian language. Sequoya (1760-1843) dreamed of giving his people the power of the written word that the Europeans used so well. It was a wild success. Every Cherokee man, woman and child saw how useful reading and writing could be. They began producing their own newspapers in Cherokee and English.

Pictographs were often painted on to hide, or carved into wood and then coloured. Some Northeastern people used this technique to make calendar sticks.

PICTOGRAPHS AND IDEOGRAPHS were used in **pre-contact** times to leave messages or records of things that had happened. Pictographs were little drawings used to represent people, animals, objects or happenings. Ideographs were symbols that stood for abstract ideas like love, longing, hate or sadness.

▲ **TRIBAL CHRONICLES** recorded the passing years by focusing on particularly important events that everybody in the group remembered. These might include an outbreak of illness or maybe the sighting of a spectacular comet. Plains peoples painted their chronicles on buffalo hides.

▲ **MAKE YOUR OWN CHRONICLE** _____

You will need: plain fabric, paints, paintbrush, pencil

1 Cut the fabric to the shape of a buffalo hide, as shown. Paint it off-white, to look like hide.

2 Make up your own symbols to remind you of important events. Choose one for each week, to sum up the main event of that week, such as playing in a match, getting measles or having a birthday.

3 Paint your symbols on the canvas, starting at the centre of a spiral as shown.

Pictographs used by the Dakota Sioux Indians:

smallpox epidemic   *shower of meteors*   *village attacked and inhabitants killed*   *peace with a rival tribe*   *successful horse raid*   *new settlement*

A spiritual life

The unseen spirit world was very real to North American Indians. They believed that the natural world and the spirit world were joined together on Earth. Everything in their lives was controlled by major and minor gods and spirits, from the rising of the sun in the morning to people's success at hunting and the health of their children. They recognized the power of these spirits in everything they did and said.

THREE WORLDS made up the universe, according to Southeastern tribes. They believed that an Upper World, a Lower World and This World were separate but linked. This World, in which man, plants and most animals lived, was a round island resting on water. It hung from the sky on four cords attached at the north, south, west and east. The Upper World was pure, perfect and predictable, and the Lower World was full of chaos and change. This World was balanced between the two. Spirits moved freely between the Worlds and people had the privilege of helping the spirits keep the Worlds in balance.

⛪ MAKE A SPIRIT MASK

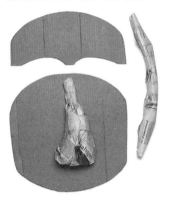

You will need: card, masking tape, old newspapers, wallpaper paste, paint, raffia, elastic, glue, Velcro

1 Cut basic shapes for the mask and forehead from card. Make a nose and brows from crumpled paper and tape into place.

2 Tape the forehead to the mask, using crumpled paper to fill it and build the forehead out. Make eye sockets from rings of folded paper, cut card ears and tape into place.

3 Paste strips of paper over the shapes. Allow to dry.

4 Paint the mask white, then add your design in colour. Glue on raffia for the hair.

5 Use card, crumpled paper and papier-mâché to build different mouth shapes. Attach them to the basic mask with Velcro dots.

▽ *The Kwakiutl made masks of the spirit Echo with a different mouth for each creature they believed he could imitate.*

basic mask

the spirit of Echo itself

an eagle or a raven

a bear

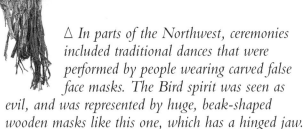

△ *In parts of the Northwest, ceremonies included traditional dances that were performed by people wearing carved false face masks. The Bird spirit was seen as evil, and was represented by huge, beak-shaped wooden masks like this one, which has a hinged jaw.*

STORIES OF HOW THE WORLD BEGAN
were told by most tribes. Pueblos believed it was the work of the Spider Grandmother. Some Northwestern tribes thought it was the Raven, while others believed that the world was made by a number of assorted spirits. Their neighbours in the Plateau region saw the world as a clever joke played by their Coyote god. Southeastern people gave the credit to the Master of Breath who lived on high.

VISION QUESTS were an attempt to get personal power from the spirits, instead of relying on the medicine man, or **shaman**. Young men went off alone, fasting, sometimes hurting themselves on purpose and keeping awake until they saw visions. These visions gave them their personal key to getting the spirits' help for the rest of their lives.

BLACK ELK said this about his visions: *"I saw more than I can tell, and I understood more than I saw; for I was seeing in a sacred manner the shapes of all things in the spirit."*

FALSE FACE MASKS were made by medicine men for the Iroquois people. They believed that illness was caused by unkind spirits with horrible faces and no bodies who lived in the forest, spreading sickness. The cure was to confuse the spirits, so medicine men cut mask shapes from living trees and gave them gruesome faces. Then they danced, while wearing the masks, until the bewildered spirits left the area.

RITES OF PASSAGE are **rituals** that mark the important stages in a person's life. For example, many people mark the birth of a child with a naming ceremony, a marriage with a wedding ceremony and a death with a funeral. For most early civilizations, the most important ceremony of all was the celebration of puberty, which is the time when a child becomes an adult. For North American Indians, this meant that young people no longer needed to be protected and could contribute fully to their group.

A BABY WAS NAMED a few days after it was born. A respected warrior would be paid, usually in horses, to name the baby. The child's given name often reflected some glorious action in the warrior's past, but it would be changed when the child made a mark for itself and earned its own name.

△ *Southwestern Hopi Indians wore* **kachina** *masks when they performed certain special festive dances.*

MAKE A KACHINA DOLL

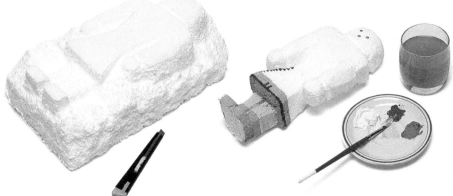

You will need: polystyrene block, PVA paints, sandpaper, craft knife, raffia, coloured wool

1 Draw an outline on the polystyrene.

2 Carve out the shape carefully with a craft knife, as shown. When the basic shape is cut, use sandpaper to smooth and round off the edges.

3 Paint a face and clothes on your doll, and add your own designs. Decorate waist and wrists with raffia and coloured wool.

BECOMING AN ADULT was tough. Boys as young as 10 would have to prove that they were made of strong stuff. In the Yuma tribe, boys had to run 15 to 25 kilometres a day for four days, with no sleep or food. Girls had to lie still, face down, on a bed of warm sand for four days while friends and relatives made long speeches.

MARRIAGE was mostly a free choice. Among Pueblo Indians, the bridegroom moved in with his wife's family, but could be sent home to his mother if things did not work out. Husbands and wives were expected to be faithful while their marriage lasted. Bridegrooms were expected to weave their bride's wedding clothes.

Tawa, who was associated with the sun

Sio Calako, a giant spirit

KACHINAS were spirits that for six months of the year were thought to inhabit the bodies of kachina impersonators – men who wore special masks and costumes in Pueblo ceremonies. Through these men, people asked for help from the spirit world. Children were given kachina dolls to help them understand the spirit world and identify kachinas.

Eototo, chief of the kachinas

AT THE END of their lives, North American Indians generally accepted death with little fuss, however it came. As it drew near, people sang their own personal death-song which they had rehearsed throughout their lives. The dead were usually cremated or buried in simple, shallow graves so they eventually blended back into the earth. Most tribes believed in a happy afterlife where the sun shone, crops ripened and hunting grounds teemed with animals.

SMOKING THE PIPE OF PRAYER was one of the most important rites. People smoked a mixture of tobacco and sweet-smelling herbs in a ceremonial pipe. They believed that the smoke was the very breath of prayer, and the pipe itself was seen as a sacred pathway to the spirit world.

Give and take

North American Indians respected nature and so did not take from it without giving something back. They hunted and fished carefully and cut down few live trees, taking only what they needed. They had a special relationship with nature and understood how important it was not to upset nature's delicate balance.

THE **INDIANS UNDERSTOOD** the world around them and knew what to expect from it. They watched the seasons come and go. They observed the movements of the stars and planets, the life cycle of plants and trees, and the regular habits and breeding seasons of the animals they hunted. They were not particularly curious to know why these things happened, because the answer was obvious to them. Everything was the work of the spirit world.

▼ MAKE A SAND PAINTING

 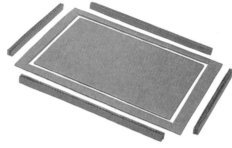 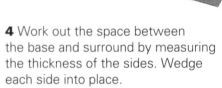

You will need: sand (silver sand is finer and easier to use than builder's sand), water-based powder paints in a variety of colours, bowl, stirring stick, thick card, pencil, craft knife, glue

1 Mix paint and a little water into a thick paste in the bowl. Add a cup of sand and stir.

2 Spoon the mixture on to a piece of card and leave in a warm place until completely dry. Repeat for all colours.

3 Make the sand painting tray. Measure and cut the card as shown. Make each side piece by cutting three identical strips of card and sticking them together.

4 Work out the space between the base and surround by measuring the thickness of the sides. Wedge each side into place.

5 Fill your tray with uncoloured sand, about half a centimetre deep. Taking a pinch of one of your coloured sands, trickle it carefully on to the base.

HEALING THE SICK was one of the main tasks of the shaman, or medicine man or woman. Healing was done with herbs and with a lot of ritual, which in itself can often help a sick person to feel better. The Indians discovered the healing properties of plants such as willow bark (which contains salicylic acid, the main ingredient of today's aspirin). Their remedies worked so well that the American government officially accepted 170 of them.

◁ *The Navajo used sacred sand paintings as their main way of treating sick people. They believed that a person's illness would be healed by the symbols in the sand. When a painting was finished, it was immediately rubbed out.*

A **CHEROKEE STORY** told that people upset the spirits of the animals because they killed them for food and crowded them out of their habitats. The animals took their revenge on humans by creating disease and sickness. But the spirits of the plants, who were people's friends, decided to help out. Each single plant, from the tallest trees down to the tiniest creeping mosses, agreed to produce a remedy that would fight and cure one of the diseases.

6 Gradually build up the different colours in your design. It is important to plan the design and colours before you begin. The design shown here is based on a sacred Navajo sand painting used to cure a sick baby. It would have been painted on the floor of the family hogan spread with a smooth layer of uncoloured sand.

SAND PAINTINGS were made by medicine men or women. Clean sand was spread for the background and then a coloured sand picture was created on top. The sick person had to sit or lie on the painting. After the ceremony, when the shaman had prayed and chanted, people took a pinch of the sand. They believed it had healing powers and could be used as a headache cure or a lucky charm. The rest of the sand was swept on to blankets and left near the sick person's house.

Looking back

Finding out how people lived in the past needs careful detective work, especially when they left no written records of their lives.

THE FIRST STEP is to gather evidence. To investigate North American Indian life, we can listen to the stories and memories of present-day Indians, passed down from one generation to the next. We can take account of travellers' tales from the earliest European explorers, who wrote about and drew what they saw. We can also investigate the findings of archaeologists, who study the objects that people have left behind, and anthropologists, who study how people lived their daily lives.

levels of soil marked to make a vertical grid

THE SECOND STEP is to use the evidence we have found to draw conclusions about how North American Indians lived many hundreds of years ago. This task may be complicated by the fact that different experts sometimes reach different conclusions. Their pictures of the past do not always match up, and every generation looks at history from a slightly different angle. The past is always much more complicated than we think.

▽ *This model is based on the archaeological dig at the Koster site in western Illinois. The site is named after the farmers on whose land the first finds were made in 1969. Since then, experts have dug through evidence of 15 settlements. The oldest, at about 10 metres below the present level, dates from 9,000 years ago.*

marker post

sorting table

top soil

A GRID SYSTEM helps archaeologists to sort out the objects they have found. They push marker posts into the ground and mark off the levels of soil in layers, so there are vertical lines through the whole site. They mark a horizontal grid on the surface, numbering the lines like grid references on a map. Every object is recorded with a reference to show where it was found and to which layer it belonged.

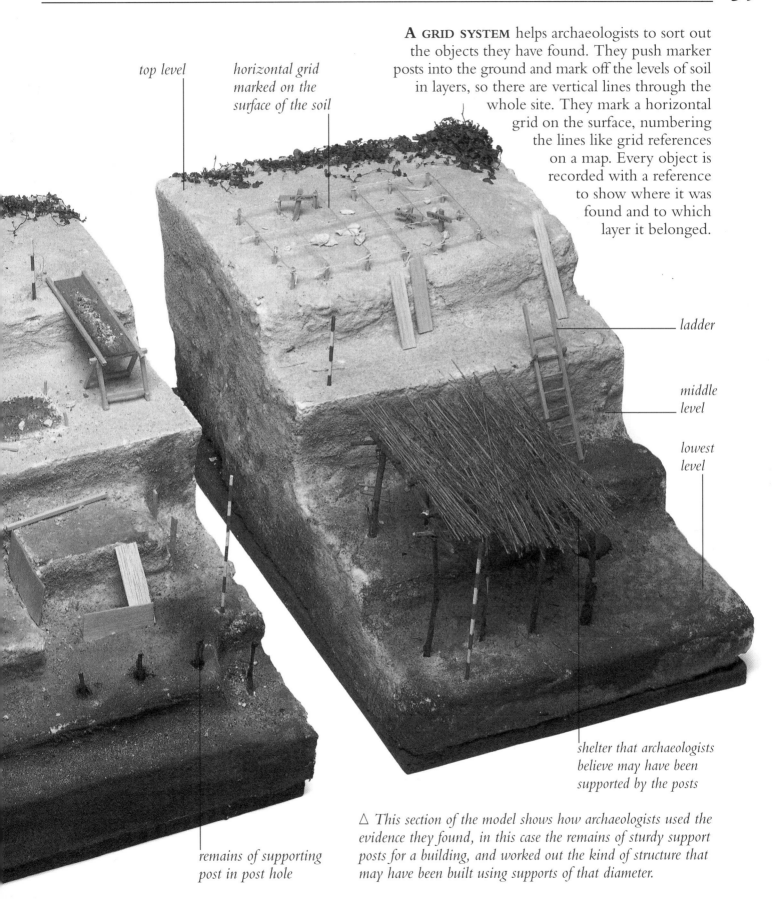

top level

horizontal grid marked on the surface of the soil

ladder

middle level

lowest level

remains of supporting post in post hole

shelter that archaeologists believe may have been supported by the posts

△ *This section of the model shows how archaeologists used the evidence they found, in this case the remains of sturdy support posts for a building, and worked out the kind of structure that may have been built using supports of that diameter.*

Post-contact times

North American Indian history spans about 50,000 years. During this time a number of different cultures have come and gone. But the greatest upheaval the Indians have ever faced was the coming of the Europeans, starting with Christopher Columbus in 1492. The Spanish, the Dutch, the French and the English arrived in waves. They landed in the east and gradually pushed the Indians further and further west. These new settlers came with guns and they believed the rich, fertile land was theirs for the taking, so they took it.

△ *Chief Red Horse, of the Sioux Indians, drew a series of pictographs representing the Battle of Little Bighorn. This pictograph shows the climax of the battle.*

THE NATIONAL POLICY STATEMENT made by the American government towards North American Indians in 1787 was full of promises that were soon broken. It said: *"The utmost good faith shall always be observed towards the Indians; their lands and property shall never be taken from them without their consent."*

THE NEW SETTLERS, whose ancestors had arrived from Europe, took territorial control from the Indians starting in the east, and gradually acquired land further to the west. Between 1776 and 1854, the North American Indians were forced back until all their land was lost, and by 1912, 48 states of America had been founded.

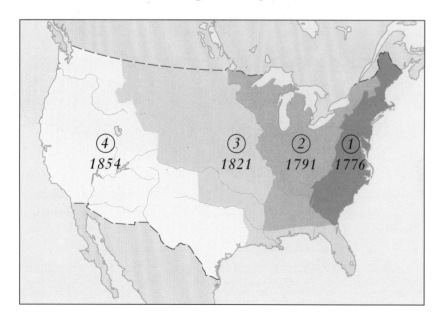

④ 1854   ③ 1821   ② 1791   ① 1776

◁ *This map shows the stages by which the new settlers took territory over from the North American Indians. Each shaded area shows the land acquired by the date shown.*

△ *Custer hoped to improve his reputation with a victory over the Sioux Indians. His troops, however, were defeated and he was killed.*

CUSTER was an American General who led his troops into many battles with the Plains Indians over their land and traditional hunting grounds. He grew to respect the North American Indian people. He published a book about his life in 1874 called *My Life on the Plains*. In it he wrote: *"When the soil which he has claimed and hunted over for so long a time is demanded by this... insatiable monster (civilization) there is no appeal; he must yield, or it will roll mercilessly over him, destroying as it advances. Destiny seems to have so willed it, and the world nods its approval."*

TWO YEARS LATER, in 1876, General Custer and one third of his cavalry regiment were killed in the Battle of Little Bighorn. They fought against the Sioux nation under its chief, Crazy Horse. This was the Indians' greatest victory against the advancing enemies, but in the end it changed nothing.

▷ *Zuni Indians still produce intricate jewellery from precious stones and silver. This picture was taken in the Southwest in 1970.*

THE LAST OF THE INDIAN WARS was at Wounded Knee in South Dakota in March 1890, when American troops opened fire on a band of Sioux men, women and children, killing 200 of them. In 1890, the last of the heartbroken Indian tribes were driven on to reservations, where land was set aside for their use but was run by the American government. In fact, more Indians died of diseases brought by the Europeans, against which they had no defence, than died in the Indian Wars.

TODAY most North American Indians live on reservations in the central and western parts of the United States and Canada. At first, reservation life was a nightmare, with Indian traditions and religions banned and children sent away to school to learn European ways. But Indians are now much more in control of their own lives. They hand on knowledge of their rich and varied traditions, and reach out to everyone with their unique record of achievements as a people. The Indians' understanding of the environment and nature's delicate balance is of great importance to people all over the world today.

Glossary

Algonquian tribes A group of Northeastern tribes who spoke the Algonquian language. There were about 50 different versions of this language.

anthropologist A person who studies the origins, development and behaviour of people.

archaeologist A person who studies remains from the past, such as buildings and possessions.

bola A rope with a weight such as a stone attached to it. Bolas were thrown as hunting weapons to bring down prey by entangling its legs, or whirled around to knock birds out of the sky.

buckskin Animal hide scraped and softened until it looks and feels like the soft, supple skin of a male deer.

canoe A thin, lightweight boat with pointed ends and no keel. Canoes are pushed through the water by paddles.

chickee A hut on stilts with no walls.

chronicle A record of events, described in the order in which they happened.

civilization A developed and organized group or nation of people.

clan A group of related families.

counting coup A North American Indian way of judging a warrior's bravery. The warrior had to come face to face with his enemy and touch him with a coup stick.

culture A group of people living at a particular time in history, who believe in the same things and share a way of life.

hogan A hexagonal or octagonal hut made from a log framework and plastered with mud.

Ice Age Throughout history there have been a number of Ice ages, when the world's climate became very cold and parts of Northern Europe, Asia and America were completely covered in ice. The last Ice age, which was fairly mild, lasted about 40,000 years and ended about 11,000 years ago.

ideograph A sign that is written down and used to represent an idea such as love or hate.

igloo A dome-shaped house built from blocks of hard snow or ice.

Iroquois tribes A group of Northeastern tribes who spoke the Iroquois language. These tribes were known in post-contact times as the five nations.

kachina Spirits of nature represented by a religious or ceremonial mask or doll-like figure.

lacrosse A team game that originated among North American Indians. It was played using sticks with rawhide nets at the end, and a ball made from hair and hide.

moccasins Shoes or boots made out of animal hide.

New World The continents of the western hemisphere: North and South America, the nearby islands, and Australia. It was known as "New" because these were the last parts of the world to be discovered by European explorers.

nomadic The way of life of groups of people who have no fixed home and wander from place to place looking for food and shelter.

Old World The continents of the eastern hemisphere: Europe, Asia and Africa. These were the parts of the world from which explorers set sail on voyages of discovery to areas that they called the New World.

pictograph A sign that is written down and used to represent a person or an object.

post-contact The time in North American Indian history after the native population had come face to face with explorers and settlers from Europe and the rest of the Old World.

potlatch A Northwestern American Indian ceremonial feast at which many gifts are given to the guests to demonstrate the host's wealth and generosity.

pre-contact The long period of time before North American Indians had any contact with people from other lands.

pueblo A village of terraced mud houses, sometimes built into the sides of hills.

rawhide Stiff animal hide that has been cleaned but is untreated.

ritual A set, ceremonial way of doing something or celebrating an important event.

roach A stiff tuft of animal hair tied on top of the head, worn for decoration.

shaman A man or woman who was believed to have a close relationship with the spirit world. People believed shamans could explain the workings of the gods to them, and make their prayers heard.

symbol A visible sign that represents an invisible idea.

tepee A portable, cone-shaped tent of animal skin or bark set over a wooden framework.

terrain The physical characteristics of an area, such as its mountains, rivers, vegetation.

tomahawk A war club with a rounded end. The word was later used to describe war-axes, introduced by Europeans.

totem pole A post that was carved and painted with symbols (usually animals) to represent family members and ancestors.

travois A trailing sledge, pulled along by dogs or, later, by horses and used for carrying possessions and people.

tribe A large group of related families.

wampum Small, white, cylindrical beads made from polished shells and used as money and expensive jewellery.

wickiup A cone-shaped hut made from grasses and rushes over a wooden frame.

wigwam A dome-shaped home made from wooden poles covered with reed or bark mats.

Index

Alaska 6
animal skins 10, 12-13, 16, 18, 23, 45
anthropologists 5, 58
archaeologists 5, 58
arts and crafts 34-39

Basket-making 34
beads 10, 12, 13, 45
beliefs 39, 52-57
Bering Strait 6
birch trees 42
bison 6
boats 40-43
 birch-bark canoes 42-43; boat-
 making tools 40; buffalo-hide
 canoes 40; plank boats 41; reed
 rafts 41; seaworthy boats 40
body paint 9
breastplates 10

Cedar trees 25, 40
Cherokee alphabet 50
chiefs and elders 22
 Black Elk 17, 53; Chief Seattle 50;
 Crazy Horse 61
children: clothing 10; learning 55;
 naming 54; play 23;
 table manners 28; travel 45
chronicle 51
clothing 8-13
corn cakes 28
counting coup 8, 46
cradleboards 45
creation stories 53
Custer, General 61

Dyes 12, 34, 36

Excavations 58
European explorers and settlers
 5, 60-61

False face masks 53
family life 23-25, 28
farming 20, 28-29
feathers 8, 12
fishing 26-27, 40
food 26-29
furniture 18-19

Gambling 30
games 30-31

Hair and headgear 9, 12-13
healing herbs 56
homes:
 chickee 15; earth lodge 15, 21;
 hogan 14; igloo 15; lean-to 14;
 longhouse 15, 20-21;
 plank house 14, 24-25; pueblo 14;
 reed house 14; tepee 14, 16-19,
 22-23, 44; wickiup 15; wigwam 15
horses 18, 44-45
hunting 22, 26-27, 46

Ice Age 6,
ideographs 50

Jewellery 12

Kachina dolls 54-55

Lacrosse 30
language 48-51

Mammoth 6
manners and customs 19, 25, 26, 28
medicine men and women 53, 57
moccasins 11
music 32-33
musical instruments 32-33

Names 49, 54

Pictographs 50-51
pipe of prayer 55
potlatch 25
pottery 35

Rituals and rites 53-55

Sand paintings 56-57
Sequoyah 50
shields 11, 47
Siberia 6
sickness and health 56-57
sign language 48
smoke signals 49
songs 32-33, 55

speeches 50, 54
spirits 52-55
 Bird spirit 53; Coyote 53; Echo 52;
 Eototo 55; Master of Breath 53;
 plant spirits 57; Raven 53;
 Sio Calako 55; Spider grandmother 53;
 Spiderwoman 39; spirit masks 55;
 Tawa 55; unkind spirits 53
symbols and colours 17, 23, 34,
 36-37, 40, 43, 44

Tattoos 9
textiles 36
totem poles 24-25
trading 40-41
travois 44-45
tribal lands 6, 7
tribes:
 Alabama 7; Aleut 6; Algonquian tribes 7,
 15, 43; Apache 6; Blackfeet 7; Caddo 7;
 Catawba 7; Cayuga 7; Cherokee 7, 47,
 50, 57; Cheyenne 7, 16, 48; Chickasaw 7;
 Chinook 6; Chumash 6, 12, 41;
 Comanche 7, 16, 48; Creek 7;
 Crow 7, 23, 48; Delaware 7; Flathead 7;
 Haida 6; Hopi 6, 28, 54; Inuit 6;
 Iroquois tribes 5, 7, 20, 28, 53;
 Kwakiutl 6, 52; Massachuset 7;
 Mohawk 7; Micmac 7; Natchez 7;
 Navajo 6, 12, 14, 21, 39, 56, 61;
 Nez Percé 5, 7, 12, 48, 49; Nootka 6;
 Oneida 7; Onondaga 7; Osage 48;
 Paiute 7; Pawnee 7, 48; Pequot 7;
 Pomo 6; Pueblo 6, 54; Seminole 7, 13;
 Seneca 7; Shoshoni 4, 7; Sioux 7, 8, 16,
 33, 44, 46, 48, 49, 51; Spokane 7;
 Tlingit 6, 12, 37, 38; Ute 7, 10, 32;
 Yahi 6, 26; Yuma 6, 54; Zuni 6, 61

Vision quests 53

War 46-47
warbonnets 8
weapons:
 blowpipes and darts 27; bola 27;
 bow and arrow 46-47; tomahawk 47;
 war club 13
weaving 38-39
wool 13